GREAT
WAR FILMS

BOOKS BY LAWRENCE J. QUIRK

GREAT WAR FILMS

LAWRENCE J. QUIRK

A CITADEL PRESS BOOK
Published by Carol Publishing Group

A Citadel Press Book
Published by Carol Publishing Group
Citadel Press is a registered trademark of Carol
    Communications, Inc.
Editorial Offices: 600 Madison Avenue, New York, N.Y. 10022
Sales and Distribution Offices: 120 Enterprise Avenue,
    Secaucus, N.J. 07094
In Canada: Canadian Manda Group, P.O. Box 920, Station U,
    Toronto, Ontario M8Z 5P9
Queries regarding rights and permissions should be addressed
to Carol Publishing Group, 600 Madison Avenue, New York,
N.Y. 10022

Carol Publishing Group books are available at special discounts
for bulk purchases, sales promotion, fund-raising, or
educational purposes. Special editions can be created to
specifications. For details, contact: Special Sales Department,
Carol Publishing Group, 120 Enterprise Avenue, Secaucus,
N.J. 07094

Designed by A. Christopher Simon

Manufactured in the United States of America
10 9 8 7 6 5 4 3 2 1

Library of Congress Cataloging-in-Publication Data

Quirk, Lawrence J.
    The great war films : from The birth of a nation to
today / by Lawrence J. Quirk.
        p. cm.
    "A Citadel Press book."
    ISBN 0-8065-1529-5 (pbk.)
    1. War films—History and criticism. I. Title.
PN1995.9.W2Q57 1994
791.43'658—dc20   94-20343
                                                              CIP

To Robert Charles Francis

February 26, 1930–July 31, 1955

Hero of the film *The Caine Mutiny*
and my army buddy in the Korean War

ACKNOWLEDGMENTS

My special thanks go to John Cocchi and Gene Massimo, who generously opened their fine still collections to me, and to Howard Mandelbaum of *Photofest* and Jerry Ohlinger's Movie Material Shop, both always sources of excellent stills. Also, great thanks to the Photo Archives of the Museum of Modern Art, New York; the British Film Institute, London; the staff of the Billy Rose Collection of the New York Public Library at Lincoln Center (Film and Theater Divisions), Library and Museum of Performing Arts, New York; the Margaret Herrick Library of the Academy of Motion Picture Arts and Sciences, Hollywood; the James R. Quirk Memorial Film Symposium and Research Service, New York.

My appreciation also to James E. Runyan, Don Koll, Arthur Tower, Doug McClelland, Barbara Barondess MacLean, Dr. Rod Bladel, Frank Rowley (the distinguished film revival theater manager), Albert B. Manski, Mike Snell, Romano Tozzi, Don Collins, Douglas Whitney, Gregory Speck, Ed Maguire, Mary Atwood, Ron Mandelbaum, John Coyle, Jim McGowan, Robert Heide, John Gilman, Mary Corliss, Herb Graff, Robert Dahdah, Lou Valentino, Bob Kent, and the various film companies and their personnel who made possible the seventy-five films included in this book. And many thanks to George Rowland, Donald Davidson, Renata Slauter, Shirley Hinkamp, Alvin Marill, and the late Howard Otway, Florence Otway and their children and personnel at New York's Theater 80, St. Mark's.

A special acknowledgment is owed to my associate, William Schoell, who with his usual insight and expertise, contributed the essays on *Birth of a Nation*, *Sergeant York*, *Retreat, Hell!*, *The Horse Soldiers*, *Wings*, *The Longest Day*, *Sands of Iwo Jima*, *The Bridge on the River Kwai*, *Three Came Home*, *Casualties of War*, and *The Red Badge of Courage*. (These essays are end-initialed *W.S.*)

And to the memory of Michael Ritzer (1949–1994), a close friend and associate for twenty-two years, and to my Korean War buddies from 1950 to 1953, living and dead, fond memories of whom inspired me to give my best to this book. God bless you all. I miss you.

And finally, the warmest kind of appreciation, as always, to my editor, Allan J. Wilson, who has been associated with me on various books for twenty-seven years.

CONTENTS

GREAT
WAR FILMS

PREFACE

While working on this book, I found myself flooded with piercing, poignant memories from over forty years back, when I served as an army sergeant during the Korean War (1950–53). I am as of this writing seventy, and I think with infinite sadness of buddies who never got past even their twenty-second birthday, and who for all these decades have lain in silence and darkness and solitude in military cemeteries here or abroad.

I think about actor Jimmy Butler, who at thirteen in the 1934 film *No Greater Glory* was my childhood hero when I was eleven. In that movie, he led a gang of boys in Budapest in defending their "fort" from a rival outfit. Poor Jimmy was to die in France as an army private in World War II; an artillery round had shattered his spine. He was twenty-four that year—1945. For some fifty years now, he has lain in grave 6704 in the military cemetery at Epinal, France. When I was last in France, I visited that sacred place. So many valiant young fighters in that terrible war lie there alongside Jimmy, their young lives unfulfilled, life roads never taken, love aspirations never realized, all hopes and dreams terminated by the exigencies of war.

In my 1989 novel *Some Lovely Image*, (also published by Carol), a chaplain broods over the deaths of young men in World War I. The year is 1918. He speculates on the ominous fates awaiting some of the green, innocent, idealistic young men to whom he has given his farewell blessing:

> I knew that many of these boys before me would pass on without friend or relative or clergyman to comfort their final agonies. They would die in the muddy filth of trenches with machine-gun fire spitting above their last gasps. Their healthy young bodies would be torn open by shrapnel, and gas would choke their lungs. These boys of tender years would scream out their last moments in this world in pain and fear and loneliness, and in the busy congress of senseless destruction all about them, their screams would go unheard. Perhaps one out of fifty would have on hand a tenderly-ministering latter-day Walt Whitman to hold their hands and close their dying young eyes, and administer a last tender kiss as the Good Gray Poet (who nursed and comforted so many so lovingly and faithfully in the military hospitals of Washington) had done so often in the Civil War.

While working on this book, I also thought often of someone I knew and loved very deeply in the long-ago—actor Robert Francis, the young hero of the 1954 movie *The Caine Mutiny,* who had earlier served with me in the United States Army and whose life was to be so tragically cut short by a plane crash in 1955. Bobby was only twenty-five. This book is dedicated to him.

When we were soldiers together, Bobby and I used to talk of how we would meet any final testings of our mettle in battlefield action, should they ever come; how we would rise to the occasion, conquer our fears, bear any wounds with fortitude, and (should it come to that) die bravely. We were lucky—we survived the war, though Bobby had but two more years of life after that left to him. But comrades "out there" had fought and died for us, and we were left feeling damned guilty, too!

Bobby Francis and I would talk of men we had served with in basic training, guys who went on to the worst of the war and never came back. I think often of a guy named George, a close buddy throughout basic with whom I pitched a pup tent on bivouac in the cold November of 1950. Our sarge was out to toughen us up all the way and didn't want to hear any sissy bullshit about the ground being icy or the pup tent freezing—so the two of us bundled up in that tiny space as best we could. George was twenty-two, a draftee; I was RA—a Regular Army man who had enlisted voluntarily during the summer that the war broke out.

George was terribly homesick. He didn't take well to army life; he missed his girl a thousand miles away in Pennsylvania, and he missed his folks and the quiet, scholarly life he had led. And on that freezing November night, as we lay huddled together in our blankets and fatigues and jackets, grateful for whatever protection our heavy stockings and strong army boots afforded our extremities, George burst into tears. "Oh God, I hope I measure up," he groaned. "When we get over there, I don't want to disappoint those I love, or let you or my other buddies down, or fail my country. And oh God, I'm so *afraid*!" I comforted him as best I could.

As it turned out, I was "lucky" (if that is the word), and he was not. I got an assignment handed me that took me away from the outfit and my pals. Shortly afterward, that same outfit was sent to Korea. George was killed a month after he got there. For a long time after that, I was to feel guilty—so damned guilty—that it happened to him and not to me.

My father, Andrew L. Quirk, served with the famous 26th (Yankee) Division in the thick of the World War I fighting in France—at Chateau Thierry, Saint-Mihiel, The Argonne. He came back shell-shocked, traumatized, and profoundly disoriented. Throughout my childhood and adolescence

he divided his time between Veterans Administration hospitals and Lynn, Massachusetts, the town we lived in, where he lost himself in violence and hell-raising in the bars. He would come home, his face all bloated from his alcoholic condition, and be abusive, brutal—a demon.

I would hear my father's vocalized nightmares as he relived the horrors of trench warfare, his buddies blown apart, the gassing, the endless, maddening shelling and machine-gun fire. Once he told me (I was ten) that he had awakened in a trench from a brief, disturbed slumber to find a severed arm lying across his chest. Another time he found himself soaked in blood and vomit and excrement and urine and flesh particles when a buddy was blown into a dozen bits.

I remember a parade in 1936, when I was thirteen; I had joined the YD Juniors—sons of (Yankee Division) veterans—and we used to march through the streets of Lynn, Massachusetts, in Memorial Day and Armistice Day parades. At the intersection of Market and Summer streets, we paused. I saw my father on the street corner, swollen and dirty and drunk. His look was infinitely sad. He came home drunk that night, as usual, but then jumped on my bed and grabbed me in his arms and repeated over and over: "If another war comes, I won't let you go—*I won't let you go!*"

My mother's idea of a summer vacation for me was sending me to visit my father at the Veterans Administration hospital at Togus, Maine, outside Augusta, where there was a small inn for visitors and patients' relatives. I spent the summers of 1933, 1934, and 1935 there. I was, at ten, eleven, twelve, a sort of mascot and pet among the disabled veterans at the hospital. Most of them were in their forties by that time, and all bore the marks of war. Some were out of their heads—raving lunatics or at least severely disturbed. Others were missing a limb or an eye; still others sat with heads shaking constantly, muscles twitching, emptily staring into space.

My father was trying hard to stay off the booze—which I realized, even at eleven, was his way of escaping those memories of 1917–18 France. Sober, he was the most wonderful, intelligent, sensitive, cultivated, well-educated, beautiful guy. When I was sick as a child, he would put cool hands on my fevered brow, hug me, read to me, feed me, nurse me, hold me close. Drunk, he was the Devil Incarnate—brutal, abusive, dangerous, unpredictable.

I used to get damned irritated with my congressman uncle's attitude toward my father. They had served together in France in the worst of the fighting, and he was himself a war hero. My father and mother had met through him. "Don't be too hard on Andy," he would say to my mother and me. "He's unfortunate, and it's too bad." One day, at age seventeen, I yelled at my uncle that my mother and I were the unfortunate ones; *he* had his escape in his wino dream world; *we* had to live with the reality. "Someday you'll understand, Larry," my uncle would say. "It was *hell* over there in France!"

When my father tried to steel himself through withdrawal, and the days of craving for booze left him maddened, he would cry himself to sleep with his arms around me, and then the nightmares of France would return, and he would verbalize them frighteningly, hugging me into so tight a vise that I thought I would suffocate—and I would relive them with him, one by one.

While working on this book, I have thought of my father so very often. For many years I had felt bitter resentment toward him because his disorientations, impracticality, alcoholism, and joblessness had doomed my mother and me to poverty and insecurity and fear—and the cruel condescensions of her more fortunately situated relatives. And then those nights at the VA hospital inn and in Lynn, when I lay frightened and sleepless in his arms while he relived the terrors, horrors, and trauma that had sealed his fate and left him one of Life's Tragic Also-Rans. And now, at seventy I realize with a belated shock, thirty-two years after his death, that I *loved* him, I *always loved him*. And now, at long last, I forgive him gladly—for all of it.

I was a 4F in World War II and worked in a defense plant for the duration. All—or almost all—my peers in the town had gone into the service, and I felt like two cents, an outsider, a loner. I was haunted by the feeling that I had missed an important area of experience, a manly rite-of-passage, an almost universal reality without which I could not think of myself as completely a man. The war ended in 1945, and I lost my defense-plant job. But five years later, in 1950, after working my way to a college degree via a night newspaper job, I got one of Life's Wonderful Second Chances. The Korean War broke out. At twenty-six in 1950, I was a much stronger and healthier guy than I had been at nineteen in 1943, and I went to the Boston Army Base and enlisted.

At first I didn't think I could take it. Nothing in my prior experience had prepared me for it. Then a wonderful young lieutenant in basic training took

me in hand: "You *want* this; you know you *want* it; you *need* it; keep going till you drop—because believe me, you *won't* drop!" I lost him a year later; he was blown to pieces in Korea. The next three years, the period of my army enlistment, brought out my finest self, my truest self. I emerged from that military experience a fully rounded human being.

The admirable author William Manchester, who wrote with such touching eloquence of his experiences in World War II, once said, "Men do not die for the flag; they die for each other." My conviction, based on my own experience, is that they die for both. I met many honestly patriotic and idealistic men during my war service—men who thought it a holy mission to fight, suffer, persevere, even die, for the democracy that had made possible their free, hopeful, positive lives.

The Korean period was an era of relative innocence. The stakes were more evident ("Communism must be contained"); the goals as we servicemen saw them were clear and unequivocal. Vietnam in the 1960s ushered in the era of cynicism, escapist drugs, the antiwar protesters who hollered about war's futility and carnage, and its carnivorous chewing-up of the lives and fortunes of the young. I have always felt that the trouble with the 1965–75 Vietnam adventure was that we did not *fight to win*—there was too much hesitation and prevarication and caution in the seats of power. We could have won that war in a year or two at most, and saved many lives, had we pushed forcefully from the start. As it was, all ended humiliatingly.

Yet even in that destructive war, amid all the suffering and woundings and drugs and death and civilian miseries, men loved it. They loved war in Vietnam as they did in World War I and II, and in Korea—and far back to the Spanish and Civil and Mexican and 1812 and Revolutionary wars, and for centuries before that—for thousands of years, in fact.

I have no love of war. I know its face. I know it is right and necessary sometimes, but at what a price! But I can understand its hold on many men's minds—and hearts. I lost part of my hearing and sustained a partial speech impairment thanks to a 55-mm howitzer round that blasted off too near me. But I came out of it all alive—oh, forgive me, George; forgive me, my buddies lost so young: *I* came out—*alive*. And I waste no time feeling any self-pity about being *seventy*-ish. Because I think of all the poor souls, including my lost George, my lost Bobby, my lost oh-so-noble-sure-and-strong lieutenant mentor—who never got out of their *twenties*.

Why have so many men loved war, despite everything about it? That male love of war is something that harks back to the innocent camaraderies of boyhood—the craving for exciting adventure, the consoling warmth of togetherness, the galvanizing male bonding that an overall purpose or pursuit requires. It has often been noted by sociologists and psychologists that American men, especially, are brought up to repress their feelings; anger comes more easily to them than love. But in war, anger and love dramatically and purgationally *coalesce*—anger toward the enemy, love for comrades—bonded in the same goal and pursuit, all-for-one-and-one-for-all, as the old saw has it.

In the more sophisticated, flexible, relativist, and aware 1990s, men have learned to express feelings toward one another more easily; they do not think of love as a vulnerability, a softening, a surrender; rather, they regard it as a galvanizing concern, a reaching-out toward others, a recognition of Our Common Human Fate. In the past only the exigencies, the tensions, the myriad tragedies, terrors, and obscenities of war elicited that element from men. Now many perceptive, sensitive, broad-spirited men who are veterans of recent wars can recognize and accept their time in the service of their country as their finest spiritual hour—a time of purgation, catharsis, a spiritual apotheosis.

I have found that each of the seventy-five films dealing with aspects of war has had something to say to me—has brought back many memories, eliciting thoughts, feelings, and people from the past—and has been easily translated into something like a universal experience. *Birth of a Nation*, an epochal, cinematic breakthrough film made in 1915, has many rousing, inspirational moments, for its creator, D. W. Griffith, was a genius. But his bias, as a Southerner, toward people of color leaves one saddened and appalled by its revelations, and implicit approval, of Ku Klux Klan cruelties (in the Reconstruction period) toward our black brothers and sisters. There is no balance here, and—even allowing for its historical context—the outcries of African-American groups against it today are eminently understandable, as are efforts to ban it in certain quarters. Treated as a kind of documentary, a museum piece, a pioneer cinematic work that in its techniques bred many imitators, it nevertheless does have merit—as African-American director John Singleton and others have stated.

Hearts of the World (1918), yet another fine Griffith war drama, this time about World War I, stars Robert Harron, the beloved son-figure to D.

W. Griffith who died mysteriously at twenty-six of a gunshot wound in 1920, and who in the film is so boyishly decent and heroic. He and Lillian Gish make the movie a memorable experience. *The Four Horsemen of the Apocalypse* made a star in 1921 of another actor who was to die young: Rudolph Valentino, who in the film is horrified by the specters of War, Famine, Pestilence, and Death—the Four Horsemen. *America*, from 1924, covers our American Revolution, and Griffith, untrammeled by his biases, directs with genius this story of the valiant fighters who guaranteed our democracy and our freedoms some two-hundred years ago. *The Big Parade* of 1925 tells it like it was where World War I France is concerned; it was my father's favorite picture. *What Price Glory* (1926) deals amusingly with the joshing camaraderie of men in war—and puts across their courage and resolution when they get down to the combat aspects. The 1927 film *Wings* showcases Buddy Rogers and Richard Arlen most touchingly as airmen male-bonding under combat conditions. And the 1930 masterpiece *All Quiet on the Western Front* offers us the German side in World War I, showing them as suffering human beings like ourselves, with the futility and terror and disillusion of war limned in ironic, disenchanted yet compassionate terms.

Journey's End (again from 1930) gives us priceless insight into the tensions of trench warfare—the waiting, the fear, the tense interrelationships. *The Dawn Patrol*, made in the same productive year, is quietly horrible as it depicts the endless chewings-up of a succession of squadrons, each new group of young hopefuls replacing, with dispatch, a previous group taken by death. And then there is the last of the 1930 crop, Howard Hughes's famous *Hell's Angels*, renowned for its aerial warfare—and with Jean Harlow for dessert. Joan Crawford is 1933's dessert in *Today We Live*—but she gets sidelined (for once) by the Gary Cooper–Robert Young—Franchot Tone male-bonding-in-war pyrotechnics. The 1936 *The Road to Glory* gives us a triple charge of war's futility, and *The Charge of the Light Brigade* whisks us back from the 1936 film's release to the 1850s and the Crimean War, and Errol Flynn and his famous—yes, charge. James Cagney and Pat O'Brien fight World War I in *The Fighting 69th* (1940), wherein Cagney learns to fight fair and clean, and O'Brien is an inspirational chaplain—and who could ask for more? Gary Cooper, by 1941 an American Dream Hero–Icon, got himself his first Oscar for that year's *Sergeant York*, a true story about a guy who starts off conscientiously objecting

and winds up kicking German butt and winning a chestful of medals for doing so.

Guadalcanal Diary, of 1943 vintage, is another tale of individual courage under fire. It followed 1942's *In Which We Serve*, in which that "effete popinjay" (so regarded in some circles) Noel Coward demonstrated for fellow Britons his fighting spirit, in his famous study of British naval heroism. Noel was no "sissy" in *that*.

So Proudly We Hail and *Cry Havoc* (the second and third of our *nine* 1943 releases) definitely belong in a book about war films, because the heroism and sacrifices of women nurses and civilians in the Pacific in World War II deserve more than a little mention—and commendation. In that same year, Humphrey Bogart and crew were cleaning up the *Sahara*, practically by themselves; and Robert Taylor, the last survivor on *Bataan*, determined he would take plenty of "Japs" with him when he checked out. Henry Fonda and Thomas Mitchell extoll soldierly virtues in *The Immortal Sergeant*, and Bogart gets into the *Action in the North Atlantic* with éclat. Ty Power does more than his best for sub warfare in *Crash Dive*, and Spencer Tracy, in *A Guy Named Joe*, comes back as a beneficent ghost to inspire Van Johnson to flying exploits (and, incidentally, gives him his own girl, Irene Dunne).

Thirty Seconds Over Tokyo, gives us more Spencer Tracy heroics. Come 1945, some brave infantrymen take that famous walk in *A Walk in the Sun*, and Robert Mitchum touchingly delineates infantry heroism as a beloved captain whose death in action is mourned in *The Story of GI Joe*. Also in 1945, Errol Flynn conquers the whole place practically on his own when he sets out on *Objective Burma!* By 1948, Clark Gable was agonizing over logistics that endanger men's lives, in *Command Decision*, and Van Johnson, during the next year, was doing his doggone best for God, country, and his buddies in *Battleground*—not to be outdone by supermacho John Wayne on the *Sands of Iwo Jima*.

Claudette Colbert, lovely and determined and courageous, is on hand yet again to remind us of the courage of women under wartime conditions, this time in a Japanese prison camp in *Three Came Home*, in 1950; while 1951 brings Audie Murphy (a genuine World War II hero) transported back to Civil War times, where he proves—according to the famous Stephen Crane novel—that a guy can start as a coward and wind up the taker of *The Red Badge of Courage*.

It's Wayne again, doing-or-dying, for *The Flying Leathernecks*, come 1951; and *Retreat, Hell!* in 1952 is the loudly shouted slogan of stalwart Frank Lovejoy and his boys. The year 1953 finds Humphrey Bogart and June Allyson tending the wounded in hospitals in *Battle Circus;* and the Pearl Harbor attack blasts lives apart and sends servicemen in Hawaii to their weapons, in *From Here to Eternity*.

In 1955, William Holden air-flaks those *Bridges at Toko-Ri*, while the guys are out for enemy blood in

15

Battle Cry. In 1956, *Attack!* is the name of the game for Jack Palance and his men. *War and Peace,* which eventually had both 1956 and 1968 versions, gives us Leo Tolstoy's literate and intelligent but blistering and realistic attitude toward—yep—war; and by 1957, Kirk Douglas was demonstrating in *Paths of Glory* that generals can be stupid, egoistic, and destructive. Wrongheaded British militarism is on telling display in *The Bridge on the River Kwai* (also 1957); and in 1958 Bradford Dillman, Robert Wagner, and Jeffrey Hunter are up to their ears *In Love and War.* In that same year, in *A Time to Love and a Time to Die,* John Gavin shows us the German side of war (again from a work by Erich Remarque).

In 1959, Gregory Peck in *Pork Chop Hill* wins, and holds, an impossible site just to assuage the vanities—and public relations—of top brass; and John Wayne and Bill Holden again lead the way for all good fighting men in *The Horse Soldiers. The Longest Day* (1962) gives us an exhaustive rerun of D-Day 1944; and *The Victors,* in 1963, takes American soldiers from Africa clear to Berlin with much suffering, death, and disillusion as their portion. The 1964 instant classic *Dr. Strangelove* shows that much truth can be spoken in jest as a war-mad general sets off World War III by being implicated in the A-bombing of a Russian missile site. *The Thin Red Line,* a 1964 "sleeper," demonstrates a love-hate relationship between a private (Keir Dullea) and a sergeant (Jack Warden) that ends up lovingly (what else?) but lethally (one dies in the other's arms in combat).

Then there's the 1965 *Battle of the Bulge,* with the Germans making their last major stand in 1944; and *The Battle of Algiers* (also from 1965), which graphically and hair-raisingly depicts Algerian revolutionists telling the French overlords to bug off, and reinforcing the message with troops and tanks and all-hell. *Beach Red* (1967) limns war unsparingly.

John Wayne (at sixty-one) is back in 1968 with *The Green Berets,* and his fight-to-win, macho approach wins the ire of the sixties antiwar crowd. *The Battle of Britain* (1969) leaves one wondering how that valiant but hapless nation held out against the Nazis in 1940–41, though hold out they did. And *Patton,* in 1970, showcases stonefaced, sadistic George C. Scott as the general the men love to hate—but he gets the damned job done.

The 1970 blockbuster *M*A*S*H* treats base hospitals as amusingly and satirically as *Battle Circus* treated them seriously, and Elliott Gould as a zany doctor walks off with the show. *Kelly's Heroes* (also

THE BIG PARADE John Gilbert's face registers the horror and disillusion of war.

1970) demonstrates the boyishly mischievous side of our troops when confronted, in World War II Germany, with a cache of Nazi bullion.

Waterloo takes us (as of 1971) to 1815 and the Napoleonic Wars, the fall of the Little Corporal, and the inauguration of some decades of (relative) peace in Europe. Rod Steiger makes a striking, method-actorish Napoleon. *A Bridge Too Far* (1977) gives more insights into the battle in the Lowlands; and 1978's *The Deer Hunter* details the horrific effects of war on men psychologically, then and forevermore. The 1978 release *The Boys in Company C* presents us with interesting (and contrasting) character studies of individual fighting men; and 1979's *Apocalypse Now* reflects the grotesque manias of Marlon Brando's film character. *The Big Red One* (1980) has the boys in intrepid, sometimes ill-advised combat action again; and *Gallipoli,* which in 1981 made Mel Gibson a star, traces a futile engagement during World War I in which no one emerged the clear winner.

16

Al Pacino fights the American Revolution of 1775–83 practically by his lonesome in—yes—*Revolution*, a 1985 film, while looking very 1929–Chicago gangsterish all through; and *Platoon* (1986) and *Full Metal Jacket* (1987) show—unsentimentally and grittily—the inroads on soldiers' character and decency that all-out war can bring about. *Casualties of War* (1989), in which a decent soldier in Vietnam, Michael J. Fox, refuses to ape his buddies' raping and foraging, (and pays the price), does much the same. Sean Penn is particularly striking in this, as a soldier who has gone animalistic.

Glory, a 1989 film about a white-led black regiment that distinguished itself in the Civil War, starred Matthew Broderick as an affectingly boyish officer with the heart of a lion, and Denzel Washington and Morgan Freeman as two of his sturdy soldiers. One of the finest war pictures ever made, *Glory* demonstrates that before any of us is white or black (or red or yellow, or whatever), we are, first and foremost, human beings. African Americans and whites were weeping and hugging each other after the showing I attended in the movie's first year.

The 1993 epic *Gettysburg* demonstrates, again in a Civil War setting, the valor and spiritual splendor of men in combat for causes they believe in with all their heart. In the cinematization of that most fateful of engagements, which turned the tide of the war in 1863, the most lasting image is the long hug that officers Jeff Daniels and C. Thomas Howell give each other at the end. Set off by their joy over their mutual survival, their male bonding is portrayed as something true and noble, platonic and innocent, and good—homoeroticism at its best and purest. One gets from that definitive scene an encapsulation of all that makes war so magnetic to so many men, despite its risks, its horrors, its wounds, and its many other traumas.

Great War Films tries to tell it all, and in all times and places and ambiences. For its author it was—profoundly, deeply, heart-wrenchingly—truly a labor of love. God bless you, buddies of my youth—I love you all.

GETTYSBURG   Jeff Daniels and Kevin Conway confer during the Little Round Top carnage.

THE FILMS

THE BIRTH OF A NATION   Black soldiers
battle a Klan raid.

1

THE BIRTH OF A NATION

D. W. GRIFFITH / HARRY E. AITKEN / EPOCH
PRODUCING CORP. (distributor)

1915

CAST:

Lillian Gish, Henry B. Walthall, Robert Harron, Mae
Marsh, Wallace Reid, Miriam Cooper, Donald Crisp,
Joseph Henabery, Raoul Walsh, Walter Long, Eugene
Pallette.

CREDITS:

D. W. Griffith, director; D. W. Griffith and Frank E.
Woods, screenplay; based on the novel *The Clansman*, by
Thomas Dixon; G. W. Bitzer, photographer. Running
time: 185 minutes.

D. W. Griffith's *The Birth of a Nation* remains one of
the most famous and influential motion pictures of
all time. It was the first great epic, and the film that
introduced many of the cinematic conventions we
take for granted today. And it is one that has been
steeped in controversy from its initial release right
up to the present day.

Birth of a Nation details the events before, during,

THE BIRTH OF A NATION   Mae Marsh looks solemn as Henry B.
Walthall displays his "banner."

and after the Civil War of 1861–65 and focuses on
two families—one Northern (the Stonemans) and
one Southern (the Camerons)—whose sons are
friends. Ben Cameron (Henry B. Walthall), known
as "The Little Colonel," falls for Elsie Stoneman
(Lillian Gish) just by looking at her picture; one of
the Stoneman boys, Phil (Robert Harron), also falls
for one of Ben's sisters, Margaret (Miriam Cooper)

But the love stories are secondary to the Civil
War action; *Birth of a Nation* features panoramic battle scenes employing thousands of extras who en-
gage in fighting in such a realistic manner that it
creates a near-documentary effect. Stoneman and
Cameron eventually meet as enemies on the battlefield, where the latter is badly wounded but suc-
cored by his new found friend, who writes to sister
Elsie, asking her to take special care of his pal in the
hospital where she is a nurse.

Cameron's reunion with his mother is touching,
as is an affecting scene when he finally comes back
home and greets his older sister on the doorstep;
the two feign a happy air at first, but eventually
both succumb to grateful tears. The assassination of
Lincoln at Ford's Theater on April 14, 1865, is
meticulously detailed. For many of the war scenes,
Griffith worked from photographs by Matthew
Brady and others to help recreate the settings and
action as authentically as possible.

The picture is initially choppy and episodic, but eventually the audience comes to know the characters and gets caught up in their stories.

The main problem with *Birth of a Nation* is that it has absolutely no perspective (thus giving it an almost comically dated quality), as it is told by Griffith—a native of the South—strictly from the Confederacy's point of view. Thus the scene that follows the title card "The master in chains before his former slaves" is not depicted as poetic justice but as the tragic downfall of a noble character (Ben Cameron, who later forms the Ku Klux Klan in response to Northern and carpetbagger-inspired Negro outrages).

The depiction of blacks in *Birth of a Nation* has always engendered much comment. On the one hand, the scenes of blacks rioting, breaking into houses, and disporting themselves in a disgraceful manner often seem disquietingly and shamefully contemporary. On the other hand, *Birth of a Nation* unmistakably suggests that the only "good blacks" are those who toe the line and remain loyal to their former masters. Virtually all of the black characters (most of whom are played by white actors in black-

THE BIRTH OF A NATION   The Little Colonel (Walthall) charges.

THE BIRTH OF A NATION   The Klan rides.

THE BIRTH OF A NATION   D.W. Griffith directs the action on the set.

THE BIRTH OF A NATION   Lincoln's assassination. Joseph Henabery as
Lincoln, slumped in box.

face) are negatively portrayed, and their Northern supporters are the worst kind of "guilty white liberals." Phil Stoneman's father is pleased to hear that his protégé, mulatto Silas Lynch, is going to marry a white woman. That is, until Stoneman learns that Lynch has designs on his own daughter—after which he is repulsed and furious. The final scenes show the "heroes" in their white hoods and raiment rushing to the rescue of the Camerons who are trapped in a cabin by crazed Negroes and Northerners. *Birth of a Nation* may be historically accurate in some respects, but it lacks *balance*.

The NAACP protested strongly against the film upon its release, and many in this era of political correctness would like to see it consigned to oblivion. Others, such as black filmmaker John Singleton (*Boyz N the Hood*), feel that *Birth of a Nation*'s artistic achievements override its political content. "It's like the Holocaust," Singleton has said. "We should never forget."—*W. S.*

THE BIRTH OF A NATION   Lee's Appomattox surrender to Grant. Donald Crisp as Grant, right, Lee: Howard Gaye seated, left.

2

HEARTS OF THE WORLD

PARAMOUNT / ARTCRAFT

1918

CAST:

Lillian Gish, Robert Harron, Dorothy Gish, Josephine Crowell, Jack Cosgrove, Adolphe Lestina, Kate Bruce, Ben Alexander, George Fawcett, George Siegmann.

CREDITS:

D. W. Griffith, director; D. W. Griffith (under an assumed name), screenplay; Billy Bitzer, photographer; James and Rose Smith, editors. Running time: 122 minutes.

Established as master of war movies, D. W. Griffith took on World War I in *Hearts of the World*. It was made at the request of the British government in 1917–18, and is as much a propaganda film as a

HEARTS OF THE WORLD   Lillian Gish on the battlefield.

drama, with much newsreel footage thrown in for good measure. But its leads (Robert Harron, Lillian Gish, and Dorothy Gish), its villain (George Siegmann), and an adorable child actor, Ben Alexander (who was to become a poignant, vulnerable soldier in *All Quiet on the Western Front* twelve years later), help greatly to put it over. And it also offers a glimpse of Noel Coward, age eighteen, pushing a wheelbarrow through a French village street.

As always in Griffith works, the battle and skirmish scenes are handled with consummate depth and force, and Bitzer's photography and James and Rose Smith's editing point up the locations—many of them authentic—shot in England and France, with later photography in Hollywood. Griffith's aptitudes with actors are also on impressive display, as he coaxes a winsome vulnerability from Lillian Gish; a manly, sensitive, but bewildered persona from Robert Harron; and a hoydenish *esprit* from Dorothy Gish, who plays a minxy type pursuing Harron, and whose title in the film (The "Little Disturber") was to be her trademark henceforth and largely shape her screen characterizations through the 1920s.

HEARTS OF THE WORLD   D. W. Griffith watches his war action on a screen.

HEARTS OF THE WORLD   D. W. confers with British soldiers.

HEARTS OF THE WORLD
Griffith (right) with
Dorothy and Lillian Gish,
abroad to make the film.

HEARTS OF THE WORLD   Getting input from officers as to
his movie "strategies."

HEARTS OF THE WORLD
Directing battle action
from an airplane at
camera with "crew"
and admiring officers
below.

Siegmann delivers in grand style as the "Bad German"; he is up to no good here—and in spades. Siegmann was to give Erich Von Stroheim a run for his money in "Bad German" parts. Even his name, "Von Strohm," was a takeoff on Von Stroheim's.

Griffith never made any bones of the fact the picture was designed to effect America's entry into the war: The project was conceived early in 1917, before the United States' engagement in the European fracas, and released in 1918, at the height of the war. The story deals with Harron, the son of an expatriate family living in France, just before the outbreak of war, next to another American family whose daughter is Lillian Gish. A romance develops between these two young people, but Dorothy Gish's high-spirited singer seeks to win Harron for herself, even though his heart is permanently Lillian's. (The romantic leads (Lillian Gish and Harron), are known throughout as "the Boy" and "the Girl.") Just as they are to marry, the war breaks out. Though he is an American, Harron feels he should enlist on principle, and joins the French army.

While Harron is off fighting, his family's village is

HEARTS OF THE WORLD   Little Ben Alexander salutes his beloved big brother, Robert Harron.

27

attacked and devastated by the Germans, and members of both expatriate families are killed. In a famous scene, Lillian, clutching her bridal gown, and deranged by her experiences, comes upon Harron—who lies seriously wounded. She sits beside him, and they spend in silence and terror (on her part) and oblivion (on his) what should have been their wedding night. When in the morning she looks for help, the Red Cross takes the wounded Harron away. She thinks him dead. Back in the village, the Little Disturber (Dorothy) now redeemed, nurses Lillian back to health.

Later, the Germans take over the village and make slave laborers of the inhabitants, including the Girl, while the Boy, who has recovered in a military hospital, becomes a spy behind German lines. He eventually makes his way back to the village in time to rescue the Lillian Gish character from a "fate worse than death" at the hands of a lustful German officer.

Such are the bones of the plot—but all is redeemed by Griffith's authoritative handling of the suspense and terror and unpredictability of war. Masterfully he guides Gish and Harron into sharp portrayals that, despite their conventional outlines, take on a poignant individuality. And the attack on the village, and other action scenes, are riveting.

Robert Harron, an actor close to Griffith during his early career, was a sensitive, handsome performer who died in 1920 in a mysterious shooting accident. He was only twenty-six. His work in *Hearts of the World,* and his other fine performances, keep him alive for audiences and commentators alike.

3

THE FOUR HORSEMEN OF THE APOCALYPSE

METRO

1921

CAST:

Rudolph Valentino, Alice Terry, Nigel de Brulier, Alan Hale, Jean Hersholt, Wallace Beery, Bowditch (Smoke) Turner, Beatrice Dominguez, John St. Polis.

CREDITS:

Rex Ingram, director; June Mathis, scenario; based on the novel by Vicente Blasco-Ibáñez; John F. Seitz, photographer. Running time: 150 minutes. (Later cut to 114 minutes.)

THE FOUR HORSEMEN OF THE APOCALYPSE   Rudolph Valentino wows all comers with his tango. Here with Pomeroy Cannon as his grandfather, and Beatrice Dominguez.

The Four Horsemen of the Apocalypse is most famous as the film that made twenty-five-year-old Rudolph Valentino a major star after some four years of also-ran Hollywood appearances. Much is made of the sensuous tango he made nationally popular and of the romantic aura he projected. But the film is also an eloquent preachment against war, the Four Horsemen of the title being War, Famine, Disease, and Death. In some brilliantly surreal scenes ably guided by director Rex Ingram and photographer John Seitz, they are seen side-by-side, running amuck. They are powerful symbols, these four horsemen, and they are used here with telling impact.

Valentino is first discovered as Julio, a spoiled, self-indulgent young man doted on by his grandfather, a rich Argentinian landowner who sees in the

handsome lad the spirit of his own lost youth. Julio
likes a good time: He dabbles lavishly in the proverbial wine, women, and song, and his tango dancing
is so sensuous and exciting that it incites the envy
of the males and the frantic desire of the females
watching.

His cousins are jealous of him. Of German blood
(his is French), they practice military games as they
sense war approaching. Though Julio expects to be
his grandfather's sole heir, when the old man dies
and the estate is divided between his two daughters
he receives less than his desired share. Fairly well-
off now, nevertheless, he drifts to Paris. He dabbles
in painting, dilettante-style, winding up teaching
the tango to various willing ladies in the
Montmartre cafés. One of his shticks during the
tango, snapping and looping a long whip with
which to draw an all-too-willing female to his side,
causes a sensation.

A deep, profound love comes to him then, in the
person of Marguerite Laurier (Alice Terry), a married woman whose husband later goes to the front
(World War I has broken out). But she later breaks
off with Julio, out of loyalty to her husband by then
blinded in battle. Julio then continues his cynical
approach to life, seeking pleasure and escape wher-

THE FOUR HORSEMEN OF THE APOCALYPSE   John St. Polis, outraged husband of Terry, glares at the trifling Valentino.

ever he can find it. Since he is an Argentine citizen, though half-French, he sees no call to duty in the French military. But when his beloved tearfully informs him that her husband has been returned to her blind, and he sees all the suffering the war has caused, his newfound hatred of the conflict causes him to enlist.

The picture is at its strongest and finest during the battle scenes, which director Rex Ingram has guided with the force and éclat that would have made D. W. Griffith proud of him—and doubtless did. A consummate irony is injected when Valentino's Julio finds himself facing one of his German cousins in a trench and dies at his relative's hand, all his dreams and hopes blasted away forever. It is right after Julio's demise that the apparition of the Four Horsemen appears yet again in the sky, masters of all they survey. War, Disease, Famine, and Death have prevailed.

The picture was a sensation in 1921, and all connected with it saw their careers vastly enhanced. Scenarist June Mathis, who reportedly was in love with Valentino though some years his senior, went all-out in her scenario to showcase him flatteringly, as did his friend Ingram's direction and Seitz's photography. Valentino is very much the star throughout—cynically exciting his female counterparts with his sensuous tango, dabbling at art in Paris,

THE FOUR HORSEMEN OF THE APOCALYPSE   The Germans take the village.

drinking his fill at the cafés, dissipating at every opportunity. And then his redemption comes, inspired by his love for Terry and his shocked awareness of what the horrors of war are doing to his Gallic friends. It is in eloquent contrast to the expected fate of the person he was before, even though in the end it brings him death. Valentino got all this across with great sensitivity and poignancy—and, though his looks and chemistry are largely credited for his stardom, in this and other films he demonstrated that he was an actor of range and virtuosity, an aspect of him that has for too long been played down.

THE FOUR HORSEMEN OF THE APOCALYPSE Sad partings. Valentino, with Bridgetta Clark, Josef Swickard, Virginia Warwick as his family.

31

4

AMERICA

D. W. GRIFFITH, INC. / UNITED ARTISTS

1924

CAST:

Neil Hamilton, Carol Dempster, Erville Alderson, Lionel Barrymore, Charles Emmett Mack, Lee Beggs, Frank McGlynn, Louis Wolheim.

CREDITS:

D. W. Griffith, director; Robert W. Chambers and John Pell, screenplay; based on the novel *The Reckoning*, by Chambers; Billy Bitzer, Hendrik Sartov, Marcel Le Picard, and Hal Sintzenich, photographers. Running time: 122 minutes (later shown at 95 minutes).

D. W. Griffith had long wanted to capture the sweep and excitement of the Revolutionary War in a film, and *America*, released in 1924, was the result. While critical opinion at the time of its release was divided, it has gained in stature in the seven decades since. As seen today, however, the picture during its first half seems to capture the breadth and prominent personages of the war but gets caught in a more narrow, localized story for the last half.

By 1924, Neil Hamilton had become Griffith's favorite male actor, and Griffith paired him with Carol Dempster, a young actress in whom he (D. W.) had taken a personal interest for some years. Lionel Barrymore was the villain of the piece. Also on hand were such powerhouse actors as Louis Wolheim, Charles Emmett Mack, and Frank McGlynn. Billy Bitzer, along with three other skilled and seasoned photographers, gave the picture sweep and variegated moods, with various locales caught truthfully and evocatively.

Acquiring the novel *The Reckoning*, by Robert W. Chambers (a well-known historical novelist of the day who dealt with just one phase of the war), D. W. expanded it to cover most of the war's major events and figures. But in the second half he more or less settled down to the Chambers story.

Lionel Barrymore is Capt. Walter Butler, a character based on a true figure, who incites the

AMERICA   Neil Hamilton and Carol Dempster have an encounter.

Iroquois Indians to raid the settlers who are Revolutionists. Griffith expanded on Butler's story, as told in Chambers's novel, and brought in more explicit and celebrated events of the time, such as the Lexington and Concord minutemen, Paul Revere's ride, Bunker Hill, George Washington at Valley Forge, and Patrick Henry's orations.

Introduced for film purposes was a romance between the lead, Neil Hamilton, and Tory scion Carol Dempster. Hamilton is a dispatch rider and message-carrier from Northern patriots who first meets Dempster in Virginia, and later at several significant

ninety-five minutes in subsequent releases. Critics felt that there was too much scurrying around, plot-wise, that the romance of Hamilton and Dempster had been dragged in by the heels, and that the lecherous, Indian-inciting Barrymore was too much the stock villain. But there was much praise for Griffith's capturing of the moods and ambiences of the period, and the battle scenes left nothing to be desired, executed as they were with Griffith's customary skill and imaginativeness.

events in Revolutionary War history. Hamilton is also maneuvered by the script into being present at Valley Forge with Washington, who later sends him with Morgan's Raiders to quell Indian uprisings incited by Barrymore's nasty Walter Butler. In the melodramatic second half, structurally more narrowed in focus, Barrymore threatens Dempster's virginity—but an imminent attack by the Indians, and the arrival of Morgan's Raiders to the rescue, deliver Dempster into Hamilton's arms.

The original running time to get across this rather turgid tale was 122 minutes; it wound up at about

AMERICA   Barrymore has designs on Dempster.

The Battle of Lexington is caught extremely well, with the men looking authentic in their uniforms and handling their weapons with historically accurate dispatch. Charles Emmett Mack is interestingly cast as the Tory brother of Dempster who turns Revolutionist and dies at Bunker Hill. Riley Hatch, as Indian Chief Joseph Brant, is another colorful character.

While not completely successful, *America* showcases Griffith at his best. His battle scenes have all

AMERICA   The battle rages.

the undiminished sweep and impact of his best work, and the rather implausible romance is sweetened by the appealing duo played by Hamilton and Dempster.

While some critics opined that Griffith was cart-ing out all his stock tricks, and had merely gone back three wars from the 1861–65 conflict to purvey them, *America* nevertheless highlights Griffith's special cinematic gifts.

AMERICA   Barrymore relishes the Indians' dancing.

5

THE BIG PARADE

METRO–GOLDWYN–MAYER

1925

CAST:

John Gilbert, Renée Adorée, Hobart Bosworth, Claire McDowell, Karl Dane, Tom O'Brien, Claire Adams.

CREDITS:

King Vidor, producer-director; Laurence Stallings and Harry Behn, screenplay; Joe Farnham, titles; John Arnold, photographer; Cedric Gibbons, art director;

THE BIG PARADE Tom O'Brien (left) and Karl Dane look on as Gilbert dozes.

THE BIG PARADE A tender scene with Gilbert and Renée Adorée.

William Axt and David Mendoza, music; Hugh Wynn, editor. Running time: 115 minutes.

The Big Parade is one of the greatest war films ever made. And it did for John Gilbert in 1925 what *The Four Horsemen of the Apocalypse* did for Rudolph Valentino in 1921: It made him a major star. The film is divided into two parts, and as seen today the second half surpasses the first. In the early reels we see the camaraderie and tomfoolery among the newly arrived American soldiers in France, their flirtations with the French girls of the villages where they are quartered enroute to the inevitable combat areas, and the growing romantic relationship between Gilbert's doughboy and Renée Adorée's pert village vixen. In one of the more charming and oft-mentioned scenes, Gilbert teaches Adorée how to chew gum.

All too soon the men are taken by truck to the front. Adorée hangs on desperately to the back of one, as if to defy time and fate, but the effort proves too much for her (a famous scene).

Then comes the truth of war as the green soldiers perceive it. It is hell and madness and futility, and Gilbert's expressive features are a mirror upon which its horrors are cast. The battle sequences are wonderfully fierce and brutal, and the contrast with the early, spring-like scenes is thereby accentuated, for in the Winter of War men change, or go mad, or suffer from wounds, or die—no springtime abides there.

King Vidor and cameraman John Arnold do not spare us in the later battle scenes. War is not glossed over; these are suffering and dying people we see. So accurately is the ambience recreated, so lifelike are the actors setting forth the griefs and horrors of combat—the tensions, the maddening waits, the hellish bursts of shellfire, the whistling bullets, the collapsing dugouts.

THE BIG PARADE   Gilbert, a pal
Harry Fleischmann (left), and
MP Ethan Laidlaw clown
with Adorée.

THE BIG PARADE   The famous
teaching-her-to-chew-gum-
scene.

In these scenes Gilbert is upfront, and there is no
trace of the dapper, but rather tame, leading man of
his earlier films. His "cute" mustache has been
shaved off, his face has been given a boyish naked-
ness and expressiveness with which to register a
variety of conflicting emotions—all of them negative. We see the fear in his expressive eyes, the
forced pride that insists he is a *man*, and as a *man*
will weather this somehow, some way—and also
on display is his disillusion, indeed his disgust, as
his lips curl and his eyes grow hooded. For a
blessed, timely *apathy* has come—an apathy that
carries him through the horrors, performing *rote* ac
tions, following *rote* instincts. Gilbert gets all this
across eloquently. He is not *acting* it; he is *living* it.
And it shows—piercingly, poignantly. If for this performance alone, John Gilbert should be counted
among the greatest actors of the screen.

The Big Parade won an even rarer accolade when
it was shown across the country; men who had actually been *there*, who *knew*, gave it their all-out
commendation, a fact that director King Vidor said
was his proudest memory—and greatest reward.

The final scene, when a crippled Gilbert struggles
to quicken his pace so that he can gather the over-
joyed Adorée into his arms, is also a memorable
episode, much admired to this day by museum and
film-school audiences.

The film is especially poignant for its revelations
of evolving character. The men who are so boyishly
playful and flirtatious with the village girls—like
happy, innocent children on a lark—in the later
episodes take on bleakly sober expressions, their

eyes mirroring the horrors they have witnessed,
their nerves and limbs shaking from reflex actions
in the face of cannon and machine-gun fire. Here
war is presented as the solemn business it is—and
King Vidor and company are not out to show it in
any other way, and don't.

The Big Parade was to win many accolades, in-

37

cluding the Photoplay Gold Medal for 1925. Had the Oscars been in existence at the time, it probably would have marched off with Academy statuettes, too. John Gilbert was to know an early death (in 1936), as did Valentino ten years before, but both actors live forever on film in roles in which they demonstrated impressive versatility and a great capacity for feeling.

THE BIG PARADE   As Dane lies wounded on O'Brien's lap, Gilbert cusses out the war.

6

WHAT PRICE GLORY

FOX

1926

CAST:

Victor McLaglen, Edmund Lowe, Dolores Del Rio, William V. Mong, Phyllis Haver, Elena Jurado, Leslie Fenton, Barry Norton, Sammy Cohen, Ted McNamara, Jack Pennick.

CREDITS:

Raoul Walsh, director; William Fox, producer; James T. O'Donohoe and Malcolm Stuart Boylan, screenplay; Barney McGill, Jack Marta and John Smith, photographers; William Darling, art director; Erno Rapee, music; Rose Smith, editor. Running time: 116 minutes.

WHAT PRICE GLORY   Victor McLaglen, Dolores Del Rio, and Edmund Lowe see trouble coming.

Laurence Stallings and Maxwell Anderson had coauthored the play *What Price Glory* that was a smash on Broadway in 1924. It made it to the screen in 1926 and was one of the biggest hits of the year. It centered around two characters, Sergeant Quirt (Edmund Lowe) and Captain Flagg (Victor McLaglen), who incessantly bicker half-humorously and half-seriously and find themselves vying for the same French village girl, Charmaine (Dolores Del Rio). Much was made of the uncensored oaths and strong language that passed between the two men. It was purveyed with raucous force and abandon in the play, and the film got away with its strong language because it was a silent one.

It was assumed that McLaglen's and Lowe's voiceless expletives would get drowned out by the background music anyway. But lip-readers around the country had a field day with the obscenities, and the boys got away with a surprising amount of it. This was just as well, because Flagg and Quirt were two tough, rough-and-tumble characters without whose language they wouldn't have been the same men. Of course, "respectable" people and bluenoses bleated—but not too loudly to spoil the fun.

The film was touted as Fox's answer to MGM's *The Big Parade*, which had opened the year before

WHAT PRICE GLORY   McLaglen indulges in a moment of affectionate badinage with Del Rio.

and was still playing to capacity audiences through 1926. But *Glory* was a bird of a different feather—more racy and raunchy, and (to at least some viewers) more realistic.

Raoul Walsh and company got across the "war is hell" message tellingly, however, because after the Far East business at the beginning—featuring an electric Phyllis Haver as the wild and woolly "Shanghai Mabel"—and the Flagg-Quirt-Charmaine scenes, the director and crew get down to the dirty business of war. And a dirty mess it was, with bombs bursting, realistic trench warfare and bayonetings, cannon fire, men being wounded, men dying, men working up a sweat in the ominous (and sometimes protracted) interludes between hell-breaking-loose action.

One often-discussed shot shows a long trench caving in after a bomb explodes. Silent film or not, one tends to imagine hearing in this sequence the terrified screams and shouts of the soldiers who disappear beneath the debris and smoke.

Although one critic commented that the grim war scenes contrast awkwardly with—and indeed go against—the humorous tone set by the first half, the truth is that *The Big Parade,* with which this film was often unfavorably compared, had a lot more comic relief and lighthearted dallying. Nonetheless, the combination of humor and tragedy in *What Price Glory* does seem offputting to some. There is a surprising scene later in the film when McLaglen's hard-boiled Captain Flagg reacts with a serious, sober, rough compassion to the death of a young "Mama's boy" under his command. Here McLaglen by his expression gets across his sense of the savage

WHAT PRICE GLORY   The soldiers march off to war.

WHAT PRICE GLORY   The soldiers reflected
in the village street.

WHAT PRICE GLORY After the battle, survivors Leslie Fenton, Lowe, and McLaglen help the wounded.

the human spirit tested in the ultimate crucible of war.

7

WINGS

PARAMOUNT

1927

CAST:

Charles Rogers, Richard Arlen, Clara Bow, Jobyna Ralston, Gary Cooper, Henry B. Walthall, Roscoe Karns, Gunboat Smith, Richard Tucker, El Brendel, Julia Swayne Gordon, Arlette Marchal.

CREDITS:

William A. Wellman, director; Lucien Hubbard, producer; Hope Loring and Louis D. Lighton, screenplay; based on a story by John Monk Saunders; Harry Perry, photographer; Julian Johnson, titles; Lucien Hubbard, editor. Running time: 139 minutes.

waste of war and the manner in which it randomly afflicts the innocent and gentle.

The picture holds the attention throughout, and has a number of effective war scenes and fine performances which have not in the least become dated. Antiwar aspects are highlighted in a number of affecting scenes, and the 1917–18 period is captured faithfully—although in 1926, "Hollywood-isms" sometimes marred the product. Not so here.

McLaglen gives the audience a full-rounded character. He is raucous, humorous, cynical, tough, and businesslike, taking himself quite seriously—and making of himself a fitting butt of Lowe's ridicule and putdowns and one-upmanship techniques. Yet both men reveal their humanity, and their reservoirs of spiritual depth and compassion (of a virile, nonsentimental kind, however) under the stresses of war. Dolores Del Rio is charming and spirited as Charmaine, the French girl, and Phyllis Haver makes something memorable of Shanghai Mabel, the foil for the guys in the early Far East sequences.

Most critics today think of *What Price Glory* (which was remade—by John Ford, 26 years later) and *The Big Parade* (which wasn't) as being "apples and oranges," both outstanding in their own right and both demonstrating the depth and potential of

Played out against a backdrop of World War I, *Wings* is essentially a love story—between two men. Jack (Charles "Buddy" Rogers) is the handsome small-town "boy next door" who seems oblivious to the charms of his pretty neighbor, Mary (Clara Bow). David (Richard Arlen), the town "rich kid," is all too aware of the charms of visitor-from-the-city Sylvia (Jobyna Ralston)—and so is Jack, to Mary's dismay. When war breaks out, both boys join the Army Air Corps, hoping to become fliers. Jack takes Sylvia's picture with him, unaware it was meant for David, while poor Mary thinks Jack is wearing her picture on the chain around his neck.

During basic training the two rivals become good friends, but only after Jack nearly beats the stuffing out of David in a boxing match. "Boy—you're game!" Jack declares when he sees how a wearied, bloodied David just refuses to give in. The two men walk off as buddies, with Jack tenderly wiping the blood off David's face.

Before long both men are on flying missions at the front, engaging in deadly dogfights with an evil German ace, Count von Kellermann (who is por-

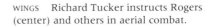

trayed as a hilarious, sneering caricature by stunt flier Frank Clarke), and his men. Meanwhile, Mary—who has joined the Women's Motor Transport Corps—helps to get a drunken Jack out of a difficult situation in Paris, although he's too blitzed to know it's she who is doing that favor.

WINGS   Roscoe Karns, Tucker, Rogers, and El Brendel decipher a certain message.

Later, David's plane is shot down and he is believed dead. When Jack learns of this, he becomes hysterical and takes to the air on a one-man mission to wipe out as many German "bastards" as he can. Unfortunately, he doesn't know that David survived his crash and has managed to commandeer a German aircraft, in which he is flying out of enemy territory. Spotting David's plane, a still-crazed Jack assumes it's the foe, and fires at his buddy. There follows the now-famous sequence during which Jack learns whom he has actually shot down, and cradles his dying friend in his arms, stroking and kissing him as he cries in guilt and remorse.

Wings is a fine picture with many memorable moments: Clara Bow's touching goodbye to her unrequited lover as he goes off to war; the poignant scene in Paris when she finds Sylvia's picture, rather than her own, in Jack's locket; David's farewell to his elderly parents—which is admittedly manipulative but nevertheless heartbreaking; and the ending, which contrasts the joy of Jack's heroic homecoming with the grief of David's parents and girlfriend. A positive aspect at the end of the film has Jack finally realizing that Mary is indeed the girl for him, and the two are happily reunited.

WINGS   Bow pensively observes the warm camaraderie of Rogers and Arlen.

Wings' battle scenes are also spectacular: the graphic and harrowing aerial combat that achieves almost a documentary feel; Jack's desperate crawl through the British trenches; the rather balletic

43

WINGS   Aerial warfare rages.

WINGS   Rogers warns Karns (right) not to monitor his dispute with Arlen.

death movements of massacred foot soldiers; and such grim details as the scene in which one soldier shoves another he thinks has stopped for a smoke, only to have him fall over dead. The attack on the massive German dirigibles is also exciting, and the aerial photography throughout is considered outstanding to this day.

Another good scene occurs early in the picture, stateside, and features Gary Cooper as a generally more experienced and particularly fatalistic cadet. When he dies in an accident before they even get overseas, David and Jack begin to realize, as they somberly go through his effects, that this is no game they are playing.

The later scenes with Clara Bow seem plugged in to give the "It" girl maximum exposure, but—aside from the dubious moments of comedy relief (she's a terrible driver)—these sequences at least make the most of the romantic angle.

Although *Wings* has been criticized for its slight storyline, the excellence of the acting and direction (and the production values) help the viewer to get caught up in the lives of these at-best-two-dimensional characters. The "love" scenes between Jack and David have raised eyebrows over these increasingly sophisticated years, but it must be remembered that in films of this period, male friendships often were innocently delineated with as much, if not more, "passion" as were relationships between men and women (*Flesh and the Devil*, another 1927 film, with a strong "male-bonding" relationship between John Gilbert and Lars Hanson, being a case in point).—*W. S.*

WINGS   Rogers senses danger.

8

ALL QUIET ON THE WESTERN FRONT

1930

CAST:

Lew Ayres, William Bakewell, Louis Wolheim, Slim Summerville, Russell Gleason, Ben Alexander, John Wray, Raymond Griffith, Beryl Mercer.

CREDITS:

Lewis Milestone, director; Carl Laemmle, Jr., producer; Maxwell Anderson, Lewis Milestone, Del Andrews, and George Abbott, screenplay; based on the novel by Erich Maria Remarque; Arthur Edeson, Karl Freund and Tony Gaudio, photographers; David Broekman, music; Edgar Adams and Milton Carruth, editors. Original running time: 140 minutes. Current running time: 130 minutes.

The greatest of pacifist, antiwar movies, director Lewis Milestone's *All Quiet on the Western Front* purveyed in 1930 a message that over sixty years later does not date: war is a savage, futile exercise which should long have been eliminated from the policy of all nations worldwide.

Based on the memorable novel by Erich Maria Remarque, *All Quiet* makes its points with chilling accuracy and poignant truth. War is portrayed here not as a glamorous, patriotic, gung-ho enterprise but as a brutal destroyer of the hopes of youths and a chilling compromise of the honor of nations. Some of the dialogue and situations on the subject of war ring true even now. As one disillusioned, battle-hardened soldier (Louis Wolheim) puts it: "At the next war let all the Kaisers, Presidents,

ALL QUIET ON THE WESTERN FRONT   Ayres contemplates his dead French counterpart, whose death he has caused.

ALL QUIET ON THE WESTERN FRONT Wolheim and Slim Summerville offer a moment of levity.

ALL QUIET ON THE WESTERN FRONT Ayres with ZaSu Pitts as his mother. Preview audiences laughed at "Zany ZaSu" making tragic, so Beryl Mercer was rushed into the part.

Generals, and diplomats go into a big field and fight it out first among themselves. That will satisfy us and keep us at home." The young soldier-hero, Paul (played touchingly and truthfully by Lew Ayres), says at one point, "We live in the trenches out there. We fight. We try not to be killed, but sometimes we are. That's all."

Told from the German side in World War I, *All*

Quiet on the Western Front graphically and unsentimentally describes war in all its terror and purposelessness from the point of view of seven Germans—each young, pliable, and impressionable—who are inspired to fight by a jingoistic schoolmaster and enlist to the sound of martial music and the sight of flags flying and crowds cheering. But combat brings no glory, no heroism—only wounds, death, and utter destruction all around them.

Lew Ayres comes home on leave to find his fellow townsmen still caught up in the "glorious fight for the Fatherland" unreality, and sets his former schoolmaster and his green students straight by telling them what war really is like. He then returns to the trenches, and in a memorable final scene, exhausted by terror and boredom, reaches out to a butterfly—only to be shot and killed. This poignant yet graphic scene concentrates on the hand as it reaches out, trembles as it registers the shot, and finally lies still.

Among the many touching scenes is Ayres's visit

46

to his dying buddy (played affectingly and boyishly by Ben Alexander) who lies in a hospital in pain, facing his imminent demise. Because one of his visiting comrades craves Alexander's new boots, Ayres brings them to him after Alexander's death. The warm affection between Ayres and Alexander, and Ayres's grief over his buddy's plight, are gotten across with considerable sensitivity. A later scene, the one in which Wolheim, the gruff veteran, is wounded and Ayres tries to carry him on his shoulders to safety as enemy planes strafe them, only to realize, when he lays him down, that the older soldier has succumbed, is also gotten across powerfully.

All of the soldiers are portrayed to perfection, with individual types limned compellingly and truthfully. Russell Gleason, William Bakewell, Ben Alexander, and Slim Summerville are especially outstanding. Lew Ayres in real life became a firm pacifist after making this film, and although he was a conscientious objector during World War II, he joined the medics, and distinguished himself heroically in his combat zones.

Bakewell and Ayres formed a lifetime friendship after making that picture together. Before his death in spring 1993, after a close association that had lasted over sixty years, Bakewell described his experiences with Alexander, Gleason, and Ayres, both in the film and in later life, as "male bonding in the finest sense of the phrase—and we learned it all from that wonderful picture!"

One interesting side note: ZaSu Pitts was originally cast as Ayres's mother, who received him on her invalid's bed when he returned on leave—but the preview audience laughed when she appeared (she was associated with comic, zany, hand-fluttering roles), so Beryl Mercer was called in to replace her.

All Quiet on the Western Front won the Academy Award as best picture, and Lewis Milestone—who, one critic enthused, directed it "in a manner reminiscent of Eisenstein and Lang"—was similarly honored. It received several other Oscar nominations, too, as well as the Photoplay Gold Medal for 1930, and other distinguished awards. *Variety*'s review of the film in 1930 deserves quoting in part: "Nothing passed up for the niceties; nothing glossed over for the women. Here exhibited is war as it is, butchery. The League of Nations could make no better investment than to buy up the master print, reproduce it in every language to be shown to every nation every year until the word war is taken out of the dictionaries."

9

JOURNEY'S END

1930

CAST:

Colin Clive, David Manners, Billy Bevan, Anthony Bushell, Robert Adair, Ian MacLaren, Charles Gerrard, Thomas Whitely, Jack Pitcairn, Werner Klinger.

CREDITS:

James Whale, director; George Pearson, producer; Joseph Moncure March and Gareth Gundrey, screenplay; from the play by R. C. Sheriff; Benjamin Kline, photographer; Hervey Libbert, art director; Claude Berkeley, editor. Running time: 120 minutes.

Journey's End (1930) was made from a successful London play of the year before. The film, a joint Anglo-American production in Hollywood because

JOURNEY'S END Colin Clive (center) and comrades Billy Bevan, Charles Gerrard, Anthony Bushell, enjoy a light moment in the midst of battle pressures.

the talkie equipment there was more advanced, tells a harrowing story of tensions among officers and men, and the stresses of fighting and dying in the trenches of 1917 France. It made an instant (and short-lived) star of Colin Clive, who headlined the London and New York stage production after an up-and-coming Laurence Olivier turned it down. Perhaps too restrained and "Britishified" for Hollywood and trans-America tastes, *Journey's End* still packs a dramatic wallop, even though today it looks primitive technologically, and the acting belongs to an era when restraint, allied to a contradictory projection (explosiveness), kept audiences off-balance.

Clive is unique and distinctive as Captain Stanhope, who presides over a grim, womanless terrain—there are no women *anywhere* in the picture, and no "civilian" scenes. His mission is to keep his men in line and fighting effectively. Stanhope is a veteran officer, three years in the trenches and holder of a Military Cross for valor. He deals with the varying temperaments of his men in an authoritative yet psychologically aware manner. Whether taking Lieutenant Hibbert over the coals for his cowardice (Anthony Bushell plays Hibbert sensitively) or expressing his distaste for Lieutenant Raleigh (David Manners), a fellow Oxonian whom

he does not feel qualified for trench warfare, Clive is nervously, electrically compelling. When he declares in high dudgeon that there were "eighteen hundred other companies" to which the detested Raleigh could have been assigned, he is angry indeed. There is a hint of some ancient schoolboy interaction of a mysterious nature between Stanhope and Raleigh, but the matter is never explored, it being tight-lipped, reticent, inhibited 1930.

Some critics felt that the styles of the actors, and indeed the approach in general, were too restrained in the British manner, but the chin-up, old-school-tie, fight-and-die-like-a-man posturings were praised by other commentators as authentic evocations of the time and its human ambience.

The movie is, of course, more successful than the play at depicting the war action that follows, and that is fierce and brutal. Raleigh is involved in an over-the-trenches raid that is gutsy and taut, as his men cut barbed wire along the post-and-wire-strewn No Man's Land, then advance to offensive positions, with the Germans whizzing machine-gun bullets at them. All this culminates in Raleigh's fatal hand-to-hand encounter with an enemy soldier. When Raleigh stumbles back to the dugout and dies in Stanhope's arms, the look of despair and futility in the latter's gaze tells it all.

As in the play, there is a strong theatrical aura to the conclusion: As the explosions proliferate, the screen turns ever darker, and finally the only sign of life is a flickering candle. There is another strong explosion, and the candle goes out. It is obvious that all have perished.

Clive, who was to go on with Whale to do *Frankenstein* the next year—after which he remained in Hollywood to specialize in neurotic, sadistic types—should have been launched into permanent stardom, so good is his performance in *Journey's End*. But something unpleasant, perverse, and odious in his personality (which suited some of his later parts perfectly) deprived him of the ultimate accolade from fans. Character player he remained until his untimely death in 1937.

Clive has many small vignettes in *Journey's End* that underline his characterizational skills: trying to make a man out of the pusillanimous Bushell; recoiling from Raleigh (a love-hate interplay is strongly suggested); and expressing a self-aware humility in admitting at one point that he is scared, too, but downs whiskey in sufficient quantities to quiet his fears.

David Manners and Anthony Bushell are effective in their roles, and Billy Bevan, as the humorous cockney, Trotter, gives the show whatever levity and relaxed moments it has—albeit of that peculiarly British kind.

10

THE DAWN PATROL

1930 and 1938 Versions

WARNER BROS.   1930

CAST:

Richard Barthelmess, Douglas Fairbanks, Jr., Neil Hamilton, William Janney, James Finlayson, Clyde Cook, Edmund Breon, Frank McHugh, Werner Klinger.

CREDITS:

Howard Hawks, director; Robert North, producer; John Monk Saunders, screenplay; based on the story *Flight Commander*, by John Monk Saunders; Ernest Haller, pho-

tographer; Leo Forbstein, music; Ray Curtiss, editor. Running time: 90 minutes.

WARNER BROS.   1938

CAST:

Errol Flynn, Basil Rathbone, David Niven, Melville Cooper, Donald Crisp, Barry Fitzgerald, Carl Esmond, Peter Willes, Michael Brooke.

CREDITS:

Edmund Goulding, director; Hal B. Wallis, producer; Seton I. Miller and Dan Totheroh, screenplay; Tony Gaudio, photographer; Max Steiner, music; Ralph Dawson, editor. Running time: 103 minutes.

The Dawn Patrol deals with a standard British fighter squadron. The title indicates the situation basic to this World War I service story. So many fighter pi-

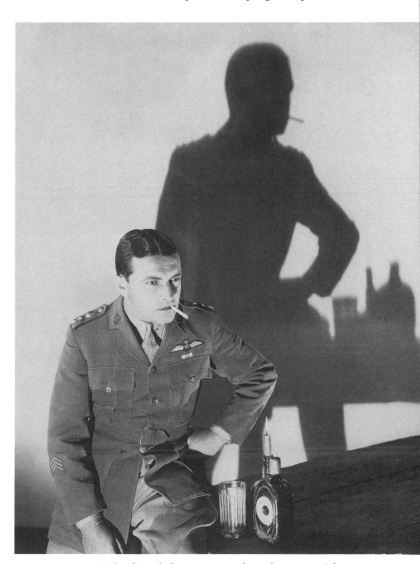

THE DAWN PATROL   Richard Barthelmess contemplates the next aerial engagement.

THE DAWN PATROL Werner Klinger (left) and Barthelmess are obviously headed for a confrontation that Edmund Breon and Neil Hamilton want to prevent.

THE DAWN PATROL A glum and saddened commander, Hamilton (second right) gives the men their orders. Douglas Fairbanks, Jr., is in the center.

THE DAWN PATROL British planes strafe the enemy.

lots are killed in action that new detachments (usually of younger, untried men) are constantly called up to replace them—to the dismay of the flight commander, played by Neil Hamilton, who takes his mission very seriously and deplores the shocking loss of lives.

The Hamilton character tries to instill disciplined methods in his men, stressing over and over that careful handling of the flights will not only implement better fighting techniques but also bring more of the fliers home in safety. Hence he finds it difficult to tolerate what he castigates as schoolboy larking in a deadly serious battle of aerial wits be-

50

tween determined Germans and cavalier Englishmen.

The picture opens rather talkily, with combat action, flying and navigating techniques, and the ethics and attitudes behind them consuming much footage unnecessarily. Part of this is due to Saunders's script as well as Hawks's direction, for in 1930, which was only the second year of the talkies, moviemakers were still unduly enthralled with human voices and wanted the actors to strut their stuff with lots of dramatic as well as expository dialogue.

But when the action finally comes, it is fast and furious, with the aerial combat scenes so effective and excitingly dynamic that they were used again in the 1938 Errol Flynn–Basil Rathbone–David

THE DAWN PATROL   Helping a wounded comrade.

Niven remake directed by Edmund Goulding. Since Goulding was primarily a "woman's director" whose talents lent themselves better to the delineation of complex emotions, masculine as well as feminine, he seems a poor choice for the remake of *The Dawn Patrol*, which was Hawks's material and métier from the word go. If the 1938 version looks better and flows more felicitously it is because the eight-year difference saw movies become more fluid, more supple, more handsomely photographed, and more painstakingly produced. But whether with Hawks or Goulding, those aerial action shots, shrewdly integrated into the 1938 version with a "planing" process so that they could approximate Tony Gaudio's rich photographic hues and nuances do pay off. (Oddly, Ernest Haller, photographer of the 1930 version, was later to outdo Gaudio in showcasing women stars to advantage, as notably in the case of Bette Davis.)

In the later version, Errol Flynn and David Niven seemed more larkish and daredevilish than did

51

THE DAWN PATROL   Action in the skies.

THE DAWN PATROL Basil Rathbone lectures David Niven and Errol Flynn on their larkish approach to war.

THE DAWN PATROL Donald Crisp (left) and Flynn (second right) try to keep the boys Carl Esmond, Peter Willes calmed down.

THE DAWN PATROL Flynn and Niven lark with director Edmund Goulding on the soundstage.

Barthelmess and Fairbanks in the 1930 original. Though Fairbanks was only twenty when he made the first *Dawn Patrol,* he had already taken on a premature manly seriousness that especially Niven had not yet arrived at, though much older. Basil Rathbone, though perhaps somewhat miscast as the 1938 commander, did get across, as well as Hamilton in the earlier version, the grief that a man in his post inevitably was to feel over and over when so many of the men he assigned did not come back.

Hamilton's commander is a very serious guy indeed. He knows that war is hell and *not* a schoolboy lark, so when Barthelmess and Fairbanks, whose egos have been affronted by German taunts on their aerial professionalism, spend more than the requisite time raining machine-gun fire on hapless Germans, and dropping more bombs than are needed to do the job, and then return with self-satisfied smirks on their faces, he lets them have it in no uncertain terms. After that, everybody gets more serious about the matters at hand—everybody who survives, that is.

In both versions the points are gotten across, and the integrity of Saunders's original vision is maintained. Stills from both the 1930 and 1938 versions are included in the accompanying photo layout because they demonstrate both the difference eight years made in photographic "polishing," and the manner in which the Saunders concept proves more important than the individual actors putting it across—granted, however, that a lush and lavish Max Steiner score gives the 1938 version yet another edge on the earlier film.

11

HELL'S ANGELS

UNITED ARTISTS—HOWARD HUGHES

1930

CAST:

Ben Lyon, James Hall, Jean Harlow, John Darrow, Lucien Prival, Roy Wilson, Douglas Gilmore, F. Schumann-Heink, Jane Winton, Wyndham Standing.

CREDITS:

Howard Hughes and James Whale, directors; Howard Hughes, producer; Howard Estabrook and Harry Behn, screenplay; from a story by Marshall Neilan and Joseph Moncure March; Tony Gaudio, Harry Perry, and E. Burton Steene, photographers; Hugo Reisenfeld, music; Frank Lawrence, Douglass Biggs, and Perry Hollingworth, editors. Running time: 135 minutes.

More than six decades after its making, *Hell's Angels* remains a classic among war films, even though it is equally renowned for making a star out of saucy, sexy, brazen Jean Harlow—whose famous line, when bedroom-vamping one of the heroes, is "Would you be shocked if I put on something more comfortable?"

Harlow and her dynamite charms aside, the picture is about two brothers, Roy and Monte Rutledge, who go from Oxford into the flying corps during World War I. James Hall (Roy) is a manly, idealistic youth with firm character and a true commitment to his duties. Ben Lyon (Monte) is a playboy and roustabout whose incessant, mountebanking mischief back at the university has not rendered him conducive to, let alone fit for, military service. They run afoul of society-girl Harlow, who plays

HELL'S ANGELS The aerial action becomes fast and furious.

both brothers against each other, though neither winds up with her on any permanent basis. A heartless trifler with men, always in search of the next man and the excitements *he* may represent, the Harlow character is no one any sensible military man (or civilian, for that matter) should be dallying with.

Soon it's away from Harlow and her drawing (and bed) rooms and on to the aerial combat, with the brothers combatting ominous-looking German dirigibles and shooting down enemy aircraft. On a suicide mission, they are captured and subject to the not-so-tender mercies of sinister German commandant Lucien Prival. Eventually Hall is forced to kill Lyon, to prevent him from revealing important strategic secrets. Prival then sends Hall off to the firing squad, grief-stricken over his brother but convinced he has committed a justifiable homicide in order to prevent dissemination of information that would cost the lives of many more comrades.

Such is the plot—but it is what Hughes and his crew do with it that makes *Hell's Angels* a perennial (and memorable) movie experience. The film was three years, on and off, in the making, initially as a

54

HELL'S ANGELS   It's time for action in the skies, hence the briefing. Roy Wilson (bald), Hall, Lyon, William B. Davidson.

silent beginning in 1927 and with Greta Nissen in the Harlow role. By 1929 sound had arrived, and Nissen's accent made her unacceptable, so Harlow, who had been languishing in small parts up to then, was drafted—though it is doubtful if her rather harsh and strident Americanese fitted anyone's conception of an English society girl.

The wonderfully-staged aerial dogfights, the masterly depiction of German zeppelin raids over London, and the boys' planes in actual combat with formidable dirigibles are alternated with shots of Oxford life (early in the film, when the brothers are students there) and a ball scene, the latter photographed in color—Hughes was determined to get everything but the kitchen sink into his pet ($4 million) film; $4 million being the equivalent of a 1990s film expenditure of, say, $100 million. The battle scenes are sometimes tinted in red hues that blur; the ball sequences (in two-color Technicolor) do not seem to sync with black-and-white ones; the general photographic effect is awkwardly varied— though the aerial scenes are so graphic and powerful that no one could quarrel with *those*. (The first officer of one of the zeppelins, incidentally, was played by the son of the great singer Ernestine Schumann-Heink.)

HELL'S ANGELS   An exciting ad for *Hell's Angels*.

One film critic of 1930 summed up the proceedings pretty well with this assessment: "It is not great, but it is as lavish as an eight-ring circus, and when you leave the theatre you will know you have seen a movie and not a tinny reproduction of a stage show."

55

HELL'S ANGELS   Harlow is driving the boys up the wall.

12

TODAY WE LIVE

METRO–GOLDWYN–MAYER

1933

CAST:

Joan Crawford, Gary Cooper, Robert Young, Franchot Tone, Roscoe Karns, Louise Closser Hale, Hilda Vaughn, Rollo Lloyd.

CREDITS:

Howard Hawks, producer-director; Dwight Taylor and Edith Fitzgerald, screenplay; based on the story "Turnabout," by William Faulkner; Oliver T. Marsh, photographer; Cedric Gibbons, art director; Edward Curtiss, editor. Running time: 115 minutes.

Though Hughes waxed ambivalent about James Whale's contribution, at one time demoting him publicly to "dialogue director," Whale (later famed for his horror movies at Universal) actually wrote and directed a great deal of the picture.

The main selling point of this movie is, and always will be, the great aerial sequences, which reflected Hughes's lifelong interest in, and passion for, aviation pursuits. His dedication pays off here, for *Hell's Angels*, even all these years later, has the emotional tension and persuasiveness of a classic labor-of-love.

James R. Quirk of *Photoplay*, the dean of film commentators in 1930, called *Hell's Angels* "masterly, compelling, a breakthrough in filming techniques."

A 1933 war picture with JOAN CRAWFORD in it? Along with a banal explication in plot terms of the title as a takeoff on the old military saw "Today we live—tomorrow we die," the implication is also set forth that a day (or night) with Miss Crawford is more than worth an eternity in an unmarked military grave—a questionable hypothesis but one millions of 1933-era Crawford admirers were willing to buy. Even in a war picture where the men—the likes of Gary Cooper and Franchot Tone—were supposed to be stealing the scenes with an assortment of military heroics. Miss Crawford takes her own peculiar liberties with the theme (sporting 1933 styles in a 1917 ambience, for instance), but she does not handicap the mainline preceedings, really. Indeed, in her own way she enhances them by providing some convincing home-fires-burning histrionics.

As uppercrust English playgirl (some critics didn't think Crawford an English type, but no matter), Crawford loves American aviator Gary Cooper even though she has a "romantic" understanding with British naval officer Robert Young. When Cooper is reported killed in aerial action, Crawford resumes with Young, though her brother (Franchot Tone) disapproves, questioning her sincerity. Then Cooper turns out not to be dead after all. The "romancing," such as it is, then transpires among the

three men (Young, Cooper, and Tone), who indulge in friendly sea-versus-air rivalries, sparked by Cooper's taking the other two for what is called "a daredevil sky ride." Tone impresses Cooper by taking him to sea on his motor launch, which he has equipped with torpedoes. Some hot and heavy sea and air action transpires, with Cooper sold at last on the equity, value wise, of sea and air.

Young, meanwhile, is blinded in action. He and Tone know that Crawford actually loves Cooper, and are determined that he shall not sacrifice—or rather jeopardize—his life yet another time. When Cooper volunteers for a dangerous air mission that involves the sinking of an enemy ship, Tone and Young (blind or no) set out to sea in *their* vessel and dispatch *that* vessel before Cooper can get to it. Of course they sacrifice both their lives in this magnanimous, albeit ill-advised, effort. So Cooper gets Crawford, and all is well—until, it is assumed, Cooper gets a daredevil yen for more heroics.

Such is the plot, and all this action and combat and bombing and hell-raising for the love of a woman—even a woman such as Miss Joan Crawford—seems unduly busy and frenetic. But the surprise of the picture is that Crawford's romantic posturings in her Adrian gowns actually play distinct second-fiddle to all the male bonding

TODAY WE LIVE
Cooper and Karns
returning Young to
Joan Crawford.

and buddy stuff and action heroics—thus constituting the only Joan Crawford picture on record that substitutes homoerotic attachments, for large stretches, for Joan-as-Target-of-Male-Romantic-Addressals. And this begs the question of why Crawford accepted such an essentially thankless role in what is obviously a men-and-war opus.

All matters of this conundrum aside, the action scenes are first-rate as directed by man's-director Howard Hawks, and photographically limned most strikingly by veteran cameraman Oliver Marsh. The three boys (Tone, Cooper, and Young) seem at their enthusiastic best when not forced to play moths to the Crawford flame, and get into the action stuff with great verve and éclat.

The air-and-sea bombing and other action scenes are really top-drawer, and Hawks makes them pay off. There is much clever crosscutting by Marsh and his editor, Edward Curtiss, and some of the scenes are harrowing in the best action tradition. The basic story orignated with William Faulkner, with Edith Fitzgerald and Dwight Taylor supplying the screenplay.

One critic wound up his summation of the film amusingly with the observation: "[The film] devotes most of its efforts to permitting Robert Young and Franchot Tone to destroy themselves gallantly so that Gary Cooper may henceforth live happily with Miss Joan Crawford. It was my suspicion that their sacrifice was too great." Gary Cooper looked ill-at-ease in the Crawford clinches, and in top form

TODAY WE LIVE   Crawford contemplates brother Tone's eventual fate in war.

and spirits in the male-bonding action heroics, which is understandable enough, given the situations.

13

THE ROAD TO GLORY

20TH CENTURY–FOX

1936

CAST:

Fredric March, Warner Baxter, Lionel Barrymore, June Lang, Gregory Ratoff, Victor Killian, Paul Stanton, John Qualen, Julius Tannen, Theodore Von Eltz, Paul Fix, Leonid Kinskey, Jacques Vanaire, Edythe Raynere, George Warrington.

CREDITS:

Howard Hawks, director; Darryl F. Zanuck, producer; Joel Sayre and William Faulkner, screenplay; based on a story by Sayre and Faulkner; Gregg Toland, photographer; Hans Peters, art director; Louis Silvers, music; Edward Curtiss, editor. Running time: 103 minutes.

The Road To Glory gives insight into the combat methods and approaches of the French in World War I, and is compellingly cast with the likes of Fredric March, Warner Baxter, and Lionel Barrymore. Baxter is the battle-hardened and weary commander of the 39th Regiment of the French army (a unit founded by Napoleon) who has become saddened and disillusioned by sending repeated waves of young soldiers to die on the battlefield. March is an initially carefree and pleasure-seeking young officer who becomes sobered and mature under the stresses of such combat. Barrymore is Baxter's father, a Franco-Prussian war veteran who insists on enlisting as a private under his son's command even though their relations are not of the best.

Then there is June Lang, a nurse caught in a tri-angle with Baxter and March, but who ends up with the latter. William Faulkner and Joel Sayre coauthored the script, which approaches war in a realistic rather than romantic way; and Howard Hawks, an old hand at this kind of subject matter, gets across all the terror and sleaze and tension of war in his usual expert style.

Most of the plot line concerns the elderly Barrymore character's relationship with his son the commander. When Barrymore falters in action, with the resultant loss of lives, Baxter, who had never wanted him in his unit, is angered. The Baxter character is later wounded and hospitalized. Blinded, and with his chastened father's help, he works his way back to an outpost, where both die while directing artillery fire against the Germans.

Little vignettes of war are tellingly introduced: Baxter effects a mercy killing on a soldier dying in agony; soldiers listen tensely to the noise of German tunnelers planting mines that will eventually blow up these hapless auditors; Baxter talks with rueful sadness to a fresh wave of recruits he knows will die in action.

THE ROAD TO GLORY Fredric March and Warner Baxter plan the upcoming strategy.

59

THE ROAD TO GLORY June Lang tries to offer Baxter comfort amid his command stresses.

March gets across powerfully the growing maturity of an initially immature character who hardens under fire and learns the assorted skills and techniques of survival, both as a soldier and as a man. Baxter, who won one of the first Academy Awards (for *In Old Arizona*), has always been an underrated actor, and in his incisive, insightful portrayal of the commander who has seen too many men suffer and die and knows chillingly the ultimate cost of war, he was never in better form. Lionel Barrymore etches one of his top characterizations as the very overaged private who "cops out" initially and then redeems himself splendidly.

Many of the soldiers in the French regiment are brought vividly to life by superb character actors: Gregory Ratoff is humorous and sanguine; Victor Killian his usual rueful self; Paul Stanton intrepid as the relief captain; John Qualen touching. Leonid Kinskey, Theodore Von Eltz, and George Warrington are also most effective.

Faulkner and his cowriter, Sayre, were not out to offer the usual derring-do, heroic, wade-through-all-obstacles-unflinchingly, win-the-battle-and-get-the-girl, standard Hollywoodized clichés: As they wrote this movie, and Hawks directed it, World War I, as the French soldier in the line knew it, was a tough, realistic, gritty, and disillusioning experience. The men in the film seem genuinely to suffer from their wounds; the trenches look dirty and dark and sinister; the whistle of rifle shots and the

THE ROAD TO GLORY
Lionel Barrymore guides blind Baxter, his son, to heroic actions.

boom of cannon and the dynamite explosions all come across realistically.

The picture was said to be a remake of an earlier French movie, *Croix de Bois* (*Wooden Crosses*), never released in the United States. Other Fox war movies had used the battle footage from this French film, but it was eschewed for *The Road to Glory* because the print used for this one did not mesh with the more grainy footage of the older treatment.

Gregg Toland's photography is impressive, and Hans Peters's art direction and Thomas Little's set work are impeccable, as is the music of Louis Silvers.

14

THE CHARGE OF THE LIGHT BRIGADE

WARNER BROS.

1936

CAST:

Errol Flynn, Olivia de Havilland, Patric Knowles, Donald Crisp, C. Aubrey Smith, David Niven, Henry Stephenson, Nigel Bruce, C. Henry Gordon, Spring Byington, E. E. Clive, Lumsden Hare, Robert Barrat, J. Carrol Naish.

CREDITS:

Michael Curtiz, director; Hal B. Wallis and Samuel Bischoff, producers; Rowland Leigh and Michel Jacoby, screenplay; from a story by Jacoby; Sol Polito and Fred Jackman, photographers; Max Steiner, music; George Amy, editor. Running time: 115 minutes.

Errol Flynn is in his element in the 1936 *Charge of the Light Brigade*, which depicts an heroic military engagement during the Crimean War of the 1850s, in which Britain defended its sovereignty and vital interests in a far-off land.

THE CHARGE OF THE LIGHT BRIGADE   Errol Flynn leads the charge.

Before the crucial engagement, however, there is a love story of sorts to be disposed of, with Flynn loving Olivia de Havilland while she, regrettably for the Flynn character, loves his younger brother, Patric Knowles.

There is a succession of sequences of British military life, with many colorful characters in both army and civilian scenes, including such heavyweight character actors as Henry Stephenson, C. Henry Gordon, Nigel Bruce, and Donald Crisp. Spring Byington takes care of the feminine side nicely—as does, of course, Miss de Havilland, who was never more beautiful and compelling in her early career as when paired with Flynn. Audiences and the movie press circa 1936 were dubbing them the most beautiful couple on the screen, and with justification, as not only their respective appearances but also their mutual chemistry complemented each other for maximum results.

But the love scenes, the triangular rivalry, and the "preparation" (or what semiliterate but brilliantly orchestrative director Michael Curtiz called the "build things up") are only the preludes to the memorable charge itself, famous in more humorous filmic lore for Curtiz's command: "Bring on the empty horses!" (meaning horses without riders).

There is stunning camera work on display from the start of this famous sequence, as mounted troops prepare for the engagement and the camera runs down the line of determined faces, their own-

ers rigid and poised upon their horses. However, sometimes there was an excess of zeal in what was subsequently choreographed, which brought on unwanted bad publicity. For instance, trip wires were used in order to get the horses to topple realistically. Quite a few broke their legs and had to be "humanely" dispatched with bullets. This sorry inevitability gave rise to a campaign on the part of the Society for the Prevention of Cruelty to Animals to terminate such practices, with the result that more attention was paid thereafter to decent treatment for onscreen animals.

The unforgettable charge, filmed near Chatsworth in the San Fernando valley, is a masterpiece of military choreography: the horses moving in unison in a straight line, the stoic yet an-

THE CHARGE OF THE LIGHT BRIGADE   Flynn and Olivia DeHavilland share a tender moment.

guished faces of their purposeful masters, the well-orchestrated falls from the horses, and the agonized deaths. It was directed not by Curtiz, but by second unit director B. Reeves Eason, who kept it all in admirable perspective, both in close-ups and in long shots. The rhythmic force of it remains deeply compelling and riveting to audiences of any era.

Some critics sneered at the famous charge as demonstrating "Butchery Done With Slick Elegance" (to quote one reviewer's headline), but all onlookers agreed that the masterly direction and choreography of what was, after all, a chaotic series of terminally lethal events, constituted an art in itself.

Flynn is cocky, amusing, debonair, and self-as-

THE CHARGE OF THE LIGHT BRIGADE   A tense meeting with Donald Crisp, George Regas, and Nick Shaid (in rear).

sured as the handsome officer who thinks he is "scoring" with lovely de Havilland, only to suffer a crushing defeat in the Tournaments of Amour at the hands of her True Love, the handsome and sensitive Patric Knowles (who deserved a far more prestigious career in films than was ever subsequently accorded him). Called by some 1936 pundits "the most handsome man in movies," Knowles (who bore a surprising resemblance to Flynn, with whom he appeared in a number of movies) gets across here a moving blend of manly valor and sensitive gentlemanliness. De Havilland, even at age nineteen, is lovely, ladylike, and impassioned enough when addressing the object of her true affections, Knowles—but the chemistry that flares between her and Flynn left audiences disappointed that they didn't wind up in an intimate embrace at the fadeout.

All the soldiers of "The Charge" are manly and lithe and purposeful in their stances and general behavior, and their uniforms are handsomely glamorous. But their loss in the horrifying carnage, while quite reasonably graphic, was castigated by some critics as Hollywoodishly choreographed. Whatever the means, however, the end is sumptuously and compellingly served in the best Warners tradition.

15

THE FIGHTING 69TH

WARNER BROS.

1940

CAST:

James Cagney, Pat O'Brien, George Brent, Jeffrey Lynn, Alan Hale, Frank McHugh, Dennis Morgan, Dick Foran, John Litel, George Reeves, Frank Coghlan, Jr.

CREDITS:

William Keighley, director; Jack L. Warner and Hal B. Wallis, producers; Norman Reilly Raine, Dean Franklin,

and Fred Niblo, Jr., screenplay; Tony Gaudio, photographer; Adolph Deutsch, music; Owen Marks, editor. Running time: 89 minutes.

This film follows the adventures of the Rainbow Division's 165th Infantry of New York in World War I, and more especially the Irish Regiment, composed mostly of descendants of the feisty Hibernian isle. James Cagney and Pat O'Brien are on hand for a reteaming, their matchless chemistry interreacting and igniting once again. Cagney is his usual vital self as a cocky street fighter and punk who turns cowardly when faced with an enemy he can't see. But before the film ends, he has become a hero. The battle scenes are staged realistically and at times poignantly in human terms, and the location work, at Warners' Calabasas Ranch, produces convincing—indeed dynamic—scenes of training at Camp Mills, the troops moving over the French countryside, and the battlefields. One knowledgeable French movie critic was to declare that the California location shots so approximated the actualities of World War I France as to be a miracle of careful research and meticulous *mise en scène*.

Cagney and O'Brien offer a more-than-usual characterizational contrast here, with once again O'Brien essaying the role of the heroic chaplain,

THE FIGHTING 69TH   (Private) James Cagney tangles with drill sergeant, Alan Hale. Sammy Cohen in center.

THE FIGHTING 69TH (Chaplain) Pat O'Brien tries to reach through to stubborn, cocky Cagney.

this time real-life Father Duffy, to whom a monument was later erected in New York's Times Square. O'Brien is unassuming but emotionally persuasive in scenes where he comforts the men, and Cagney has a field day with his Bad-Boy-Turned-Coward-Turned-Eventual-Hero personality pyrotechnics. His self-confident, grating behavior in training camp doesn't win him many friends, and he is even less popular in the downbeat midsection, but in the best Hollywood tradition, redeems himself in the grand finale that all war pictures regard as mandatory.

While adept in conveying his character's successive evolvements, Cagney was up against a script that gave him rapid transitions of personality and mood, and it is a tribute to the art that two years later was to win him an Oscar (as George M. Cohan in *Yankee Doodle Dandy,* 1942) that he makes it come off convincingly.

Pat O'Brien, on the other hand, is almost inescapably one-dimensional as "heroic, saintly" Father Duffy—but, since he took on a type much admired circa 1940, he manages to save the day with it, looking wise, earnest, compassionate, reproving, and inspiring in successive stages.

While the Irish humor and sentiment and mischief-making is piled on in equal doses of mawkishness and semibrutality, the film makes its points

THE FIGHTING 69TH   Cagney comes to a stricken O'Brien's aid.

to 1940 audiences concerning the timeless virtues of honor, loyalty, camaraderie, team spirit, and duty. As is usual in such films, each actor limns a distinctive type: Jeffrey Lynn, handsome and sensitive, makes the poet Joyce Kilmer (who wrote the poem "Trees") a manly and touching figure whose doom is telegraphed throughout. George Brent is the stoical, no-nonsense officer who is a Rock of Gibraltar for his men. Frank McHugh and Alan Hale offer humor, high spirits, and humanistic relief from the gathering tensions among the men as they get down to the real business of battlefield engagement; and William Lundigan, Dick Foran, Guinn Williams, DeWolf Hopper, and Sammy Cohen offer standard but humanly recognizable types who complain and falter and grouse and sulk, but rise to the Grand Occasion when called upon.

William Keighley, directing from a screenplay by Norman Reilly Raine, Fred Niblo, Jr., and Dean Franklin, keeps the proceedings at a fast pace and ably choreographs the assorted heroics, deaths, advances, retreats, and hunkering-downs. One of his more surprising feats is the individualizing of various soldier types in a series of fast brush strokes that keep some faces in the memory. The poignancy of woundings and deaths, and the tension and honest fear some of the soldiers display, are highlighted ably.

The Fighting 69th, opening as it did in early 1940,

fit right in with President Roosevelt's efforts, subtle and overt, to condition the United States populace to the facts of war, kindling a patriotic spirit, and indicating what FDR felt was the inevitability of our eventual engagement in the great European war that had broken out in 1939. The theme was popular—Darryl Zanuck had planned to make the same story, but deferred to Warners on it—and, with its popular stars and snappy action, the film scored heavily.

16
____

SERGEANT YORK

WARNER BROS.

1941

CAST:

Gary Cooper, Joan Leslie, Walter Brennan, George Tobias, David Bruce, Stanley Ridges, Margaret Wycherly, Dickie Moore, Ward Bond.

CREDITS:

Howard Hawks, director; Jesse Lasky and Hal B. Wallis, producers; Abem Finkel, Harry Chandlee, Howard Koch, John Huston, screenplay; Sol Polito and Arthur Edeson, photographers; Max Steiner, music; William Holmes, editor. Running time: 134 minutes.

Adapted from the diary of a real-life World War I hero, *Sergeant York* is the story of Alvin C. York, who grew up in the hills of Tennessee and was always causing folks to shake their heads over his carousing, fighting, and wild carryings-on. That this fellow would ever grow up to be a pacifist seems unlikely, but that's exactly what happens. On his way to "put paid" to a man who cheated him out of the land he feels is rightfully his, York is almost struck by a bolt of lightning near a church, and sees this as a sign. In the next moment he gets religion, and before long is reading the Good Book night and day when he isn't working.

Then comes the problematic situation of World War I. York refuses to enlist because the Bible says

SERGEANT YORK Gearing up for combat George Tobias is at left, Joe Sawyer at right.

SERGEANT YORK   Ward Bond, Walter Brennan, and Noah Beery, Jr., keep Gary Cooper in line.

that it is wrong to kill. The town pastor, Rosier Pile (Walter Brennan), tries to get York a conscientious-objector exemption, but his little ramshackle congregation isn't accepted as a bona fide church. Drafted into the army, York is given an understanding talking-to by a major (Stanley Ridges), who tells him that America's is a "heritage worth fighting for."

After a brief furlough, York comes to the same conclusion and is seen involved in trench warfare in France. In the Argonne, he routs a nest of "Heinie" snipers virtually by his lonesome, and with eight other men—all that's left of his regiment—captures 132 German soldiers. To do this he uses the same techniques that made him a great hunter and target-shooter back in the hills of Tennessee.

Sergeant York was basically brought out as a propaganda film on the eve of the United States' entering World War II, and because of this the thought-provoking subject matter is somewhat trivialized. The approach to York is far too reverent; his every action is taken at face value, and his motives are never even remotely questioned. Everything is one-dimensional, and frequently unconvincing. In spite of all this, however, *Sergeant York* remains a very entertaining and well-made

SERGEANT YORK   Bond tries to reason with Cooper.

67

SERGEANT YORK   Out on the shoot with Dickie Moore.

motion picture, clearly more of an "action" film than one that simply says "War is Hell."

Gary Cooper won the first of his two Oscars for playing Alvin York, but he was actually much too old at forty to be playing a youthful hell-raiser. Considering the simplistic nature of the script (John Huston was one of a battery of credited writers), Cooper manages to be surprisingly effective at times—but his performance can hardly be classified as great acting. Walter Brennan (Oscar-nominated as the pastor), Joan Leslie as York's girlfriend Gracie, and Margaret Wycherly as Ma York, all hit the right notes, however.

Some of the battle scenes are extremely well-staged and harrowing, including one in which York and comrades stand in a trench listening to the whistle of approaching shells and trying to remain devil-may-care while wondering exactly where the missiles will land. And York's heroic assault on the German snipers is thrilling. There is an occasional stab at showing horror and death, but this is kept to a minimum, considering the producers' suspicions that American boys would soon be off fighting in another world war, and that the picture was seeking an atmosphere of patriotic fervor more than anything else.

One major flaw is that York's first killings aren't handled with the proper dramatic emphasis, con-

SERGEANT YORK   In the thick of things, with Tobias (standing at center) and comrades.

sidering that he was supposed to be a pacifist and surely must have felt *some* anguish inside, *none* of which is mirrored on Cooper's face. It makes sense that York would realize he had to "take lives to save lives," but no sense at all that he would seem so utterly unaffected.

Director Howard Hawks, photographer Sol Polito, and composer Max Steiner all were clearly inspired to do their best with the material they were given.—*W. S.*

CREDITS:

Noel Coward, producer-director; David Lean, associate director; Ronald Neame, photographer; Noel Coward, music; Thelma Myers, editor. Running time: 114 minutes.

Noel Coward was probably the last noted figure in England who could be expected to provide a rousing, trenchant, inspirational war drama, but pro-

17

IN WHICH WE SERVE

RANK / TWO CITIES / UNITED ARTISTS

1942

CAST:

Noel Coward, Bernard Miles, John Mills, Richard Attenborough, Celia Johnson, Kay Walsh, Joyce Carey, Michael Wilding, Penelope Dudley Ward, James Donald, George Carney.

IN WHICH WE SERVE   John Mills.

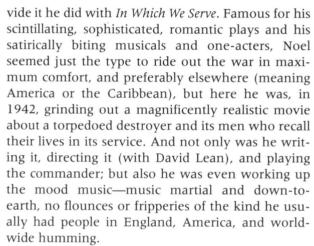

IN WHICH WE SERVE   (Above) Noel Coward, Celia Johnson.
(Below) Joyce Carey, Bernard Miles.

vide it he did with *In Which We Serve*. Famous for his scintillating, sophisticated, romantic plays and his satirically biting musicals and one-acters, Noel seemed just the type to ride out the war in maximum comfort, and preferably elsewhere (meaning America or the Caribbean), but here he was, in 1942, grinding out a magnificently realistic movie about a torpedoed destroyer and its men who recall their lives in its service. And not only was he writing it, directing it (with David Lean), and playing the commander; but also he was even working up the mood music—music martial and down-to-earth, no flounces or fripperies of the kind he usually had people in England, America, and worldwide humming.

Forty-three at the time he did *In Which We Serve*, Coward was technically (if not spiritually) middle-aged and could have ducked the assignment on those grounds, too. He had endured a brief term in the British armed forces when he was nineteen or so (in World War I) and, wanting to get his part in it over with quickly, had won no medals for valor. But *In Which We Serve* demonstrated to his fellow Britishers and the world alike that there was another Coward, and that one tough, patriotic Brit was he. His picture won widespread praise, and went on to earn an Oscar nomination for his screenwriting.

Coward had on hand a supporting cast—for in any Coward production everyone else *was* "supporting"—even though many of them were stars in their own right. These included such luminaries of stage and screen as John Mills, Bernard Miles, and Celia Johnson; and all got into the spirit of the doings. The word around London theatrical and film

circles was that when Noel was good he was very, very good, and when he was patriotic he was—well, even better!

Some of the Coward writing evidenced in *In Which We Serve* is as good as anything he had ever done; and it was terse, concise, and realistic—as when he tells about how his ship, *Torrin*, had been in one scrap after another, and how, though men were killed, they got the old girl back, those survivors did. He tells how the ship they all loved and served on happily and vigorously lies 150 fathoms deep now, with half their shipmates, and if those fellows had to die, what a grand way to go! They lie with the ship they love, and they're in very good company. The survivors? "Each of us knows twice as much about fighting and each of us has twice as good a reason to fight!"

Reviews for *In Which We Serve* were highly laudatory on both sides of the Atlantic, with the *New York Herald-Tribune* declaring, "Never at any time has there been a reconstruction of human experience

IN WHICH WE SERVE
Coward (center) and mates
are tiring but game.

which could touch the savage grandeur and compassion of this production."

The story and the character that Coward so memorably delineated were based on the experiences of Lord Louis Mountbatten, whose ship, HMS *Kelly*, had been sunk from under him. Coward set out to tell the tale of a British destroyer, following her from her launch to a Mediterranean engagement with the Germans during which she goes down. The personal stories of the men are told intimately and affectingly. The film, made in collaboration with the British Ministry of Information and the Royal Navy, won special commendations from such as King George VI, Winston Churchill, and Eleanor Roosevelt.

Coward sets the tone in his opening voiceover: "This is the story of a ship. But it is more: It is the story of man's heroic soul and the selfless, indomitable spirit by which a whole nation endures." Among the more notable scenes are those of survival in the ocean after the ship sinks, leaving men afloat only by virtue of their hanging on to inflated tubes. All the actors give it their very best. "Chin up" is a mild way to describe the valiant performances in this valiant film.

IN WHICH WE SERVE   Coward and his boys hang on for dear life.
Miles, center; Mills, right.

71

18

GUADALCANAL DIARY

20TH CENTURY–FOX

1943

CAST:

Preston Foster, Lloyd Nolan, William Bendix, Richard Conte, Anthony Quinn, Richard Jaeckel, Roy Roberts, Minor Watson, Ralph Byrd, Lionel Stander, John Archer, Miles Mander.

CREDITS:

Lewis Seiler, director; Bryan Foy, producer; Lamar Trotti, screenplay; based on the book by Richard Tregaskis; Charles G. Clarke, photographer; David Buttolph, music; Fred Allen, editor. Running time: 93 minutes.

Richard Tregaskis was a famed war correspondent who wrote a bestseller about marines fighting for a vital Pacific base. His book, *Guadalcanal Diary,* was acquired by Darryl F. Zanuck and translated faith-fully to the screen. The action shots are particularly outstanding, presented as they are with no holds barred and all the horror of war fully delineated.

Preston Foster, Lloyd Nolan, William Bendix, Richard Conte, Anthony Quinn, and others all get very much into the spirit of the proceedings, and they are about as unactorish as one can get under Lewis Seiler's tough-yet-sensitive direction.

We see the marines on shipboard getting their instructions and repeated briefings. Then it's into the landing craft and onto the beaches for weeks of fighting and assorted survival techniques. By the time the army comes to offer needed and welcome relief, the men are as hardened as combat veterans can get—and any former boys among them are boys no longer. This is war as Tregaskis conveyed it, and Hollywood proved humble this time, remaining true to the essential spirit of his book—merely rearranging settings and situations so as to extract the maximum drama while leaving the basic Tregaskis spirit and approach alone.

Lewis Seiler, the film's intrepid director, later told an interviewer that they were after realism, and

GUADALCANAL DIARY   Planes fly overhead.

wanted to keep Tregaskis's message loud and clear and untrammeled: "Sometimes movies tamper too much with the original realities," he said. "We wanted the reality, yes; what it needed was a minimal but definite dramatic framework. From then on, our aim was to get to the truth of that original material, without frills or theatricalisms of any kind."

The types limned throughout the action are recognizable yet graphically individual. There is Preston Foster (an underrated actor in his time) as a chaplain as pragmatically aware and alert as he is spiritually focused on positives. Lloyd Nolan is the tough sergeant who knows all the angles and puts up with no bull. The men fear to cross him but they respect him, too, and look for guidance from him when the tight situations arise. William Bendix, as a Brooklyn cabbie, is brash and comical and winning; he is out for laughs to relieve the tension, and his grateful buddies respond heartily. Anthony Quinn is the Mexican-American private who survives. And (in his first film) Richard Jaeckel is the young, green, and untried leatherneck who is *proud*

GUADALCANAL DIARY   Preston Foster reads to a wounded comrade.

GUADALCANAL DIARY   William Bendix confers with officers. Minor Watson, center.

GUADALCANAL DIARY   Fighting and dying on the beach.

of being a marine and is determined to demonstrate that pride any way he can.

There are no women in *Guadalcanal Diary;* given the goings-on, they would have seemed blatantly out-of-place. No early flirtations and romantic gaucheries are on display here, to be contrasted later with brutal fighting, suffering, and dying. It's man-action all the way; deadly serious, deeply professional, profoundly determined.

Some critics felt that the earlier scenes went on too long—the lighter, more playful ones, with

marines cutting up and clowning—and that the initial buildup failed to carry over into the later scenes. But as seen fifty years later, the professionalism and purposefulness can be clearly discerned. Seiler and his boys were out for the kill—a believable, authentic film.

True, there is a documentary feel to some of the footage, and so one-note is the mission at hand that the light and shade, the active and passive of dramatic ambience, are short-changed. But as the picture approaches its denouement, it is apparent that the tone set by Seiler is all of one piece—"Get on with the business, and the devil take the hindmost" is the tone set and held.

Another critic, in this case Bosley Crowther of the *New York Times*, remarked that "It seems too fortuitous that the four or five marines we stay with most enjoy a miraculous immunity from death—except for one, just at the end." But however this cookie crumbled plotwise, the result was a realistic, compelling tension throughout.

19

SO PROUDLY WE HAIL

PARAMOUNT

1943

CAST:

Claudette Colbert, Paulette Goddard, Veronica Lake, Sonny Tufts, Barbara Britton, Walter Abel, George Reeves, Ted Hecht, Mary Servoss, Dick Hogan, James Bell, Lorna Gray (later Adrian Booth), Dr. H. H. Chang, Kitty Kelly, Bill Goodwin, Byron Foulger, Richard Crane.

CREDITS:

Mark Sandrich, producer-director; Allan Scott, screenplay; Charles Lang, photographer; Miklos Rozsa, music; Ellsworth Hoagland, editor. Running time: 125 minutes.

While criticized by some for its "Hollywoodish" touches, and sneered at for glamour puss Claudette

SO PROUDLY WE HAIL   Goddard is a battle-hardened nurse.

Colbert and other ladies seeming artificial even with smudges on their faces and uniforms, *So Proudly We Hail* is actually a strong and powerful depiction of the struggles and occasional triumphs of World War II combat nurses in the Pacific. The story takes place in the midst of conflict against the Japanese in the Philippines. Set against a background of Corregidor and Bataan, and with sea sequences, the picture was actually studio-bound, even though realistically portrayed.

Colbert is joined by Paulette Goddard and Veronica Lake, and all try to come through with a sense of the gritty realism appropriate to the circumstances. All are individual types. Colbert is the warm and womanly one, who has a romance with handsome soldier George Reeves during the proceedings. Goddard is more earthy and humorous—and newcomer Sonny Tufts, handsome but buffoonish, is a perfect foil for her. Veronica Lake is a Pearl Harbor widow—solemn, serious, detached, determined—who lets her celebrated hairdo show only when she sets out to blow up some Japanese soldiers (and herself into the bargain).

There are many graphic scenes that any war picture would be proud of, and Mark Sandrich does

not stint on those involving wounded soldiers; pain from wounds; delirium; the truncated medical and hospital facilities implemented amidst chaos; bombings; reshufflings; and retreats. Throughout the film, the nurses work faithfully to comfort and succor their patients, even when the Japanese attack is at its fiercest. And, when the beaches at Bataan are evacuated under horrific conditions, the nurses are there to help, even with the enemy bombarding the hell out of the terrain.

So Proudly We Hail was the first of two 1943 pictures that set out to realistically depict the role of women in war; the other was *Cry Havoc* (see elsewhere in this book). The former was a Paramount picture; the latter an MGM effort. Obviously two major Hollywood studios saw Women in War as a subject worthy of respectful and major attention.

The courage of the nurses is exemplary, and while the criticism that the ladies might have besmudged and begrimed themselves more thoroughly and acted their roles more grittily and

SO PROUDLY WE HAIL   Lake is dedicated to her work.

SO PROUDLY WE HAIL
Claudette Colbert and
Goddard (center) prepare for
a sudden emergency. Ann
Doran and Lorna Gray
(Adrian Booth) in truck.

SO PROUDLY WE HAIL   Dorothy Adams, Colbert, Goddard, and
the other ladies get bad news by radio. Barbara Britton, Lorna
Gray lean on radio.

glamour-free may hold some water, a reviewing of
the picture fifty years later indicates quite clearly
that the Claudette–Paulette–Veronica combine tried
sincerely to give creditable performances—howso-
ever tailored, admittedly, to their differing personalities.

Certainly the picture must have heartened many
women on the home front, whether working in defense plants or homemaking, keeping a light in the
window for soldiers who might not return. It
demonstrated that the so-called weaker sex was
every bit as much a part of the upfront war action
as the more assertive and combative males. News
reports of the time indicated that there were many
war casualties among the nurses. Disease too was
a constant threat, given for example the climate
and conditions in the Bataan–Corregidor area.

Feminists of the 1990s will find much to cheer in
this film even while allowing for some of its dated
aspects. True, glamour—or at least a hint of the
same—rears its lovely but admittedly inappropriate
head, what with Colbert and George Reeves spoon-
ing about on their honeymoon night; and
Goddard's flirtatious, humorous scenes with Tufts;
and even Lake, when she makes a human mine of
herself to trap enemy soldiers (who, it would appear, did have a yen for her famous one-forelock-
down-the-face hairdo), is somewhat posturing and
actress-ish just before she blows herself and her
Oriental admirers to perdition. But, on balance,
Sandrich and screenwriter Allan Scott succeeded in

showing women in World War II as essentially decent, dignified, and nurturing creatures who held up under combat stress every bit as well as did the men they were to find themselves aiding and abetting (and/or abedding).

Photographer Charles Lang and mood-music genius Miklos Rozsa deserve special honors for creating an ambience at once realistic and poignant.

20

CRY HAVOC

METRO–GOLDWYN MAYER

1943

CAST:

Margaret Sullavan, Joan Blondell, Ann Sothern, Fay Bainter, Marsha Hunt, Ella Raines, Frances Gifford, Diana Lewis, Heather Angel, Connie Gilchrist.

CREDITS:

Richard Thorpe, director; Edwin Knopf, producer; Paul Osborn, screenplay; adapted from the play *Proof Through the Night* by Allan Kenward; Karl Freund, photographer; Daniele Amfitheatrof, music; Ralph E. Winters, editor. Running time: 97 minutes.

Obviously determined not to be outdone by Paramount in effectively depicting the roles of Women in War, MGM paraded its *Cry Havoc* within two months of *So Proudly We Hail*—the first film premiering in September of 1943 and the second in November.

This time Margaret Sullavan, Ann Sothern, and Joan Blondell took the spotlight, in a story of nurses and other women volunteers weathering the Bataan–Corregidor–Philippines disaster. This was very much a woman's picture, though not the usual offering, and such variegated distaff personalities as Fay Bainter (in a sizable role), Marsha Hunt, Ella Raines, Frances Gifford, Heather Angel, and Connie Gilchrist gave able support to the upfront histrionics of the Sullavan–Sothern–Blondell trio.

In this case the story dealt with problems between "regular army" nurses and volunteers. After

CRY HAVOC   Ann Sothern and Marsha Hunt distracted by a barracks quarrel.

CRY HAVOC   Director Richard Thorpe discusses a scene with Fay Bainter.

CRY HAVOC Ella Raines, Fely Franquelli, and Ann Sothern watch as Joan Blondell tries to get a message through.

CRY HAVOC Hunt and Sothern have a confidential talk.

some initial henfights and fuss-and-feathers, the volunteers show themselves a real asset to the proceedings. There is much tearjerker emotion generated as the nurses gradually realize that they are as doomed as the fighting men they are trying to comfort and save.

Though based on a Broadway play by Allan Kenward that some critics thought artificial, stagy, and posturing, as directed for the screen by journeyman Richard Thorpe, the proceedings are laid out realistically, indeed bitingly. The nursing of dying and seriously wounded men (one of whom is, fleetingly, Robert Mitchum in a very early role), and the gradually growing camaraderie among the nurses and volunteers who come to realize that they are totally—and, it appears, terminally—bonded in a common cause, are gotten across with point, purpose, and considerable poignancy. Director Thorpe and writer Paul Osborn wisely avoided sentimentality, making The Mission and Its Accomplishment the all-important thing—that being to save lives, and clean up the mess of the Bataan engagement, as well as human fallibility and daunting circumstances might permit.

Margaret Sullavan proves herself the equal of Claudette Colbert in *So Proudly We Hail*—offering a characterization that is a wonderful combination of common sense and compassion. Urged by another head nurse, Fay Bainter, to take more rest, she maintains the attitude throughout that rest is at the bottom of her priorities. Joan Blondell offers some amusing moments as a volunteer who is an ex-burlesque queen; she even regales her cohorts with some turns from her old shows. The rest of the nurses are either shy or outgoing types; some are fearful of their circumstances while others are philosophically resigned; still others are trying to find laughs where tears come more easily.

Since this is primarily a woman's picture, the males make relatively few appearances, and at that usually only to die in one or another of the nurses' arms—notably the young Mitchum. Even in this bit, however, he indicates what his future in films will be.

When *Cry Havoc* is compared with *So Proudly We Hail* in the areas of realism, guts, and the full addressing of the realities of time and locale, the answer by consensus is apples and oranges. Possibly the less glamorous and more forthright Sullavan set the tone for a more businesslike and down-to-earth treatment of the subject than did Colbert, which is not to fault the latter actress's sincere rendition. There seem to be more comedy relief and lighter moments in *Cry Havoc*, but both pictures have their distinctive merits.

After finishing the picture (she was not to do another movie for seven years), Sullavan returned to the Broadway stage. She later said that *Cry Havoc* had been her last of a six-picture MGM contract and that she had taken it because leading an ensemble of talented ladies represented less work than carrying a whole picture by herself or with a costar. In any event, it showcases her most creditably—as it also does Sothern, Blondell, and Bainter, and the able supporting cast.

21

ACTION IN THE NORTH ATLANTIC

WARNER BROS.

1943

CAST:

Humphrey Bogart, Raymond Massey, Julie Bishop, Dane Clark, Alan Hale, Ruth Gordon, Sam Levene, Charles Trowbridge, Peter Whitney, Kane Richmond, Dick Hogan, J. M. Kerrigan, Ludwig Stossel, Dick Wessel, Iris Adrian, Don Douglas.

CREDITS:

Lloyd Bacon, director; Jerry Wald, producer; John Howard Lawson, screenplay, with additional dialogue by W. R. Burnett and A. I. Bezzerides; based on a story by Guy Gilpatric; Ted McCord, photographer; Adolph Deutsch, music; Thomas Pratt and George Amy, editors. Running time: 127 minutes.

This story of a World War II American convoy attacked by German U-boats is rousing, riveting, exciting, suspenseful, and (although overlong) rich in human characterizations. *Action in the North Atlantic* was one of the hits of 1943, and deservedly so. The men, purposes, achievements, and grace under fire of the U.S. Merchant Marine all are put on display with great impact by director Lloyd Bacon, an old hand at screen excitement. The photography is excellent, and while it is a studio-bound product (shot in its entirety at the Warner studio in Burbank), it manages to suggest a much wider panorama and field of action.

Humphrey Bogart is there as a merchant marine officer, and his saturnine, purposeful performance gives the picture strength and cohesion. He is ably complemented by Raymond Massey as his superior, and a host of seasoned actors from the Warners

ACTION IN THE NORTH ATLANTIC Kane Richmond, Humphrey Bogart, and Raymond Massey survey the sky scene.

ACTION IN THE NORTH ATLANTIC
Sam Levene, Bogart, and Alan Hale check on a laid-low Massey.

ACTION IN THE NORTH ATLANTIC
Ad for *Action in the North Atlantic.*

80

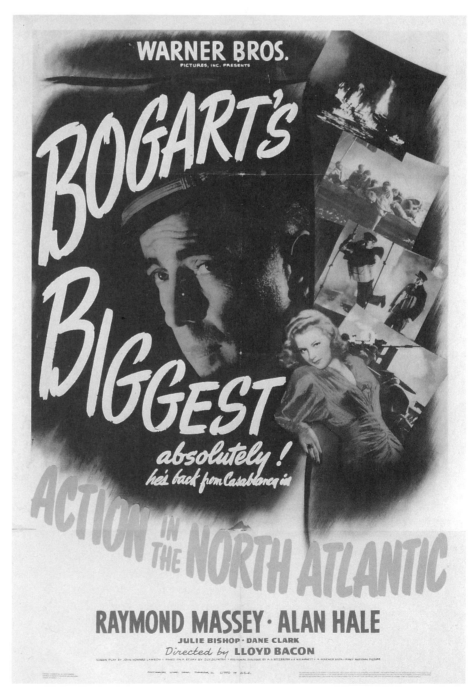

stock company playing seamen—these including Dane Clark (zesty and troublesome as ever), Alan Hale (an old salt with pepper added), Dick Hogan, Kane Richmond, Sam Levene, and Chick Chandler.

The task of the merchant marines was never an easy one. Commissioned to get crucial materials to the Allies in Europe, they had to cope with erratic weather conditions in the North Atlantic, the omnipresent danger of U-boats and other tools of German surveillance, and the varying physical condition of the ships they sailed. To say nothing of an erratic, sometimes unpredictable collection of varying human temperaments, all more or less finely tuned—not always successfully—to work in unison to achieve the overall objective.

The crafty maneuverings of the U-boats, the bleak weather conditions, the suspense, and sometimes the terror, on board all are welded together in John Howard Lawson's screenplay. True, at times the flag-waving chauvinism and wade-through-all-obstacles-unflinchingly attitudes get to smack more of needed (though admittedly rousing) war propaganda than of honestly depicted human vicissitudes under difficult wartime conditions, but all winds up well, thanks to the fast-paced action sequences,

taut direction, and sound characterizations.

Fresh from his *Casablanca* triumph, Bogart seems oddly miscast as a derring-do marine officer; his personality is too gloomy and cerebral for the role, though his cynical looks and stances do add *some* bite to the heroics. He is given a bit of perfunctory romancing with a cabaret singer (Julie Bishop), but his main thrust remains getting the wares to Murmansk—even though, in every sequence, he seems to be walking through the role. Yet his innate professionalism carries the day for him anyway. The fires and torpedoings and man-overboard hysterias seem authentic to a point, but sometimes display a tempest-in-a-teapot fussiness that keep one *reminded* that it was all shot in the studio tank at Burbank.

Countering mate Bogart's cynicism and cryptic manner is Raymond Massey's intrepid merchant marine commander, who is all purposeful intensity and stoical intrepidity. The two men contrast admirably: Both dedicated to the same goal (Deliver that cargo—and U-boat torpedoes and other assorted harassments be damned!), they go about their business as per their individual temperaments. Yet, beneath their detached interplay, a

ACTION IN THE NORTH ATLANTIC   Julie Bishop charms Massey and Bogart.

sense of camaraderie and mutual understanding shines through.

The action sequences are exceptional; the tension mounts as the Germans give their best shots to sinking the cargo so badly needed by the Allies; it is all a paralyzingly frightening panoply of sinking boats, crafts afire, men bailing out, commanders shouting orders (sometimes heeded, sometimes disregarded by the hysterical crew); and inevitable but hard-won triumphs over almost insuperable odds. Ted McCord's photography is first-rate in getting all this across.

22

BATAAN

METRO–GOLDWYN–MAYER

1943

CAST:

Robert Taylor, George Murphy, Thomas Mitchell, Lloyd Nolan, Lee Bowman, Robert Walker, Desi Arnaz, Barry Nelson, Phillip Terry, Roque Espiritu, Kenneth Spencer, Tom Dugan, Donald Curtis.

CREDITS:

Tay Garnett, director; Irving Starr, producer; Robert D. Andrews, screenplay; based partly on the 1934 film *The Lost Patrol*; Sidney Wagner, photographer; Cedric Gibbons, art director; Bronislau Kaper, music; George White, editor. Running time: 114 minutes.

Bataan, a well-received war film of 1943, focused on a single American patrol against the Japanese early in World War II when the Pacific peninsula in western Luzon was overrun. The men are all doomed to die, but they fight heroically—in this case literally to the last combatant. The usual mix of personalities and ethnic types is on display: Robert Taylor as the hard-bitten sergeant; Lee Bowman as the intrepid captain (the first to die, from a sniper's bullet); George Murphy as a quietly dependable air corps officer; Thomas Mitchell, a dedicated career soldier; Lloyd Nolan, wisecracking but understand-

ing and generous; Robert Walker (in his major film debut) winning all hearts as a sensitive, vulnerable young sailor ridden with homesickness; Barry Nelson as the competent, determined type; and Desi Arnaz—lovable, humorous, and definitely Hispanic. All die one-by-one, and the row of graves lengthens. At last Taylor, now the lone combatant, digs his own grave beside the others, knowing that his body will fall into it as he fires his last shots and gets a lethal return from the advancing enemy.

BATAAN   To slow the Japanese advance, American soldiers blast a huge bridge.

Though the entire action was shot on an MGM soundstage, no effort was spared to make the setting as realistic as possible. The captain (Bowman) is a dedicated officer, but he has the humility and balance to recognize that Taylor's sergeant is a more seasoned veteran with thorough knowledge of the terrain on which they are fighting, and defers to him when it comes to crucial decisions. His death scene is a moving one as his men look up from his body toward the Japanese, a grim determination

BATAAN   Sergeant Robert Taylor and (Cpl.) Lloyd Nolan disagree as to combat strategy.

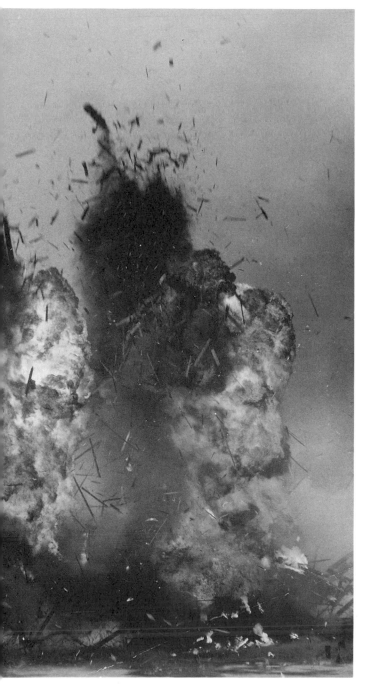

etched on their faces—they are thenceforth hell-bent on making the enemy pay heavily for each of the inevitable deaths among them that will follow.

Bataan, while loosely based on the 1934 John Ford film *The Lost Patrol*, had a character and ambience uniquely its own, thanks to the trenchant, sure direction of Tay Garnett; Sidney Wagner's graphic yet eloquent photographic nuances; the realistic art direction of Cedric Gibbons; and the riveting, exciting special effects provided by Arnold Gillespie and Warren Newcombe. Bronislau Kaper's musical scoring was especially apt, heightening the action sequences but not sentimentalizing or "hero-icizing" them. As each man dies, and is buried in his at-the-ready grave, the horror and futility of war is encapsulized in the individual tragedies.

BATAAN   Taylor determines to fight to the end.

The camaraderie and mutual protectiveness of men under fire, men who know that they are certainly doomed, is underlined poignantly but unsentimentally: Lloyd Nolan and George Murphy are models of stoically admirable fighting men; Robert Walker is touchingly sensitive yet with a valor all his own; Thomas Mitchell, a hardened veteran, is compelling as a man who has seen it all and is resigned to the inevitable.

Taylor gives one of his best performances. Long eager to overcome, or at least underplay, his exceptional good looks when roles he was assigned made it possible for him to emphasize characterization and depth, he had his best opportunity here, before going into the service himself (to great distinction). His performance as Sgt. Bill Dane is intrepid and forceful, yet compassionate and understanding. And though he is deeply concerned for his men, knowing that they are all doomed, he also is determined that their deaths will serve a worthwhile purpose. The famed saying, "Love in action is a harsh and dreadful thing compared to love in dreams," finds an apt exemplar in Taylor's character, as he shores up his men, buries each sorrowfully, and then prepares for his own inevitable ending as the enemy draws ever closer.

Director Tay Garnett has several times declared for public print that Taylor was a far better actor than the excessive concentration on his good looks allowed most critics and audiences to discern. He was determined to be a good actor rather than a glamorous star. That he only partly succeeded in furthering this impression was due more to critics' and audiences' tendency to typecast than to any failure of effort on his part. *Bataan* does showcase Taylor the actor.

BATAAN   Phillip Terry (Joan Crawfords' husband), Lloyd Nolan, George Murphy, Robert Taylor, Thomas Mitchell, Desi Arnaz, Lee Bowman, Barry Nelson, Kenneth Spencer, Rogue Espiritu. The boys in a gung-ho stance.

BATAAN Getting ready for the inevitable attack. (Left to right) Tom Dugan, Kenneth Spencer, Robert Walker, Taylor, Thomas Mitchell, and Nolan.

23

THE IMMORTAL SERGEANT

20TH CENTURY–FOX

1943

CAST:

Henry Fonda, Thomas Mitchell, Maureen O'Hara, Allyn Joslyn, Reginald Gardiner, Melville Cooper, Bramwell Fletcher, Morton Lowry, Donald Stuart, Jean Prescott, Heather Wilde.

CREDITS:

John Stahl, director; Lamar Trotti, producer-screenplay; based on the novel by John Brophy; Arthur Miller, photographer; David Buttolph, music; James B. Clark, editor. Running time: 90 minutes.

A stirring, yet often poetic story of the North African campaign in World War II, *The Immortal Sergeant* is the tale of the intrepid NCO, Thomas Mitchell, with the singular gift of inspiring raw recruits into approximating his own ideals of soldiering in war. When the Mitchell character dies in ac-

THE IMMORTAL SERGEANT
Henry Fonda ponders
his next move.

THE IMMORTAL SERGEANT   Fonda and Thomas Mitchell confer
while Allyn Joslyn looks on.

tion, his sterling example carries Henry Fonda, as a
hitherto meek corporal, of a psychologically civilian
stripe, to the heights of battlefield heroism, culminating in an officer's commission and the
Distinguished Service Cross.

Fonda gets across tellingly the corporal's evolvement into a consummate fighting man. At the beginning he is timid, insecure, and mooning over his
lost love (Maureen O'Hara) back home, who has
promised to wait for him. He is the least promising
of raw recruits. But when he falls under Mitchell's
charismatic spell, he learns the true psychology of
soldiering. Under the tutelage of "The Immortal
Sergeant" he learns, along with other hitherto-
green-and-timid recruits, that anything worth
doing at all is worth doing well; that among the
highest ideals of soldiering is Getting the Job Done,
as well as one can, for God, country, and the loved
ones back home.

Some critics thought the film's theme rather
high-flown and pseudopoetic, even manipulative—
but others felt it had all the galvanizingly inspirational ingredients (along with the gritty action
scenes) necessary to a first-class war film. There
also was some exception taken to the earlier scenes
with Fonda and O'Hara–what was known as the

"Love–Girl–Home Fires" stuff. But once Fonda moves into the manly business of fighting a war and getting its aims both set forth properly and bravely accomplished, the film settles into a graphic, telling study of war, its uses and purposes, and its aims and the means of achieving them.

Thomas Mitchell's electric, inspirational sergeant is one of his finest portrayals. Faced with a bevy of young men who are the least likely candidates for fighting-man status, he hectors, bullies, shames, inspires, rouses, and instills in them the desire to give the essence of their manhood to what he describes as the greatest of causes: protecting one's country and loved ones. Fonda's corporal, unsure of himself and with no defined aims, purposes, or ideals, hardens and grows and learns and spiritually profits from all that Mitchell has to teach—and when the sergeant meets his death on the battlefield, this boy-become-a-man, kneeling beside him, is prepared to pick up the torch and distinguish himself

in a manner that his mentor would have been proud of.

Some critics refused to be impressed by *The Immortal Sergeant*, one dubbing it "an inspirational war drama quite neatly done but a shade embarrassed by its own poetic leanings." *Time* magazine intoned: "By the time the first soldier has bit the sand, the film identifies itself; it is none other than Hollywood's old friend, the Foreign Legion of *Beau Geste* vintage, jerked from the shelf and clothed in a new uniform."

Time's 1943 evaluation, some fifty years later, seems in retrospect a bit dismissive and unfair. Fresh viewings of the film show that it took a stance very much its own, and was far less derivative of Foreign Legion posturings of old than had been previously believed. Trotti's screenplay, faithfully following the basic premise of the John Brophy novel, limns compellingly the gradual transmogrification of the characters of men un-

THE IMMORTAL SERGEANT Fonda, Melville Cooper, and Joslyn get the bad news.

formed in psychology and life-motivations, and demonstrates cogently the strong power of an exceptional masculine-military role model when it comes to redirecting the lives and interior makeup of his men.

The Immortal Sergeant has its full share of strongly delineated combat scenes; its action and battles are in the best tradition of such films. But its basic message could never be sufficiently repeated: One strong leader can turn faithful followers into admirable developers of their own individual potentialities.

24

SAHARA

COLUMBIA

1943

CAST:

Humphrey Bogart, Bruce Bennett, Lloyd Bridges, Rex Ingram, J. Carrol Naish, Dan Duryea, Kurt Krueger, Guy Kingsford, Hans Schumm, John Wengraf.

CREDITS:

Zoltan Korda, director; Harry Joe Brown, producer; John Howard Lawson and Zoltan Korda, screenplay; Rudolph Maté, photographer; Miklos Rozsa, music; Charles Nelson, editor. Running time: 85 minutes.

Humphrey Bogart as the saturnine, battle-worn commander of a twenty-eight ton tank he has named Lulu Belle. The merciless Sahara desert in wartime 1942, replete with sand, heat, and windstorms. To say nothing of wartime conflict and tension. Who could ask for more?

Who could indeed, as Bogart's American tank crew, which is trying to rejoin the British Eighth Army to which it is attached, sets off across the Libyan Desert? Along the way, Bogart and crew pick up five British hangers-on, a man from the Free French forces, a Sudanese corporal with his Italian prisoner in tow, and a downed German pilot. A motley company they make, and the as-

sorted internecine tensions create enough excitement for ten movies.

Adapted from an incident in the Soviet film *The Thirteen*, this Bogart beauty has spawned a host of imitators, but few as successful, trenchant, and gritty as the 1943 original. The name of the game with this disparate gang is water—the need for it, the search for it, the imminent danger of life-extinguishing thirst. When the men reach the well at an old fort, they find the water almost gone. Then an advance scout-car team tips them off that the Germans are water-short, too, and in search of the same well (which by now is a dry hole indeed after the crew-of-all-nations has gotten through with it).

Bogart and company, deciding to make a stand against the advancing enemy, are picked off one by one until few remain for the Allies but Bogie and one British soldier, both about out of ammo. But there is an offbeat *and* upbeat finish in the offing as the Germans, victimized by their pervasive thirst, beg for water—and throw down their arms! The ironic ending is that the well, having received direct hits from German shelling, has just been shaken into pouring out fresh water. (The presumption is that the two Allies not only have captured the entire German force, but also will manage to keep

SAHARA   Humphrey Bogart checks out a suspicious scene. Bruce Bennett, Richard Nugent, Hans Schumm, Henry Rowland.

SAHARA   Jumping into the fray.

SAHARA   Bogart lends a helping hand to prisoner J. Carrol Naish.

SAHARA A cup-of-cheer exchange with Naish. Bogart, Carl Harbord, Nugent, Louis Mercier, right.

them from retrieving their dropped but loaded weapons—not to mention further using their other, bigger toys to their rear. But this is, after all, just a movie.)

The supporting cast offers a collection of distinctive types, including Rex Ingram and his Sudanese prisoner (played strikingly and vividly by J. Carrol Naish), and Kurt Krueger as the fox-in-the-woodpile Nazi pilot.

James O'Hanlon's script makes a fine starting point for Zoltan Korda's pithy direction. The suspense keeps building and the action is fast and furious. Though no women appear, they are not particularly missed; all this fighting and dying and thirsting and scrounging and surviving is strictly men's work—and work they do.

Not only were the supporting characters different and individual, but also an American battalion from Camp Young that was undergoing tough strategic training prior to overseas assignment was drafted to sub for German soldiers who enter the action at the final crucial moment. Americans all, they look mighty convincing in their German outfits, and since few of them get to speak so much as a single word, their German accents (had they *had* them) are *not* missed.

But there is little time for talk, in any or all accents, as Bogart and cohorts Bruce Bennett, Lloyd Bridges, and Dan Duryea, among others, push and push across that desert, and slop and soak up what little water is left as if their lives depended on it—which they did.

Bogart was sent out on loan to Columbia for this film, after which it was back to Warners and his standard fare there. Though the 1942 *Casablanca* had made him a star, Bogart was to find himself in actioners both at his home studio and on this Columbia excursion. One reason for this was the absence of younger Hollywood leading men, as they had gone off to war, and thus real-life fighting, in various combat theaters East and West. Bogart in 1943 was forty-three (he was as old as the century—even in fact a little older, having been born at Christmastime 1899—but he had already done a navy stint at nineteen in World War I). Lined, offhand, sarcastic, and offputting, Bogart was an acquired taste in action heroes. And that taste got acquired fast by moviegoers across America who liked what they saw: Bogart as Movie Star Supreme, out to rival Gable, Power, Flynn—anyone you might chance to name.

25

CRASH DIVE

20TH CENTURY–FOX

1943

CAST:

Tyrone Power, Anne Baxter, Dana Andrews, James Gleason, Dame May Whitty, Henry (Harry) Morgan, Charles Tannen, Frank Conroy, Ben Carter, John Archer, Minor Watson, David Bacon, Paul Burns, Thurston Hall, Gene Rizzi.

CREDITS:

Archie Mayo, director; Milton Sperling, producer; Jo Swerling, screenplay; based on an original story by W. R. Burnett; Leon Shamroy, photographer; David Buttolph, music; Fred Sersen, special effects; Walter Thompson and Ray Curtiss, editors. Running time: 105 minutes. (Technicolor.)

Crash Dive, released in April 1943, was to be Tyrone Power's final film before entering the United States Marines. Some critics who snipped that Ty was too "sensitive" and "pretty" for such onscreen heroics as limned in *Crash Dive* were to eat their words later when he won for himself a distinguished service career. Not to be seen again on the screen for three years (*The Razor's Edge* was his postwar "comeback" film in 1946), he went away with honor and credit in this movie, for *Crash Dive* is a hard-hitting story of submarines and PT boats weathering the German naval onslaught in the North Atlantic.

As was standard in 1943 action pictures, there is a romantic subplot that takes up much of the early footage; here it features Anne Baxter in a love triangle with Power and his commanding officer, Dana Andrews. But later there is some rousing naval action, with boats getting set on fire, and sea rescues, and submariners sustaining wounds that are either lethal or nonlethal—whichever the situation warrants.

The entire mechanics, panoply, and logistics of PT boat and submarine warfare in the North Atlantic is ably orchestrated by director Archie Mayo and a special-effects team that won an Oscar for its efforts, with Leon Shamroy's photography especially effective. The subs are carefully observed as to inner fittings and details, and when one of them attacks an enemy base toward the close of the action, there is an eloquently forceful and suspenseful interplay of fiery seas, buffeted boats, and helmeted

CRASH DIVE   Tyrone Power in a solemn confab with James Gleason, as Henry (Harry) Morgan (second left), David Bacon (rear), and other mates look on.

men poised for combat in rather fragile craft that threaten to topple them into the briny at any moment.

All the cast members deliver in fine style, and director Mayo even manages to etch sharp and individual characterizations from most of them, including: Dana Andrews as the intrepid submarine commander who loses the girl (naturally) to Power, and who figures in the final heroics tellingly; James Gleason, as usual rather superannuated for combat heroics but delivering with his customary pizzazz; and stalwarts John Archer, Ben Carter, George Holmes, and David Bacon—who, along with other reliable types, rally to their ship stoically and courageously.

Early in the picture there are handsome uniformed troop maneuvers and paradings, with white-capped sailors following their officers in rigid formation. Later, the scenes of the burning seas, and of flimsy but sturdy craft holding men from the submarines who are out to get a little "land action" against the enemy, are rousing; and the Technicolor process splendidly gets across the realness of the water and blood (and mud) of the engagements in

CRASH DIVE   In the thick of the fighting.

CRASH DIVE Power Romeo-ing with Anne Baxter's Juliet, as Florence Lake looks on.

hues that are vivid and masculine rather than muted and feminine—as in the romantic scenes.

Anne Baxter is fine as Power's love interest, but some critics registered impatience with the time taken up for her woo-pitching with Power on land. Dame May Whitty, the fine English character actress, is included in the cast for no good reason, but does offer a pleasant reminder of her Lady Beldon in the famed *Mrs. Miniver* of the year before. Henry (Harry) Morgan, always a dependable character performer, adds heft to some of the combat training and action scenes.

Tyrone Power, who was about to go to war himself, considered *Crash Dive* a worthy terminal piece for his pre-service career, and told a magazine writer that he had tried to make his portrayal authentic, adding, "Watch the dirt on my face and on my pants—I really got into It!" One critic opined that the film also served "to eulogize a branch of our armed services that has had less than its deserved share of Hollywood's attention."

Crash Dive was one of 20th-Fox's big 1943 moneymakers, providing a formula which, in that war-blended-with-romance year, pleased audiences mightily.

CRASH DIVE Power and crew rescue survivors.

George Folsey and Karl Freund, photographers; Cedric Gibbons, art director; Herbert Stothart, music; Frank Sullivan, editor. Running time: 120 minutes.

26

A GUY NAMED JOE

METRO–GOLDWYN–MAYER

1943

CAST:

Spencer Tracy, Irene Dunne, Van Johnson, Lionel Barrymore, James Gleason, Barry Nelson, Don DeFore, Henry O'Neill, Esther Williams, Ward Bond.

CREDITS:

Victor Fleming, director; Everett Riskin, producer; Dalton Trumbo, screenplay; from an original story by Chandler Sprague, Frederick H. Brennan, and David Boehm;

It took the combined talents of Spencer Tracy, Irene Dunne, director Victor Fleming, and winning newcomer Van Johnson to make *A Guy Named Joe* minimally palatable. Dalton Trumbo concocted a highly sentimental screenplay, from an original story by Chandler Sprague. Such fine character actors as James Gleason, Lionel Barrymore, and Ward Bond seem merely along for the ride, but do their job like the pros they are. The best thing about the film is the aerial combat material, which features some lively, hair-raising action.

The story deals with the men of the Army Air Corps (as it was called in 1943). The "Guy Named Joe" can be anyone in the corps, as long as he is a good guy by corps standards. Tracy gets himself killed in a well-staged air fight early in the film, when his daredevil piloting smacks more of

A GUY NAMED JOE   James Gleason, Addison Richards, and others watch a combat plane land.

Hollywood melodrama than of authentic war maneuvering. Still, as shot, it is very convincing in a posturing way. Mr. Big in the Sky, Lionel Barrymore as God (and in full uniform, too) sends Tracy back to earth with another dead corpsman, Barry Nelson (a sort of guiding angel), to keep his eye on the new airmen and guide them to efficient air achievements—and outright heroism, provided they have the stuff. Meanwhile, down on earth, Tracy's old girlfriend, Irene Dunne, continues to mourn him until distracted by the boyish charms of young Van Johnson, a fledgling pilot who comes under Tracy's ectoplasmic wing. There is a triangle-of-sorts in the offing—for a while—with Tracy upset over the Dunne-Johnson romantic teaming; but all is straightened out, and Tracy goes off into the wild blue yonder forever after giving them his blessing.

There is a confused plot turn in which Dunne, fearful that Johnson will meet Tracy's fate if he goes off on a dangerous mission, takes the plane's controls herself, with Tracy guiding her to a successful engagement and landing. While a servicewoman, Dunne is not hitherto featured as a topnotch pilot, yet under Tracy's supernatural guidance she brings home the bacon. This seems pure Hollywood invention by any standards, and a lush typically

A GUY NAMED JOE   Spencer Tracy spiritually counsels Irene Dunne as she sets off on a combat mission (Ward Bond in background).

A GUY NAMED JOE   Lionel Barrymore, as the Chief in the Sky, sends Tracy back with Barry Nelson to do what good he can with young fliers.

MGM music score wafts it out onto clouds of added romantic unreality.

Still, *A Guy Named Joe* qualifies as one of the more "heartening" (if that is the word) war films of the era, as it is bathed in home-front valor, is even a bit ahead of its time in suggesting that a woman (even a supernaturally guided one) can fly a successful combat mission, and showcases, in their only teaming, the charismatic and celebrated Tracy-Dunne duo. (Then-still-starlet Esther Williams even gets a scene or two.)

Victor Fleming, man's-man director that he is, keeps the action focused, for the most part, on the guys named Joe-or-Whomever and their combat expertise. Dunne pleases her women audiences by sporting—her only time in the film out of uniform—a ravishing evening gown, and is even allowed one song, her singing voice being one of her more publicized charms in this period. The fact that in 1943 she was forty-five and Tracy was forty-three seems to have inspired the photographer and makeup artists to make them seem younger, but Tracy's flab and Dunne's quite mature (if hand-some) features make them unlikely candidates for the title of Top Screen Lovers of the Year. Also, since Van Johnson in 1943 was something like twenty-six to Dunne's forty-five, their pairing seemed a bit unrealistic (unless he had a mother complex). But Jimmy Gleason and Ward Bond, as tough, no-nonsense servicemen, made welcome efforts to keep the macho fires burning.

Van Johnson sustained serious facial cuts and abrasions in a near-fatal automobile accident halfway through shooting. There was talk of replacing him, but Tracy supposedly held up the picture while Johnson recovered (or so the MGM publicity flacks reported). A more likely reason was that most of the footage of Johnson was in the can at the time of the accident, and it was cheaper to await his recovery and finish the film with him. The change in his facial features is fairly noticeable, but good makeup covers up the worst of it. The large slash-scar across his forehead defied all cosmetic efforts, however.

As an uneasy blend of romance and fighter-pilot heroics (and Lionel Barrymore cast as God in the

A GUY NAMED JOE
Tracy keeps spiritual watch on a thoughtful, sad Dunne.

bargain!), *A Guy Named Joe* heartened many women in the audience—1943 featured some severe casualties, militarily—and was given the full MGM treatment, including more-than-intrusive mood music and lush mounting. That sort of thing kept wartime audiences mighty happy.

27

THIRTY SECONDS OVER TOKYO

METRO–GOLDWYN–MAYER

1944

CAST:

Spencer Tracy, Van Johnson, Robert Walker, Phyllis Thaxter, Scott McKay, Robert Mitchum, Don DeFore,

A GUY NAMED JOE   Ghosts Nelson and Tracy look on while Johnson and Dunne have it out (Bond is at right).

THIRTY SECONDS OVER TOKYO   Van Johnson romances Phyllis Thaxter.

THIRTY SECONDS OVER TOKYO Johnson welcomes Robert Mitchum to the squadron as Douglas Cowan (left), Don DeFore, and John R. Reilly watch.

Horace (Stephen) McNally, Louis Jean Heydt, Leon Ames, Paul Langton, Donald Curtis.

CREDITS:

Mervyn LeRoy, director; Sam Zimbalist, producer; Dalton Trumbo, screenplay; based on the book by Ted W. Lawson and Robert Considine; Harold Rosson and Robert Surtees, photographers; Cedric Gibbons and Paul Groesse, art directors; Herbert Stothart, music; Frank Sullivan, editor. Running time: 138 minutes.

Since registering with Spencer Tracy and Irene Dunne in *A Guy Named Joe* the year before, Van Johnson had become MGM's most popular younger-generation purveyor of war heroics. And with most of the standard MGM "heroes" off to the real war, Johnson, who had been rejected for the service, was drafted to lead the onscreen action. The facial injury that he had sustained smack in the middle of *A Guy Named Joe* in an auto accident had given his youthful face more character, and the wide slash across his forehead seemed to underline the dangers and hazards facing servicemen.

THIRTY SECONDS OVER TOKYO Don DeFore and the boys indulge in some barrack-room hijinks. Reilly is standing (center), and Douglas Cowan, Johnson, Mitchum, and Gordon MacDonald are seated at right.

Again he finds himself in a picture with Spencer Tracy, who shines as always in a cameo as Gen. Jimmy Doolittle, who orchestrated the first American bombing raid over Japan in April 1942.

There was criticism that the film's heroics, as well as its private scenes of devotion between the Johnson real-life character and his wife, Phyllis Thaxter, were tales told not twice or three times but a score of times—yet the sincere acting of the principals helped give the film solidity and balance.

There is a solid look to the training sequences, and the advance briefings and orchestrations for the historic raid are imparted with an authenticity and thoroughness that do credit to Dalton Trumbo's screenplay based carefully on the book by Capt. Ted W. Lawson (the character played by Johnson) and Robert W. Considine.

Again there is an assortment of types among the men, all carefully directed and highlighted by Mervyn LeRoy. Robert Walker is the "sensitive" flier who ably does his duty, with Robert Mitchum (in his pre-starring period) a more stoic incarnation. Louis Jean Heydt and Don DeFore limn smaller roles with relish and a characterizationally authentic feel, and Horace (Stephen) McNally and Leon Ames are their usual reliable selves. Phyllis Thaxter is touching as Johnson's wife; it was her first film role, and she delivered well. The scenes in which the Japanese locations are effectively bombed are hair-raisingly tense, with the men registering varied reactions to the extraordinary circumstances and the split-second timing and concentration necessary to accomplish the mission successfully.

Van Johnson, age twenty-eight in 1944, is at his best in the harrowing sequences when one of his legs is seriously injured and he must face amputation as a lifesaving measure. He gets across all the anguish, stoicism, self-control, and tolerance of pain and uncertainty that the role calls for. There was some criticism in 1944 of the sugary domestic-devotion scenes between Johnson and Thaxter, but as seen fifty years later they actually offer a nice, neat, poignant contrast to the more gritty and incisive action sequences.

Tracy as guest star finds himself with much less to do than usual, but at forty-four he is a solid presence in his few scenes, and conveys General Doolittle's razor-sharp perceptions and quiet, fierce determination most tellingly.

Thirty Seconds Over Tokyo utilized the Pensacola (Florida) Naval Air Station for much of its actual shooting, and the authenticity shows nicely. The

THIRTY SECONDS OVER TOKYO Peter Varney portrays one of the Tokyo raiders.

training given the men is portrayed convincingly, and the care and effort that went into this historic raid are underlined throughout. The scenes in the aircraft on the way to Japan and the actual raid are shot and directed very effectively. Mervyn LeRoy was to say long after the picture's release that he wanted to convey human qualities among the men and did not want them to seem mere stereotypes. Considering that the main action—the planning, the intermediate steps, the execution—dominates the film, LeRoy does well in portraying the individual types.

Some critics felt that every conceivable World War II bromide had been busily enlisted for this movie. Others commented that there was an inescapable sameness dramatically, no matter how well-intentioned director and actors and photographer might be, to most (if not all) military-service films—which, of course, almost uniformly featured preparation scenes, action scenes, dramatic-resolution sequences, etc.—all of which followed in what some felt was deadly (in more ways than one) inevitability. Van Johnson performs quite creditably, and, in the scenes where he sustains the crucial leg wound and faces amputation, gets across an admirable synthesis of vulnerability and stoicism.

Franz Waxman, music; George Amy, editor. Running time: 142 minutes.

28

OBJECTIVE BURMA!

WARNER BROS.

1945

CAST:

Errol Flynn, James Brown, William Prince, George Tobias, Henry Hull, Warner Anderson, John Alvin, Stephen Richards (Mark Stevens), Dick Erdman, Tony Caruso.

CREDITS:

Raoul Walsh, director; Jerry Wald, producer; Ranald MacDougall and Lester Cole, screenplay; based on a story by Alvah Bessie; James Wong Howe, photographer;

Objective Burma! ran an abnormally long 142 minutes which many critics felt could have been cut by a healthy half-hour. It also displayed Errol Flynn, in one of his gung-ho, highly Hollywoodish incarnations, as an intrepid leader of paratroops out to destroy a Japanese post in Burma. Flynn is ably supported by such as William Prince, Henry Hull, and George Tobias, and all the troops in his command come across, under Raoul Walsh's rigorous direction, as genuine fighting men with individual natures, well-delineated. The British were to take offense because the operation was made to seem an entirely American one, and in fact the movie was not to be released in England until 1951, six years after it was made, and then with an apology tacked on.

Already there was a certain amount of ridicule afoot concerning Flynn's onscreen war heroics, first because he was in actuality a 4F living a plush civilian life, and second because his well-publicized sex

OBJECTIVE BURMA! Errol Flynn leads his men on patrol.

trials involving teenage girls were a standard joke of the war years. Yet no one could fault the intrepid Flynn for his war heroics onscreen, as he made them surprisingly forceful and convincing—which is why Warners kept him busy dishing them out.

As Captain Nelson, Flynn leads fifty paratroopers in a dangerous operation across the Burmese terrain, and with full awareness of the lethal intents—both overt and covert—of the Japanese enemy. Their objective is an enemy radar station of great strategic importance. Nearly two-hundred miles behind enemy lines, the band of men risk life and limb to further their objective, roused to intrepid action again and again by the charismatic Flynn character.

The mission accomplished, they await an airlift that will take them back to safety. But the Japanese attack suddenly, and no aircraft can land. Flynn's men then choose an alternative: fight their way through some 150 miles of Burmese jungle to the outside world and safety—or at least *relative* safety. Of the fifty men in the original paratroop detachment, only about a dozen survive. The final action finds them defending, in last-ditch style, a hill surrounded by the advancing enemy. But then comes the usual (and more often than not as anticipated by wartime audiences) Hollywoodian finale: The Allies finally launch their all-out air strike against

Burma—or rather its Japanese occupants—and wave after wave of paratroops, bombers, and so on signal liberation of the survivors. By this time, however, the latter are so depleted by battle tensions and jungle fevers that they respond with only the barest appreciation—joy seeming an irrelevant (and indeed anachronistic) reaction after all they

101

have suffered and survived, and after all the cruel deaths among them.

Time magazine's critic, not unduly impressed with the picture, snickered: "At the rate Errol Flynn and Co. knock off the Japanese, it may make you wonder why there is any good reason for the war to outlast next weekend." But the reviewers for the most part praised all the hard work, special effects, acting, and trenchant direction by Raoul Walsh that gave the picture its special brand of tension and force.

Flynn is colorful and heroic as usual, though his men, ably portrayed by the best character actors on the Warner lot, hog a large share of the heroic doings—and the footage. Nevertheless, when allowed to plan and maneuver and lead and inspire and egg the troops on to larger-than-life heroics, there is no man better equipped than Flynn. He has the look and stance and chemistry and brazenness to be a Leader Extraordinaire (at least in pictures like this), and he utilizes all those qualifications tellingly.

One critic of 1945 opined that had Flynn not been declared 4F, he might well have gone on to duplicate his screen heroics very tellingly in actual combat situations. The truth of this assumption we shall of course never know.

29

A WALK IN THE SUN

20TH CENTURY–FOX

1945

CAST:

Dana Andrews, Richard Conte, Sterling Holloway, George Tyne, John Ireland, Herbert Rudley, Richard Benedict, Lloyd Bridges, Norman Lloyd, Huntz Hall, James Cardwell, Chris Drake, George Offerman, Jr., Danny Desmond, Victor Cutler, Steve Brodie, Al Hammer, Matt Willis, Anthony Dante, Robert Lowell, Burgess Meredith (narrator).

CREDITS:

Lewis Milestone, producer-director; Robert Rossen, screenplay; based on the novel by Harry Brown; Russell Harlan, photographer; Fredric Efrem Rich, music; W. Duncan Mansfield, editor. Running time: 117 minutes.

One of the more honored films of World War II, *A Walk in the Sun* was directed by Lewis Milestone, who also produced. Milestone fifteen years earlier had guided one of the greatest of war films, *All Quiet on the Western Front,* and this one adheres to the standard he had set.

The story deals with a platoon of American infantry as they establish a beachhead on Italian soil after the 1943 Salerno engagement. As the men move toward a farmhouse occupied by the Germans, their fabled "walk in the sun," their individual natures, as well as their fighting skills, are incisively probed. The gunfire, the bursting of bombs, the general fear and the chilling suspense, all are tellingly gotten across—as are the men's reactions to one of the more terrifying and life-endangering incidents in their Italian engagement.

In zeroing in on this one platoon—its men, its battle potential, its weapons—Milestone has shown both war in miniature and war as symbol, succeeding on both counts. Howard Barnes of the *New York Herald-Tribune* said of *A Walk in the Sun:* "Of all our top directors, Milestone is the one who knows best how to couple imagery and dialogue in a fascinating film fugue. The camera always accents the insistent and terrible consequences of [even] a minor maneuver."

Dana Andrews is particularly fine as the sergeant, playing with quiet and eloquent square-jawed intensity a man who realizes he has responsibility for others as well as himself as he draws ever nearer the fortified farmhouse in which the lethal enemy tensely awaits their arrival. The deaths are depicted with what can only be termed an eloquent realism—and the flexibility and resourcefulness of the men are also forcefully and sensitively delineated. The innermost thoughts and feelings of the men are gotten across as vividly as are their actions.

Among the cast, Richard Conte is the essence of soldierly stolidity; Sterling Holloway comes on initially flibberty-jibbet in his usual style, but soon displays that his soldiering and military flexibilities are to be honored, however individualistically purveyed. John Ireland, Lloyd Bridges, Huntz Hall, and Norman Lloyd enact varying types with skill and precision, and the entire excruciating operation, as the hapless yet determined platoon draws ever nearer its waterloo, seems in essence a microcosm

A WALK IN THE SUN   Ad for *A Walk in the Sun.*

of small engagements throughout the war and on all fronts.

As seen again nearly a half century later, the film's assets are all the more tellingly displayed. Milestone was after high standards here, and—daring nothing less than a work of art—he was largely successful in realizing his aims. The camaraderie of the men is portrayed touchingly and truthfully: They know that Death awaits many of them, but Duty and Mutual Protectiveness carry them onward despite their own fears, and in the full knowledge that their deaths will bring great sorrow to their loved ones far away.

Andrews as their leader is the perfect battle-scarred yet battle-hardened fighting man—balanced, sensitive to his men, determined to do his duty, yet saddened by the horrifying costs entailed. His men sense his capacity for leadership; they do not want to let him (or themselves) down, and they follow him onward despite all inner trepidations and reservations.

A WALK IN THE SUN   Dana Andrews talks sense to an over-wrought Lloyd Bridges.

The combat action sequences are superb, but so also are the pauses—the slow, introspective, silent, eloquent stances and attitudes of the men when given a moment to rest and reflect. Lloyd Bridges and John Ireland are particularly fine as soldiers determined to do their duty yet unashamed to articulate their fears and concerns.

Harry Brown was a former army private who knew what he was writing about, and his novel, upon which the film was based, was a true and honest portrait of both the exterior and the interior lives of American fighting men. Milestone's film adaptation offered an indeed worthy follow-up to his benchmark masterpiece, *All Quiet on the Western Front*.

A WALK IN THE SUN   Taking their walk in the sun.

30

THE STORY OF GI JOE

UNITED ARTISTS

1945

CAST:

Robert Mitchum, Burgess Meredith, Freddie Steele, Wally Cassell, Jimmy Lloyd, Jack Reilly, Bill Murphy.

CREDITS:

William A. Wellman, director; Lester Cowan, producer; Leopold Atlas, Guy Endore, and Philip Stevenson, screenwriters; based on the book by Ernie Pyle; Russell Metty, photographer; Ann Ronell and Louis Applebaum, music; Robert Aldrich, assistant director; Otho Lovering, editor. Running time: 108 minutes.

The Story of GI Joe, released in 1945, was one of the most exceptional of war films, as it was true, deglamorized, realistic—and all the more poignant for the events and human sufferings it described. The story line is built around famed war correspondent Ernie Pyle's determination to live among the boys who were the backbone of his acclaimed writings, infantrymen in combat in Italy. He shares every aspect of their days, and exposes himself, along with them, to every conceivable vicissitude that infantry life involves. As the gifted actor Burgess Meredith envisioned and portrayed him, Ernie Pyle emphathized deeply with the men, incorporating their collective experience as his own—and thus emerged with a deeply moving human as well as military document.

William A. Wellman, who directed the famous *Wings*, delves into the psyches and experiences of the men in telling detail, and—as more than one critic observed—tells his story more in documentary than dramatic style. Eschewing the usual Hollywood clichés, he makes facts, stark and forceful as they turn out to be, substitute for the usual trumped-up heroics and story turns that often emerged more colorful than truthful.

Army film clips were used during action sequences, and these graphic depictions of the actual fighting in Italy greatly heightened the cinematized dramatic and human experiences of the screenplay. As one commentator noted, when the men of the U.S. Fifth Army who had actually undergone the brutalities and sufferings of actual combat in Italy saw *The Story of GI Joe*, their reaction was: "This was it!" The film went on to win a special commendation from Gen. Dwight D. Eisenhower, who pronounced it "the greatest war picture I've ever seen!"

Time led the parade of critical admirers of the film, stating in part: "[It was] an attempt to picture the infantryman's war as the late Ernie Pyle saw it. Pyle himself and nine fellow correspondents supervised and vouched for the film's hard-bitten authenticity. The result is far and away the least glam-

THE STORY OF GI JOE   Freddie Steele, Robert Mitchum and Burgess Meredith in the thick of the action.

THE STORY OF GI JOE   The troops fight their way into a German stronghold.

THE STORY OF GI JOE   The patient, slogging infantry marches past an overturned army vehicle.

THE STORY OF GI JOE   Mitchum talks with Steele during a lull in the fighting.

orous war picture ever made. It is a movie without a single false note. It is not 'entertainment' in the usual sense." *New York Times* critic Thomas M. Pryor called *The Story of GI Joe* "humorous, poignant, and tragic, earnestly human reflection of a stern life and the dignity of man."

The picture made Robert Mitchum. (It gave him his only Oscar nomination.) As an intrepid, no-nonsense, but compassionate and protective leader idolized by his men, he is quietly forceful, fitting his essentially unassuming performance into the documentary-style, honest realism that Wellman and his screenwriters were after. So authentic-looking-and -sounding is Mitchum in the dramatized scenes that one expects to see him in the documentary footage also. He is so real, so true, that he even imparts a documentary quality to the filmed work by Wellman and Russell Metty, whose camera lingers on him and his comrades with a brooding intentness, as if to say: Here is the true, unvarnished face of war and the men who fight it!

In a particularly poignant and moving scene—all the more racking for its superb, underplayed restraint—the men receive back Mitchum's body after he has been killed, and hold their own form of wake for him. He symbolizes all they have followed, fought for, believed in—and as they brood over his silent, stony features and inert form, they inpart not only a sense of chilling loss, but also the more heartening sense of continuity. They will go on fighting as he did, remembering him for his morale-building, his quiet courage, his persistence, his protectiveness—his concern for those in his charge.

Burgess Meredith is excellent as Ernie Pyle: compassionate, understanding, empathizing, with the outsized intuitive sense of an artist, he shares the stoic, silent sufferings of infantrymen who see their duty and do it; he asks not—and pauses, not to reason why—but accepts his fate and does what must be done.

31

COMMAND DECISION

METRO–GOLDWYN–MAYER

1948

CAST:

Clark Gable, Walter Pidgeon, Van Johnson, Brian Donlevy, John Hodiak, Charles Bickford, Edward Arnold, Marshall Thompson, Richard Quine, Cameron Mitchell, Clinton Sundberg, Ray Collins, John McIntire, John Ridgely, Warner Anderson, Moroni Olsen.

CREDITS:

Sam Wood, director; Sidney Franklin, producer; William R. Laidlaw and George Froeschel, screenplay; based on the play by William Wister Haines; Harold Rosson, photographer; Miklos Rozsa, music; Harold Kress, editor. Running time: 111 minutes.

Clark Gable, in his first substantial role after returning from World War II, makes the most of his characterization of Brig. Gen. K. C. ("Casey") Dennis, who from his British air force base orders wave after wave of bombing missions over Germany while fully aware of the cost in human lives. He also knows that the raids are vital if the United States is to be victorious, and the picture incisively delineates the inner mental suffering and emotional strain Dennis undergoes due to knowing that his decisions, while right for the overall design—winning the war—are exacting a heartbreakingly terrible cost in truncated destinies and lost future potential represented by the men who never come back.

Gable was following a tough act here, for Paul Kelly had made a tremendous hit in the role on the Broadway stage. While Gable was not up to Kelly's superior standards, he did demonstrate that his own service career in World War II had lent him an added depth and maturity of character, and at forty-seven he was in fine fettle. Nor did he shortchange his audiences in the later scenes, when his reaction to the outraged protests directed at him by others of his command result in his own sorrow and guilt and outrage at the waste of war—and through his tough veneer comes a human and touching awareness of the anguish that his decisions, necessary though they were, have caused.

William Wister Haines's 1947 play had gotten across most effectively the torment and ambivalence of spirit suffered by many officers in top commands who were forced to traffic in human lives to achieve ultimate objectives. As directed on film by the able and prescient Sam Wood, from a screenplay by William R. Laidlaw and George Froeschel, *Command Decision* emerged as a triumph for all hands, won considerable respect from the 1948 movie critics, and presented a new Clark Gable—a less "Hollywoodishly glamorous" and more moving, believable figure than in the past.

Walter Pidgeon gives Gable some tough competition as Major General Kane, who is a consummate politician and operates from sheer expediency and ends-justify-the-means attitudes, firmly and inexorably held. His characterization contrasts—and meshes—nicely with Gable's, and the scenes between the two have a trenchancy and sharpness that are among the best things in the film.

Van Johnson is on hand in a dependable, if not too well fleshed out, role, and Brian Donlevy is stolidly authoritative as another officer with the best of intentions who understands intimately the horrors of "command decisions." John Hodiak as another senior officer, Edward Arnold as a blustering congressman, Charles Bickford as a skeptical war correspondent, Cameron Mitchell as a bom-

COMMAND DECISION   Checking out the aircraft. (From right) Brian Donlevy, Clark
Gable, Walter Pidgeon, Charles Bickford, Clinton Sundberg, and Warner Anderson.

bardier whose pilot and copilot have been killed, Marshall Thompson, and others, all get their characterizations across with individualism and force.

Some critics and some audiences admittedly felt that the men who did the actual "dirty work"—the piloting and surveying and bombing—were first, last, and always the heroes of World War II, with the senior "command decision" types the ones who gave the orders for others to "do and die" while evading any imminent risks themselves. But the dual points, of both play and film are that the guilt and sorrow and remorse and human vulnerability are *always* inwardly at war with purpose and discipline and pursuit of inevitable objectives—and their oft-tragic results. *And* (point two) that this toll on human sensibilities, even in the cases of trained officers who are experts in "mind control" (their own *and* others'), often takes a pathological form that sooner or later crops up in peacetime: It does so in the spirits and minds of officers who performed their duty admirably in expedientist, war-dictated terms, yet eventually have to live with the

COMMAND DECISION   Pidgeon tells Bickford, Donlevy, and Gable of his faith in air power.

COMMAND DECISION   A congressman (Edward Arnold) points out where he feels targets should be to overseas bomber-base officers. (From left) Sundberg, Donlevy (seated), Pidgeon, Moroni Olsen, Bickford, Ray Collins, and Gable.

ghosts and lost potential of the very men they sent to premature death.

Both Clark Gable and Walter Pidgeon later went on record as regarding their roles in *Command Decision* as the most challenging of their careers. Certainly it showcased new acting potentials in both, Gable having been previously a rather shallow, even if dashing, figure in various adventure films, and Pidgeon having been largely confined to husbanding Greer Garson and making himself inconspicuous and benevolently innocuous in role after role. Here was a new challenge and both met it head-on.

32

BATTLEGROUND

METRO–GOLDWYN-MAYER

1949

CAST:

Van Johnson, John Hodiak, Ricardo Montalban, George Murphy, Marshall Thompson, Denise Darcel, James Whitmore, Richard Jaeckel, James Arness, Scotty Beckett, Douglas Fowley, Leon Ames.

CREDITS:

William A. Wellman, director; Dore Schary, producer; Robert Pirosh, screenplay; Paul C. Vogel, photographer; Cedric Gibbons and Hans Peters, art directors; Lennie Hayton, music; John Dunning, editor. Running time: 118 minutes.

The Battle of the Bulge has been a popular subject for war films, and *Battleground*, the MGM opus of 1949, was no exception, proving a smash box-office draw. Such contractees as Van Johnson, George Murphy, John Hodiak, and Ricardo Montalban gave it their best shot, with James Whitmore (most memorably), Marshall Thompson, Jerome Courtland, and Leon Ames in solid support.

The film won its share of recognition, garnering Oscars for screenwriter Robert Pirosh and photographer Paul C. Vogel, as well as nominations for best picture, director William Wellman, and supporting actor Whitmore.

The tension, suspense, battle chaos, and assorted individual heroisms all are piled on thick, but with entertaining and often persuasive results. The growing desperation of the platoon, which is making its way through enemy-infested territory as the Germans rally for one last stand, is gotten across forcefully and convincingly—and, in individual cases, often poignantly.

True, the individual characters of the men tend to be reminiscent of types in numerous war films of the past, but Pirosh gives them a coating of freshness, and at times striking insight. Opportunistic Van Johnson is the hail-fellow-well-met extrovert with an eye for the French girls encountered along the way, and when he runs into Denise Darcel, war's pressures and stresses are relieved, for a time—a moment, really, given war's exigencies and unpredictabilities.

Then there is writer John Hodiak, serious and intense and something of an intellectual, who passes

BATTLEGROUND   Ricardo Montalban, John Hodiak, and Van Johnson plan strategy.

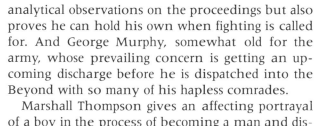

BATTLEGROUND   James Whitmore (standing, second left) and his men Johnson, James Whitmore, Bruce Cowling, Marshall Thompson seated, left. Montalban, Hodiak, Richard Jaeckel, Jerome Courtland keeping warm as best they can.

analytical observations on the proceedings but also proves he can hold his own when fighting is called for. And George Murphy, somewhat old for the army, whose prevailing concern is getting an upcoming discharge before he is dispatched into the Beyond with so many of his hapless comrades.

Marshall Thompson gives an affecting portrayal of a boy in the process of becoming a man and discovering that, in war, manhood's maturities and disciplines come at a price. And James Whitmore, who made a name for himself as the compassionate and understanding yet complex and hard-bitten sergeant, inspires those about him with his take-charge behavior amid battle chaos. Too, Leon Ames is on hand as an army chaplain who repeatedly reminds the men that the cause they are fighting *for* and the enemy (Fascism) they are fighting *against* give their efforts an imperative dignity and purpose.

There are a number of compelling cinematic images: the soldiers marching stolidly yet warily through snowy fields and woods; the stresses and strains registered by all as the skirmishes and battles force the best out of the already tired men; the crack of pistols and the rat-tat-tat of machine guns; bomb bursts filling the air with light and ominous shadow.

The stresses that come to men under fire, their quiet heroism, the discipline and unity of spirit that keep them following orders despite the evident

BATTLEGROUND Johnson, Montalban, and Hodiak encounter some white-flag-carrying Germans, John Mylong, Henry Rowland, Ivan Triesault.

dangers, all are set forth tellingly. Wellman's direction and Vogel's photography work in a fine sync, as accurate and well-paced as if guided by a metronome.

Louis B. Mayer, two years from the end of his association with Metro-Goldwyn-Mayer, had not been keen on doing yet another war film; he felt that, four years after the end of World War II, the public was sated with material of this kind. But he had to reckon with the strong opinions of Dore Schary, who in 1948 had been put in charge of the studio production team. Schary had purchased the screen rights to *Battleground* while still at RKO—where he had also headed production—and believed in the project. He also believed in Pirosh and Wellman, and maintained that the *treatment* of the subject, even if familiar, was what mattered. Schary's judgment was proved justified when the picture scored well with both public and critics—*and* the Oscar voters.

Van Johnson is persuasive in the lead—happy-go-lucky at the start, a serious fighter in the latter half. John Hodiak and George Murphy and (especially) James Whitmore make worthy contributions to the overall positives of a well-mounted, well-executed film.

33

SANDS OF IWO JIMA

REPUBLIC PICTURES

1949

CAST:

John Wayne, John Agar, Forrest Tucker, Adele Mara, Arthur Franz, Richard Webb, Wally Cassell, James Brown, Julie Bishop, James Holden, Peter Coe, Richard Jaeckel, Martin Milner, Bill Murphy.

CREDITS:

Allan Dwan, director; Herbert J. Yates, producer; Harry Brown and James Edward Grant, screenplay; from a story by Harry Brown; Reggie Lanning, photographer; Victor Young, music; Richard Van Enger, editor; Howard and Theodore Lydecker, special effects. Running time: 110 minutes.

This extremely popular 1949 film was dedicated "to the United States Marine Corps, whose exploits and valor have left a lasting impression on the world and in the hearts of their countrymen." A legend also notes that "The first American flag was raised on Mount Suribachi by the late Sgt. Ernest L. Thomas, Jr., USMC, on the morning of February 23rd, 1945."

Sands of Iwo Jima is a stirring tribute to the marine heroes of World War II, detailing their heroism in an effective manner but never being accused of not humanizing its soldiers. Sergeant Stryker (John Wayne), who is determined to whip his men into shape, frequently drinks himself into oblivion because his wife left him and took their young son with her. Peter Conway (John Agar), whose father was a war hero and in whose eyes he feels he can never measure up, hates Stryker because he reminds him of his old man—and therefore has a massive chip on his shoulder. "I'm a civilian," he tells Stryker, "in here strictly for tradition." Al Thomas (Forrest Tucker) has a big grudge against Stryker for turning him in for one-too-many infractions. These men are not, at first glance, a pleasant bunch.

This all changes when the shooting starts, however, and we see how heroic these (and other) characters can be when faced with almost insurmountable odds. A lot of actual combat footage is blended in with re-created battle scenes, to convey a fairly realistic and vivid depiction of what it must

SANDS OF IWO JIMA   John Wayne in fighting trim.

SANDS OF IWO JIMA   Richard Jaeckel tries to play down his wounds to Wayne, Bill Murphy, and John Agar.

113

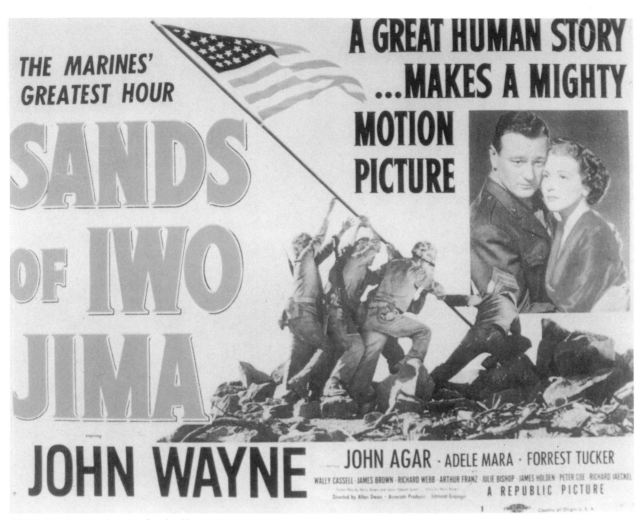

SANDS OF IWO JIMA   A poster for the film.

have been like for these men in the trenches, slogging through mud, and advancing uphill amid heavy enemy fire. The battle sequences are not especially cinematic or well-staged (there is no "pretty" cinematography to speak of), but the effect is realistically gritty, cluttered, and busy nonetheless.

Wayne's performance as Stryker garnered him his first Oscar nomination. He fully deserved it. Stryker, a part that Wayne was born to play, makes full use of the actor's tough, cynical, world-weary—and at times surprisingly tender—persona. Whether telling off a friend who warns him that he drinks too much ("You've got an old maid's failings—you worry!") or playfully dismissing a woman's promise that she'll pray for him ("Let's not get religion!"), Wayne is every inch the complex, raw, likable character he's playing.

The film contains several excellent sequences. In a battle that takes place before the climactic Iwo

Jima landing, Wayne and his men are in a foxhole at night when Agar hears a soldier crying out in the distance. He wants to go to his aid, but the more experienced sergeant knows that it could be a "Nip trick" and is afraid Agar will give away their position to the enemy and doom them all. But the camera plays across Wayne's face as he agonizes over his decision to refuse to let Agar leave, and wonders if it was the right one. The scene is very tense and disturbing.

Two interludes show Stryker's contradictory nature. In one he goes home with a woman he meets in a bar who asks him for money to buy booze. Along with a bottle of whiskey, she buys a can of pablum for the baby she has hidden in the next room. It was basically the child's welfare she was thinking of, all along—not "romance." Instead of getting angry, Stryker gives her most of his money and departs. Later on, learning that Al Thomas (Tucker) caused a man's death in the trenches be-

114

cause he delayed bringing needed ammo to him, Stryker gives him a beating in the best John Wayne tradition. Forrest Tucker also turns in an excellent performance.

The most poignant sequences deal with the deaths of men we've come to care about. Green recruit McCue (Martin Milner), barely eighteen years old, is one of the first to die when the marines hit the beaches of Iwo Jima; in his chest pocket is a paperback copy of *Our Hearts Were Young and Gay*. But the most affecting death is that of Wayne, who is shot in a deceptively quiet moment at the end of the picture. Surrounding his body, the comrades who loved him read aloud the letter he almost finished composing to the five-year-old son he knew he might never live to see again. It is an undeniably manipulative moment—but also a movingly effective one, because it rings true.

SANDS OF IWO JIMA   John Wayne with his troops.

SANDS OF IWO JIMA
Approaching Iwo Jima.

Sands is a fine picture for portraying human heroes who have flaws and insecurities, for showing both the fear and vulnerability of the men and their tenderness toward one another, and especially for having the courage to allow the outsized Wayne to expire at the film's conclusion instead of riding off into the sunset like some invulnerable icon. Furthermore, the dialogue in the screenplay by Harry Brown and James Edward Grant often lifts the picture above a macho breast-beating level in such scenes as when John Agar insists his son will "read Shakespeare, not the marine manual," and that he'll be "intelligent instead of tough"; and when Forrest Tucker muses "That's war—trading real estate for men." Although there are no graphically bloody scenes, the film still manages to get across the terror and insanity of battle, and emerges as a credible filmic document.

SANDS OF IWO JIMA   Murphy, James Holden, and Jaeckel fight.

Sands of Iwo Jima was not only Wayne's finest hour—but also, even if in a crude way, one of the finest war films ever made.—*W. S.*

34

THREE CAME HOME

20TH CENTURY–FOX

1950

CAST:

Claudette Colbert, Patric Knowles, Florence Desmond, Sessue Hayakawa, Sylvia Andrew, Phyllis Morris.

CREDITS:

Jean Negulesco, director; Nunnally Johnson, producer-screenplay; based on the book by Agnes Newton Keith; Milton Krasner, photographer; Hugo Friedhofer, music; Lionel Newman, musical director; Dorothy Spencer, editor. Running time: 106 minutes.

Three Came Home is a devastating picture based on a nonfiction account of a woman's stay in a prisoner-of-war camp with her little boy after Japanese forces invade Borneo in World War II. (Her husband has been imprisoned in a separate camp for men.) While events have undoubtedly been diluted a bit, this is still a hard-hitting, unglamorized depiction of the noncombat agonies of wartime, focusing on the physical and (more especially) emotional anguish of female prisoners, who must endure not only rigorous hardships but also constant concern as to whether they will ever see their husbands again. Claudette Colbert quickly jettisons the Hollywood mannerisms of her early scenes and gives one of her strongest performances. In a grim, uncompromising confrontation that shows her at her best (and is light years from her lightweight comedies), she is tortured by her captors for daring to report nearly being raped.

Although Patric Knowles as Colbert's husband is an inept leading man in this film, Sessue Hayakawa strikes just the right note as a sympathetic commandant who loses his family when the United States drops The Bomb on Hiroshima. (In 1957, Hayakawa was again to play an officer in charge of a camp, in *The Bridge on the River Kwai*.) Colbert's scene with him after Japan has surrendered is dramatically effective, but is perhaps the only moment in the film that doesn't ring true; it seems contrived in order to give two fine actors another chance to emote.

Except for a manipulative but strong finale when husband and wife are reunited, *Three Came Home* never hits you over the head with pathos, but the emotional tone is very high and sustained throughout, and indeed there are times when the film is unbearably moving. A particularly powerful scene occurs when the captured husbands and wives are allowed to tender each other a last farewell before imprisonment but aren't allowed to touch, the men on one side of a wide, muddy trench and the women on the other. Colbert is of course justly afraid that she'll never see her husband again. The most heartbreaking moment comes when a young woman runs up and down the line, staring across at the men, desperately looking for her husband but

THREE CAME HOME   Courageous Claudette Colbert comforts her child.

116

THREE CAME HOME   Running into trouble with the enemy.

THREE CAME HOME   Colbert and Patric Knowles sense trouble.

THREE CAME HOME   Sessue Hayakawa is a baleful figure as the camp commandant.

not finding him. She tries to put a brave face on it, rationalizing that he may be ill or somehow occupied elsewhere—but we later learn, of course, that he was killed by the Japanese. The scene is so well-acted and so painful that is is actually hard to endure.

Pulling very few punches, *Three Came Home* reminds us that the suffering during wartime was not limited either to men in combat or to their women waiting at home. The film maintains a consistent, almost palpable sense of loss and desolation, detailing unflinchingly the awful effects of war and the emotional attritions of separation from every last one of those you love whose fate is uncertain.

Colbert's expert thesping, Nunnally Johnson's moving script, and Jean Negulesco's telling direction combine to make a haunting and powerful motion picture—an undeservedly neglected classic—*W. S.*

117

35

THE RED BADGE OF COURAGE

METRO–GOLDWYN–MAYER

1951

CAST:

Audie Murphy, Bill Mauldin, Douglas Dick, Royal Dano, John Dierkes, Andy Devine, Arthur Hunnicutt.

CREDITS:

John Huston, director-screenplay; Gottfried Reinhardt, producer; based on the novel by Stephen Crane; Harold Rosson, photographer; Cedric Gibbons, art director; Bronislau Kaper, music; Ben Lewis, editor. Running time: 69 minutes.

John Huston directed this ambitious adaptation of Stephen Crane's famous 1894 novel, but was furi-

ous when the studio cut the film down to little over an hour, reportedly to make it more commercial. (Lillian Ross's well-known book *Picture* recounts the making of this movie.) While it is an admirable film in many ways, the question remains as to whether or not its missing footage would have made that much difference.

As did the novel, *The Red Badge of Courage* attempts to see inside the psyche of a young Civil War recruit who—far from being gung-ho and unrealistically macho about fighting—recognizes the terrible danger he is in, and is quite justifiably scared. However, Huston's film doesn't *quite* capture the stark terror and gruesome brutality of war as many other films have done.

The young Union soldier, Henry Fleming, is portrayed by Audie Murphy, a real-life war hero who was later to play himself in *To Hell and Back* (1955), a less distinguished film based on his autobiography. In *Red Badge*, Murphy proves himself a sensitive and capable (if limited) actor. Bill Mauldin, the noted World War II cartoonist, is also excellent as his buddy Tom Wilson, and John Dierkes really scores as a fellow soldier who dies midway through the film, while marching away from the battle with other injured Yankees. The entire cast, in fact, acquits itself with distinction.

Henry manages to get through the first wave of his initial major battle, but later, when the Rebel forces come charging at his regiment through a ghostly roil of cannonball smoke—like dreadful spectres emerging from storm clouds—he bolts in

THE RED BADGE OF COURAGE
Audie Murphy tells Bill Mauldin of his feelings about war.

THE RED BADGE OF COURAGE Officers guide their men in the thick of battle. Douglas Dick aids James Dobson.

fear and runs away from the fighting. Reunited ultimately with his buddies who thought he was dead, he points to an injury given him by another fleeing soldier and claims he was shot by the enemy and became disoriented.

Realizing that no one is aware of his secret shame, he becomes cocky and puts up a ready-to-fight front. Then "front" becomes reality when he gets so angry at seeing how the Rebs are mowing down his fellow soldiers that he leads the charge into battle and becomes a bona fide hero.

While it is true that anger can briefly overcome a person's fear, Fleming's abrupt change of character never really seems convincing, as it may have been in the novel. An essentially "cowardly" person (even if only cowardly because he has the imagination to realize what might really happen to him—and in graphic detail) might rise to the occasion and do his job as competently and bravely as others, but having Fleming switch from Milquetoast to Rambo is a little hard to swallow.

Ironically, at the end of the picture, Fleming

THE RED BADGE OF COURAGE Murphy finally shaping up as a fighting man.

119

learns that his best buddy, Tom Wilson, also briefly deserted during the previous battle.

Nevertheless, *The Red Badge of Courage* is an interesting slice-of-war with many good scenes. One that particularly stays in the memory is a shot of a Union officer, safely on horseback and hanging back from the fighting, ordering his men into a suicide run into the thick of battle—all sabers, blood, and bombs—and calling *them* cowards when they quite sensibly run for their lives.

Harold Rosson's striking photography makes the picture pleasant to look at, and Bronislau Kaper's musical score is generally rich and unusual. The narration was done, stirringly and eloquently, by James Whitmore.—*W. S.*

36
FLYING LEATHERNECKS

RKO PICTURES

1951

CAST:

John Wayne, Robert Ryan, Janis Carter, Don Taylor, Jay C. Flippen, William Harrigan, James Bell.

CREDITS:

Nicholas Ray, director; Edmund Grainger, producer; James Edward Grant, screenplay; from a story by Kenneth Gamet; William E. Synder, photographer; Roy Webb, music; Sherman Todd, editor. Running time: 102 minutes. (Technicolor.)

John Wayne and Robert Ryan make an interesting costarring duo in this story of marine fighter pilots in the South Pacific during World War II. Wayne's peppery, macho forthrightness is contrasted effectively with Ryan's saturnine, grim mannerisms, and the two fight a running battle all through the film— Wayne bossing his men around with what Ryan considers totally insensitive boorishness, and Ryan

weathering Wayne's scorn for what Wayne conceives to be Ryan's cerebral approach to matters that call for hands-on action—and speedy action at that.

This small squadron composed of men known as Flying Leathernecks is isolated somewhere in the Pacific arena of war, and as the story progresses it comes out that Ryan is not so distinterested after all, since he had originally been recommended for the command post now so abrasively and gratingly (in Ryan's view) filled by Wayne.

There is a lull in this feud, and in the aerial action in general, when Wayne takes a furlough to spend time with wife Janis Carter and their small son back home. But soon Wayne is back in action, the domestic interlude having demonstrated that though he is an essentially caring husband and dad, derring-do with fellow males in tight situations is his real metier and absorbing interest. (But then, can one imagine a John Wayne picture being otherwise?) And the Ryan-Wayne conflict continues to build, if only because Ryan's mystique onscreen has never been one that plays second fiddle to that of

FLYING LEATHERNECKS   In the thick of the fighting.

120

FLYING LEATHERNECKS
Robert Ryan tries to cheer up the men.

FLYING LEATHERNECKS
Wayne comforts an injured comrade, Maurice Jara.

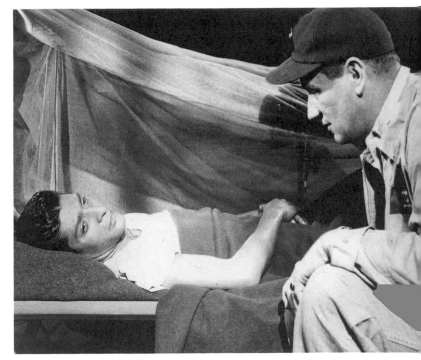

any other actor, and he doesn't come off second here, either.

There is a plethora of sickening violence, strong for 1951—and later—standards, but Wayne and company seem to mightily enjoy dishing it out. On hand to subserve the Wayne purposes are a gaggle

121

FLYING LEATHERNECKS   The tank lets loose.

37

RETREAT, HELL!

WARNER BROS.

1952

CAST:

Frank Lovejoy, Richard Carlson, Anita Louise, Russ Tamblyn, Ned Young, Lamont Johnson, Dorothy Patrick.

CREDITS:

Joseph H. Lewis, director; Milton Sperling, producer; Milton Sperling and Ted Sherdeman, screenplay; Warren Lynch, photographer; William Lava, music; Folmar Blangsted, editor. Running time: 95 minutes.

of types of the usual Wayne-actioner persuasion, including Jay C. Flippen as a crew chief who knows his onions—a sly fellow who is every bit a match for Wayne. Also in on the melee are such worthies doing their marine duties as Don Taylor, Brett King, and Carleton Young—who, when they are not bitching at Wayne's totalitarian rule, are finding such consolations as the locale permits (and they are not many).

The aerial action scenes are the best thing in the film, staged with excitement and fine pacing and with a realistic look. Sometimes the action seems to swoop right out on the audience, so graphic is it, and the well-applied color helps heighten its reality. (The Technicolor footage employed in this Howard Hughes presentation is impressive in its evocation of the ambience of aerial conflict, in part because, for felicitous results, studio shots were mixed in with actual color footage of battle action.)

Janis Carter is fine as Wayne's patient wife, back in the States, who sees the situation and her place in it. No combative feminist is she, and in the best 1951 tradition she is content to play wife and mother while Wayne wings away thousands of miles off to do his macho thing.

An interesting Wayne-Ryan interactioner and a graphic aerial-combat film—such is *Flying Leathernecks*.

The title for this excellent Korean War film comes from a scene late in the picture when the marines are told to effect a strategic withdrawal from their area because of the threatened onslaught of 100,000 Chinese soldiers. "Does this mean we're retreating, sir?" one of the men asks Colonel Corbett (Frank Lovejoy). "Retreat, Hell!" he snaps back. "We're just attacking from another direction!"

The film commences with marine training at Camp Pendleton. Corbett is concerned about the reliability of Captain Hanson (Richard Carlson), a World War II veteran who doesn't seem to have the right attitude anymore. "Hanson's got a wife and two children," Corbett declares. "He's gonna play it safe—too safe!" Then there's the green recruit Jimmy McDermott (Russ Tamblyn) who is always eager to volunteer—his brother is also a marine, and Jimmy wants to demonstrate that he can do as well, but is unprepared for what he must face when the fighting truly begins.

The battalion's assignment is to retake the South Korean capital of Seoul. Just as McDermott is about to climb up and out of their landing craft, the man ahead of him is shot, and his dead body drops into McDermott's arms. Then, facing a hail of bullets on the beach, the young marine is so scared that all he can do is claw the sand and cry in terror as the others race on to their fate. These early scenes are interesting because we see them from McDermott's

RETREAT, HELL! The boys mean business. Carlson, Tamblyn, Lovejoy.

123

point of view, and can feel sympathetic toward him and appreciate the fear he is undergoing. Soon after, however, the film drops this approach in favor of the standard scenario, when McDermott overcomes his terror and becomes a hero by lobbing a grenade at a sniper in a building—thus saving the day.

Captain Hanson also shows that he still "has the stuff" and that Corbett need not have worried about him. The only worry is the unexpected presence of tens of thousands of Chinese troops who surround the men and begin systematically mowing them down. Then comes that "strategic withdrawal." Corbett is determined that no marine will be left behind, so small groups go up into the hills to both search for injured comrades and pick off the snipers who are continually picking *them* off with both bullets and grenades as the marines laboriously make their way back along the road they came upon.

McDermott—in one of the search parties—nearly freezes to death in the snow of the hills, but Hanson finds him and the two manage to make it to the airfield, where a hospital plane is waiting. Meanwhile,

Corbett and the survivors are doubly determined to take Seoul, come hell or high water. The picture ends at this point.

Although some actual combat footage is used, most of the picture consists of gritty, well-staged Hollywood action scenes, such as the aforementioned sniper incident, and a superb sequence which depicts a night raid by the Chinese on the ramshackle marine headquarters. In these eerie and suspenseful minutes, thousands of enemy soldiers swarm down the hills toward the trenches, where the Americans find they are rapidly running out of ammo and will be forced to fight with fixed bayonets. Before long, scores of bodies line the sweeping, moonlit hills—a horrific and unforgettable image. Another memorable scene has a tank busting out of a quiet, ostensibly deserted roadside cabin, to fire on the battalion until McDermott, Hanson, and Corbett take it out of action via their combined efforts.

There are also effective noncombat scenes, as when McDermott goes to find his brother and is told by a hardened marine that he'll find him "around the corner." Around the corner in an al-

RETREAT, HELL! Lovejoy and men under siege at the convoy.

RETREAT, HELL! Tough leatherneck Lovejoy intends to get his men out of a tight spot.

leyway, McDermott finds a score of bodies covered with blankets. One of the dead is his brother. "I guess it's all right to hold him now" he says tearfully. (Tamblyn's performance as the sensitive, yet brave and durable, young marine is consistently excellent.) Later, when a rumor is spread that the men might be home in time for Christmas, two pals give each other an exuberant, joyful hug that is all the more poignant because of the likelihood that neither may even survive the week, let alone until Christmas.

One of the rare amusing moments has Corbett passing by a tent at Camp Pendleton where some men are singing Bette Davis's famous number from the 1943 film *Thank Your Lucky Stars*, "They're Either Too Young or Too Old." (Apparently Davis had her share of fans among the macho marines.) Corbett just smiles and shakes his head, then walks on.

Much of the credit for the success of *Retreat, Hell!* has to go to director Joseph H. Lewis, who keeps the picture moving briskly and brings the battle scenes to life with real cinematic know-how.—*W. S.*

38

BATTLE CIRCUS

METRO–GOLDWYN–MAYER

1953

CAST:

Humphrey Bogart, June Allyson, Keenan Wynn, Robert Keith, William Campbell, Perry Sheehan, Patricia Tiernan, Adele Longmire, Steve Forrest, Jeff Richards, Dick Simmons, Danny Chang, Philip Ahn, Ann Morrison.

CREDITS:

Richard Brooks, director-screenplay; based on an original story by Allen Rivkin and Laura Kerr; John Alton, photographer; Lennie Hayton, music; George Boemler, editor. Running time: 90 minutes.

Battle Circus is one of the more unusual—and unlikely—Humphrey Bogart movies. He is essentially miscast as a major running a mobile field hospital

125

near the front lines in Korea. The film was also a rare appearance for Bogart at Metro-Goldwyn-Mayer, and furthermore, he found himself uncomfortably saddled with one of the MGM female luminaries—June Allyson—as costar. Her sugar blends very badly indeed with his salt, and their pairing, considering the total lack of chemistry between them (at the time he was fifty-three and she was only pushing thirty-five) seems inexplicable today. Moreover, director Richard Brooks, who had made miracles with admittedly far better material earlier in his career, did not seem galvanized to any extraordinary efforts when faced with the unlikely Bogart-Allyson duo. He even allowed such Bogie sallies as "Three World Wars in one lifetime. Maybe whiskey's as much a part of our life as war."

Today *Battle Circus* is in its several aspects seen to be a hilarious/serious jape of the later *M*A*S*H*, and its solemnities and pretenses only heighten the joke. Allyson plays a dedicated army relief nurse, all patriotic jingoism and Florence Nightingale-ish attitudes (and illusions). Bogart, half-attracted to and half-contemptuous of this pernicious innocent, makes passes at her while wising her up on the gritty, grisly procedures at the hospital that make realistic, feet-on-the-ground approaches a must. The Bogart character is also one who can drink anyone under the table, and this makes the supervising colonel, Robert Keith, very uptight indeed. Soon Bogie is being threatened with transfer if he

BATTLE CIRCUS   June Allyson and Humphrey Bogart dance it slow and easy. . .

BATTLE CIRCUS   . . . and later get down to serious talk.

BATTLE CIRCUS   Bogart and Allyson tending the wounded.

doesn't lay off the booze. All this and starry-eyed June Allyson, too! But marriage he does *not* want, which leaves her very sad. All turns out well in the end, however—though *why* defies logic.

Keenan Wynn is amusing and salty and down-to-earth as the sergeant in charge of pitching the field hospital at various sites forced upon them by the changing fortunes of battle. Allyson proves her mettle to Bogart by disarming a Korean prisoner making tough with a hand grenade. Some medically needy front-line wounded are picked up in a fancy helicopter maneuver. All proceeds as usual.

The *M*A*S*H* comparisons notwithstanding, there are serious, solid moments to the film (it was studio-bound, no location shooting) and Bogart handles the operating knives as slickly and nonchalantly as he orchestrates the movings-around, the rescues, and the combat action—into which he injects himself if and when required. Certainly he is more convincing waging war than making love to dainty June. (Whoever at MGM worked up the idea of casting Bogie and June as lovers was out to lunch *that* day.) The same could probably be said of teaming Robert Mitchum with Ann Blyth in *One Minute to Zero* (also about the Korean War) around the same time.

BATTLE CIRCUS   Bogart looks to Patricia Tiernan for help with a zonked Allyson.

127

All of the supporting actors are so good that they make the field-hospital doings look fairly rational—yes, even in darkest Korea with the enemy snapping at their heels at every turn. Robert Keith is a fatherly, stern superior officer who first dithers with discipline and then clamps down. Keenan Wynn injects cynical levity into his role, and—lest the point be missed—is on one occasion labeled a former circus roustabout.

When the action sequences come around, Brooks does not fail his viewers, and Bogart shows himself surprisingly lithe when he deigns to exert himself for God (?), Country (Maybe), June (*also* maybe), and a chance to get back to his steady drinking (certainly).

Danny Chang and Philip Ahn play standard Orientals, William Campbell is a no-nonsense chaplain, Jeff Richards is a stalwart lieutenant, Adele Longmire and Ann Morrison are intrepid officers in the medical corps, and the other performers manage to look and act real, despite the surreal ambiences and influences. And of course there are the casualties, with whom we get acquainted from time to time. *Battle Circus* is fun, once you get in sync with its rhythm—but that comparison to *M*A*S*H* is likely to stick nonetheless.

39

FROM HERE TO ETERNITY

COLUMBIA

1953

CAST:

Burt Lancaster, Deborah Kerr, Montgomery Clift, Frank Sinatra, Donna Reed, Ernest Borgnine, Philip Ober, Mickey Shaughnessy, Jack Warden, Claude Akins, George Reeves.

CREDITS:

Fred Zinnemann, director; Buddy Adler, producer; Daniel Taradash, screenplay; based on the novel by James Jones; Burnett Guffey, photographer; George Duning, music; William Lyon, editor. Running time: 118 minutes.

From Here to Eternity is a now-celebrated film about the regular army in the period largely before Pearl Harbor. The action takes place at Schofield Barracks, near Honolulu, lending the film unchallengeable authenticity. Packed with star power, it features Burt Lancaster as the tough Sergeant Warden. Montgomery Clift, a compelling Pvt. Robert E. Lee Prewitt, is a gung-ho regular-army bugler who falls in love with prostitute Donna Reed. Lancaster gets romantically involved with his commander's unfulfilled wife (Deborah Kerr), resulting in a now-famous beach scene in which they make love on the sand while the waves pour over them.

FROM HERE TO ETERNITY   The famous Lancaster-Kerr beach scene.

Frank Sinatra fought for the role of Private Maggio, which won him a supporting Oscar for 1953 and revitalized his career. (Originally, Eli Wallach had a lock on the part.) The casual cruelty and negations of army life are exemplified by the brutal, burly Fatso (Ernest Borgnine), who runs the base stockade and who torments Maggio.

The original James Jones novel emphasized the sexual frustrations and rampages of the bored and mischievous soldiers, and much of its grit and cynicism was retained for the film. The action sequences form an important part of the footage, and when Pearl Harbor finally is bombed and chaos erupts at Schofield, the soldiers all get a chance to make use of their military training. In fact, the sudden exigencies of a wartime situation seem to bring out the best in all concerned, providing as it does a

FROM HERE TO ETERNITY
Ernest Borgnine and Frank Sinatra square off, as Burt Lancaster intervenes.

FROM HERE TO ETERNITY
Montgomery Clift proves his manhood via fisticuffs, here with John Dennis.

FROM HERE TO ETERNITY   Clift's bugle tootling beguiles his buddies, including Sinatra (right).

130

FROM HERE TO ETERNITY   Burt Lancaster rallies his men after the Pearl Harbor attack.

therapeutic energy expenditure for all the pent-up feelings on display throughout the earlier parts of the picture.

Academy Award winner as Best Picture of 1953, *From Here to Eternity* also took a number of other Oscars, including the supporting awards to Sinatra and Donna Reed, and statuettes to director Fred Zinnemann and screenwriter Daniel Taradash.

Zinnemann was obviously determined, as was writer Taradash, to portray army men with unsentimental, truthful realism. The film was made some eight years after World War II, by which time flag-waving, gung-ho depictions of the conflict had largely gone out of fashion, even though some were still to be found among the more blatantly commercial product of the early and mid-fifties.

Lancaster's character is a basically good guy turned cynical by his army experiences, including the less-than-admirable human interplay between officers and men. Nor does he take women that se-

riously, and his adulterous affair with restless and unhappy Kerr, whose officer husband (Philip Ober) seems a deadly-dull person to be married to, is one he initially conducts with his usual jaded approach to everything in his life. Jarred into sincerity—of a kind—by the affair, Lancaster later reverts to his true, take-charge self when the Pearl Harbor attack rallies the military.

Monty Clift limns a character who is simple on the surface, yet complex within. True, his bugle, his army service, and his not-so-pure girl are his primary interests, but he also gives evidence of being a thoughtful, introspective person who has found the military a refuge against the world's complexities—though its disciplines come naturally to his nature, which is one of basic integrity. His scenes with Donna Reed, who is lonely and longing to get back to the States and a quiet, financially secure life even while purveying her charms to all comers, ring quite true. She and Clift pool their individual-

FROM HERE TO ETERNITY   Clift and Donna Reed in an introspective moment.

ized needs, and Clift's famous line "Nobody ever lies when they say they're lonely" rings a bell for both.

Philip Ober is the consummate duty-obsessed officer who can however be human at times; Borgnine's Fatso Judson symbolizes and embodies all the obtuse, animalistic insensitive bullies of time immemorial; and Sinatra's vulnerable, besieged, yet defensively combative Maggio gets beneath the skin of that character and makes him live.

When Pearl Harbor Day finally hits the hitherto quiet post, and hell breaks loose, director Zinnemann shows himself as adept at picturing defensive military confusion, and belated but effective rallying, as at portraying the inner emotions that his characters had earlier left largely unresolved. *From Here to Eternity* is an accurate reflection of life as it is really lived—unglamorous, yet compelling.

40

BATTLE CRY

WARNER BROS.

1955

CAST:

Van Heflin, Aldo Ray, Mona Freeman, Tab Hunter, Dorothy Malone, Raymond Massey, Anne Francis, Nancy Olson, James Whitmore, John Lupton, Perry Lopez, William Campbell, Fess Parker, Rhys Williams, Justus McQueen (later L. Q. Jones), Felix Noriego, Allyn Ann McLerie.

CREDITS:

Raoul Walsh, director; Leon Uris, screenplay, based on his novel; Sid Hickox, photographer; Max Steiner, music; William Ziegler, editor. Running time: 149 minutes. (CinemaScope / Warner Color.)

With a tough, hard-hitting screenplay by Leon Uris, based on his pungent novel, and directed with his usual brio by Raoul Walsh, *Battle Cry* was given the all-out Warner treatment in 1955, being photographed in CinemaScope and WarnerColor, and with a lush Max Steiner score. The entire enterprise ran a long but fast-paced 149 minutes.

Yet another story of fighting marines in the Pacific, this effort was redeemed by some good act-ing, especially on the part of Van Heflin as the colonel who mixes toughlove with compassion, James Whitmore as the gruff but sympathetic top sergeant, and Raymond Massey as a commanding general who knows how to be flexible when the occasion calls for it. Then there's Aldo Ray as the rugged marine who gets involved with nice-girl Nancy Olson, and an opposites-attract pair they do make. Not so lucky is innocent, romance-minded Tab Hunter, who works up steam for navy wife Dorothy Malone, a man-devourer par excellence. Then there's nice kid John Lupton, all bespectacled

BATTLE CRY   Van Heflin and his sergeant, James Whitmore, confer on strategy.

133

hopes by distinguishing themselves in combat—though with some winding up severely wounded, others dead, and still others wishing fervently that they had remained in the training phase. Had they heard Massey's observation about "a hell of a way to make a living," they doubtless could not have agreed more.

L. Q. Jones (originally Justus McQueen) is on hand for his filmic debut here. He decided to take the name of his *character*—yes, L. Q. Jones—because he felt it was distinctive and attention-getting. He was right. Perry Lopez, Fess ("Davy Crockett") Parker, John Lupton, and Victor Millan, among others, get across their individual character types sharply under Walsh's knowing direction; and when the action gets hot and heavy, photographer Sid Hickox is giving it all he's got. Max Steiner offers up a musical treatment that makes the goings-on sound like a great epic, which *Battle Cry* is

BATTLE CRY   Ray, Felix Noriego, Tab Hunter, and Whitmore assess the situation.

sensitivity, who gets himself killed and is mourned by pal Perry Lopez. Heflin also gets knocked off at the end. Popular with his men, he is greatly mourned. But the fight, laid in the Pacific in 1944, goes on—and on.

Heflin doesn't want his battalion held passive in reserve status, so appeals to his commanding officer, Massey, to let the boys get in there and fight, as he says they long to do (his is a really gung-ho gang of leathernecks). A reluctant Massey, having reconsidered the overall strategy, accedes, authorizing (with the rueful observation, "It's a hell of a way to make a living!") Heflin to take his boys into action.

Meanwhile, Heflin and Whitmore have kept their troops training hard for that Big Opportunity in combat—but Whitmore has to rein in Heflin's humanitarian impulses when the latter signs furlough papers for Hunter so that the kid can straighten out his personal problems. Whitmore thus gives his superior some straight-from-the-shoulder advice about not getting involved in certain men's personal lives.

But these are side issues, definitely. Most of the running time is taken up with tough, disciplined training, and the men redeem their commanders'

134

BATTLE CRY Heflin asks General Snipes (Raymond Massey) to let his battalion fight.

BATTLE CRY Dorothy Malone is Hunter's *femme fatale*—and then some!

BATTLE CRY Victor Millan, Whitmore, and Aldo Ray consider the fighting odds.

not—but Steiner was a wise old hand at juicing up picture moods and ambiences with his memorable melodies.

Sexy Dorothy pours it on as the bad-gal type (married, too) who takes pretty-boy Tab on an emotional toboggan ride. Cynical, rueful, essentially destructive, and consummately self-centered, the Malone character showcases her as a type she was later to do interesting variations on (as in the 1956 *Written on the Wind*). Up against vividly vixenish Malone, Nancy Olson, Mona Freeman, and Anne Francis seem weak tea indeed, although they do pretty much what they can with what the script accords them. But this is a guy's picture all the way, and with the veteran Raoul Walsh to guide them, the guys give their all to the battle fireworks.

41

THE BRIDGES AT TOKO-RI

PARAMOUNT

1955

CAST:

William Holden, Fredric March, Grace Kelly, Mickey Rooney, Robert Strauss, Charles McGraw, Keiko Awaji, Earl Holliman, Richard Shannon, Willis E. Bouchey, Charles Tannen, Teru Shimada.

CREDITS:

Mark Robson, director; William Perlberg, producer; Valentine Davies, screenplay; adapted from the novel by James A. Michener; Loyal Griggs, photographer; Charles G. Clarke, aerial photography; Lyn Murray, music; Alma Macrorie, editor. Running time: 102 minutes. (Technicolor.)

While William Holden in 1955, at age thirty-seven, is somewhat old for the derring-do exploits he essays in *The Bridges at Toko-Ri*, his action heroics do reinforce the matinee-idol status he had attained by that time. And with Grace Kelly on hand as Mrs.

Loving-and-Loyal, what man could ask for more? The vital-to-the-enemy bridges of the title are in North Korea, and Holden has to bomb them—a premise that leads one to wonder why his character has abandoned (as per the script) a thriving legal practice in Denver to risk his life in such a manner. But logic plays second fiddle to action thrills in such pictures, so it is not for us to wonder why, merely to watch and sigh—and occasionally cheer—for Holden's relentless bombings, followed

THE BRIDGES AT TOKO-RI Hell breaks loose in the vicinity of the bridge.

by his returns to the "tiny speck of deck in a wild, angry sea." This peculiar devotion to duty becomes a subject of considerable discourses on the part of philosophical Adm. Fredric March, who must send such men off to fight in the air over hostile territory, then mourn fittingly when they fail to return (as Holden initially does), and finally ask himself where the navy ever found such men.

It never seems to occur to the March character that, though he pays for it with his life in the end,

THE BRIDGES AT TOKO-RI   William Holden and Mickey Rooney run for their lives.

the Holden character is fighting dangerously over North Korea because he was probably bored stiff in Denver—his philosophy having obviously been: A short life with some kick in it is worth a long life of routine tedium. In one extended sequence, he's down behind enemy lines and has to be rescued by helicopter jockey Mickey Rooney, though both fail to survive. Whatever his motivations, Holden's airman-bomber *par excellence* is an action figure to conjure with.

The aerial and bombing shots, the best thing in the picture, are introduced excitingly at the beginning by those uncertain plane takeoffs from tossing decks. One is given cause to wonder why more bomber pilots didn't bail out from air-sea sickness *before* they got off the deck, but intact they are, as they do their man's work in the face of enemy fire.

True, there is perhaps too much time taken out for philosophical musings, especially on the part of the March character; and Holden's bomber boy gets into a lot of picture-slowing conversational mus-

137

ings himself; and then there is the matter of doing his husbandly duty with the lovely Grace Kelly when she visits him in Tokyo—but the later action sequences make up for all this. The aerial photography of Charles G. Clarke is superb, and the audience is left with the definite impression that the photographers took as many risks as did the men doing the fighting. Credit is also due second-unit photographers Wallace Kelley and Thomas Tutweiler, who make the action intimate, real, and compelling.

Mark Robson brought bite and conviction to the proceedings, adapted as they were from James Michener's novel. The scenes of Holden's preliminary self-psyching as he prepares to board his plane for a flight from which he may not come back (he doesn't), the nerve-racking takeoff from the quavery deck, the silent time in the air just before the real action commences, the emergence through the clouds of the strategic North Korean bridges of the title, the tense moments before the bombs are released, and the subsequent conflagration and chaos, all are carried out to perfection. Yes, it is all flag-waving, rabble-rousing, superficial patrioposturing (to coin a new word), and forty years later seems dated and simplistic. However, respect certainly was (and is) due for all the technical work

138

THE BRIDGES AT TOKO-RI   Fredric March as the intrepid commander.

that went into making these raids convincing, the highly professional blending of direction and photography, and the mise-en-scène.

Robson was later to say that when directing a war epic of this kind, the director and the photographers and their second-unit crews have a highly intricate working relationship, and that the director of such a film can fairly take credit singly for what is a directorial–photographic partnership. In any event, the result is seamless professionalism, with more than enough credit to go around to every field of endeavor connected with the film.

42

ATTACK!

ASSOCIATES AND ALDRICH / UNITED ARTISTS

1956

CAST:

Jack Palance, Eddie Albert, Lee Marvin, Robert Strauss, Richard Jaeckel, William Smithers, Buddy Ebsen, Peter Van Eyck, Steven Geray, Strother Martin.

CREDITS:

Robert Aldrich, producer-director; James Poe, screenplay; based on the play *Fragile Fox*, by Norman Brooks; Joseph Biroc, photographer; Frank De Vol, music, Michael Luciano, editor. Running time: 104 minutes.

When he is in a trenchantly truth-telling mood, Robert Aldrich can always be depended on to leave his audiences both drained and enlightened. His splendid war film *Attack!* is set during the 1944 Battle of the Bulge. On the march through Belgium, Jack Palance is increasingly disgusted with the procrastinations and overall cowardice of his superior officer, Eddie Albert. These deadly flaws in the senior officer's character and personality have led to some heavy casualties. The picture traces Palance's gradually growing anger, horror, and final near-derangement as he seeks to save what is left of his infantry detachment by fair

ATTACK! Jack Palance ready to attack.

means or foul—meaning emphasis on the latter.

In one of his best performances, Palance gets across all the desperation and disgust of a well-meaning fighting man who must combat the forces of privilege and special influence. It seems that Albert's father back in the States has a giant share of political pull, so the cowardly commandant's superiors studiously ignore his many shortcomings as a military leader, and turn a blind eye to the evident cowardice and diffidence in the personality of a man temperamentally unfit to lead.

And this is the cold, unsentimental, to-the-point premise of *Attack!*—namely, that in the military, as in civilian life, power, rank, privilege, "pull," and/or connections often subvert the finest planning, and make mockery of the brave efforts of common soldiers and NCOs who, left to their own devices, might otherwise have turned the inevitable defeats brought about by chain-of-command intrigues into shining victories.

As the story develops, a manic Palance determines to counteract all this negation; the lives of his men become his paramount consideration. The action, and the personality projections, take on, in time, a surreal, hallucinatory quality as morale and mental health itself give way to frantic self-preservational methods and a vicious flaunting of established chain-of-command rules.

Albert, seldom better, sketches cleverly and subtly the pusillanimous nature of an officer technically in command but hopelessly out of his depth, fearful and weak. So good is Albert's performance

ATTACK! Palance holds the rifle aloft.

ATTACK! Palance aids a dying comrade.

ATTACK! Moving into the field.

140

that he almost evokes a condescending pity for this contemptible man—a pity that finally dissolves as the audience joins Palance in disgust and horror at what this man's weak nature brings about: the loss of lives, a slowing-down of the advance, deteriorating morale among the men.

The Battle of the Bulge being the background (the famous 1944 engagement in which the Germans made a remarkable surprise stand and counterattack as the Allied forces swept ever nearer to Germany's major cities), there is some fine choreographing of battles, and portrayal of the tense wait between ambitious military forays. Lee Marvin, hard and forceful as always, and Robert Strauss and Richard Jaeckel, both in fine fettle, get across the military professionalism of troops who are trying to fulfill their mission yet sense (in some instances fatally) that the real enemy is not coming at them from the German side but from the command above—that very command that they look to for safety, support, and morale enhancement.

In several interviews, Robert Aldrich set forth his motivation for making this film. He said he wanted to show all the waste and attrition that came from the wrongful assigning of incompetent officers due to "pull" and "headquarters pressure" and pernicious connections going back to the seats of power in Washington—where, he added, corrupt congressmen on the "right" committees could make or break the best-laid plans of the military. Some critics thought the film overfrantic, with one of them declaring, "[It] does not so much tackle a subject as hammer it down," and another declaring it was "violent and very effective [though] by the end we seem to be in the company of raving lunatics rather than soldiers."

43

WAR AND PEACE

1956 and 1968 Versions

PONTI / DELAURENTIIS / PARAMOUNT
(U.S. / ITALY)   1956

CAST:
Audrey Hepburn, Henry Fonda, Mel Ferrer, Herbert Lom, John Mills, Oscar Homolka, Wilfred Lawson, Vittorio Gassman, Anita Ekberg, Helmut Dantine, Milly Vitale, Barry Jones,

CREDITS:
King Vidor, director; Dino DeLaurentiis and Carlo Ponti, producers; King Vidor, Bridget Roland, Robert Westerby, Mario Camerini, Ivo Perelli, and Ennio de Concini, screenplay; based on the novel by Count Leo Tolstoy; Jack Cardiff, photographer; Mario Soldati, director of battle scenes; Aldo Tonti, photographer of battle scenes; Nino Rota, music; Stuart Gilmore, supervising editor. Running time: 208 minutes. (Technicolor / VistaVision.)

SOVFILM / KINO

1968

CAST:
Ludmila Savelyeva, Vyacheslav Tikhonov, Sergei Bondarchuk (he acted in his film), Irina Skobtseva, Giuli Chokhonelidze, Boris Zakhava.

141

WAR AND PEACE   Herbert Lom, as Napoleon, ponders his future.

CREDITS:

Sergei Bondarchuk, director; Vasili Solovyov and Sergei Bondarchuk, screenplay; Anatoli Petrifsky and Dmitri Korzhikhin, photographers; Vyacheslav Ovchinnikov, music; Tatiana Likhacheva, editor. Running time: 507 minutes. (Shown in 2 parts; also in 4 parts.)

The American and Russian versions of Leo Tolstoy's world-famous novel were released in the U.S. in 1956 and 1968 respectively. The lavish production from the USSR is infinitely superior—not merely because of the novel's locale, but because the Russian director and actors and crew understood Tolstoy's original intentions far better, and gave the film a faithful transcription of the saga, one filled with intellectual and emotional depth, and faithful evocations of the period. The war scenes in the Russian version also are far superior; indeed, the entire film has an *authentic, true* look to it which the Hollywoodisms and simplicities of the story line of the American (actually Italian) film do not even begin to approximate.

War and Peace, written 1865–69, is one of the keystones of world literature. It is not so much a novel of plot, characterization, and situations (though it is that, too) but a work that delineates historical progression. It deals with Russia during the Napoleonic wars from 1805 to 1812, and also depicts the military and political aspects of the broader European scene. Against this background, Tolstoy posed many fictional characters. The three who dominate the novel, and thus the films, are Prince Andrei, his friend Pierre Bezukhov, and Natasha Rostov. Andrei is an idealist; he is dismayed by the corruption all about him; we see him through the Battle of Austerlitz, the death of his first wife in childbirth, and his unfortunate love for the beautiful Natasha. Pierre Bezukhov, heir to a great fortune, is an amiable but bumbling fellow who weathers, in desultory fashion, the Napoleonic invasion of Russia, a bad marriage, and capture by the French when they besiege Moscow, surviving all vicissitudes to marry Natasha. The two who were from the beginning designed for each other finally achieve togetherness.

The novel also covers a vast cross-section of Russian society, from Czar Alexander I to General Kutuzov, who triumphs over Napoleon. Napoleon himself is shown by Tolstoy as the fallible human being he was; no hero is on display here. To Tolstoy, history is a sweeping, immutable force which makes mockery of the designs of men, Napoleon being the prime victim of his self-delusions.

Which brings us to the two films. The 1956 version was a Ponti / De Laurentiis production with an American release and many Americans in the cast,

WAR AND PEACE   Hepburn at the ball.

WAR AND PEACE   Hepburn and Ferrer dance.

as well as an American director, King Vidor. It does fairly well in the battle sequences (especially the Battle of Borodino), but drags and falls flat in the personal aspects. Audrey Hepburn is a charming Natasha, but Henry Fonda at fifty-one was too old for Pierre Bezukhov, and both looked and acted it. Mel Ferrer is Prince Andrei, who perishes after a battle, leaving the other two to find their way to each other. He is personable but rather department-store-dummyish, more or less relegated to looking great in his uniforms. An impressive cast—among them Herbert Lom (as Napoleon), Oscar Homolka (as Kutuzov), John Mills, Wilfred Lawson, Vittorio Gassman, Anita Ekberg, and Helmut Dantine—attempt to invest their characters with life and indi-

viduality, but the script (by six—count 'em—writers, including director Vidor) is too muddling to accommodate them, and the direction and general handling too tedious.

One critic stated, "The film has no more warmth than pictures in an art gallery." And Henry Fonda, exasperated with the result, declared later, "When I first agreed to do it, the screenplay by Irwin Shaw was fine, but what happened? King Vidor used to go home nights with his wife and rewrite it. All the genius of Tolstoy went out the window!"

Vidor in his own defense stated that he had done the best he could with the picture, considering the many European locations, interference from the producers, and "troubles with temperamental ac-

144

WAR AND PEACE   Napoleon (Vladislav Strzhelchik) planning strategy.

tors who wanted their parts built up at the expense of other cast members." He later congratulated himself for having gotten through what wound up as a 208-minute film in one piece, sans heart attack or stroke.

The Russian version, for reasons already given, was far more respected by critics, and far more successful with audiences. Sergei Bondarchuk directed, wrote the script (with Vasili Solovyov), and portrayed Bezukhov. The photography by Anatoli Petritsky and Dmitri Korzhikhin is evocative and haunting, and the music by Vyacheslav Ovchinnikov is just right for the period and the Russian setting. Mario Soldati, who directed the battle scenes for the 1956 version, and photographer Jack Cardiff, who shot them, were competent and professional, but not in the same league as their Russian counterparts.

The Russian film took five years to produce and wound up costing between fifty and seventy mil-

WAR AND PEACE   Reviewing the troops headed for war.

145

WAR AND PEACE   Giuli Chokhonelidze as Bagratin confers with Boris Zahava's Kutuzov.

WAR AND PEACE   Fighting in the snow.

lion dollars. It won an Academy Award for Best Foreign Film. The cast, headed by such as Ludmila Savelyeva as Natasha, and Vyacheslav Tikhonov as Andrei, also seemed more authentic, more true and real in their roles, than their 1956 counterparts. Running originally at 507 minutes, the film was harmed by careless English dubbing in theaters. Released originally in the Soviet Union in four parts, it was shown in two parts in the United States.

The battle scenes are creditable, but the depiction of the Battle of Borodino and of Napoleon's engagements against Kutuzov, hailed as the Savior of Russia, are spectacular and totally engaging. The soldiers fight with lifelike addressal, the wounded seem *really* wounded, the dead *really* dead. The

WAR AND PEACE   Digging a comrade's grave.

WAR AND PEACE   Peasant good cheer amid the conflict.

147

choreography of the military doings is masterly—and one gets the sense of being there, in 1812, living, loving, and fighting along with the protagonists of *War and Peace*.

44

BATTLE HYMN

UNIVERSAL-INTERNATIONAL

1957

CAST:

Rock Hudson, Martha Hyer, Dan Duryea, Don DeFore, Anna Kashfi, James Edwards, Jock Mahoney, Carl Benton Reid, Alan Hale, Jr., Richard Loo, Philip Ahn, Phil Harvey, Stanley Cha.

CREDITS:

Douglas Sirk, director; Ross Hunter, producer; Charles Grayson and Vincent B. Evans, screenplay; Russell Metty, photographer; Frank Skinner, music; Russell Schoengarth, editor. Running time: 108 minutes. (CinemaScope / Technicolor.)

Battle Hymn offers a fairly unusual story against a war background. It seems that clergyman Rock Hudson, a World War II veteran, has resumed his military career five years later, this time for the Korean War. He is a gentle, sensitive, caring type put in charge of training fighter pilots. But this intrepid, stalwart boy scout of an Air Force officer has a guilty secret in his World War II past, and it keeps on festering like an open wound. For in the course of one of his flying missions over Germany, he had bombed an orphanage, and the deaths of those young innocents haunts him obsessively.

Then Life—and Fate—give this man, named Dean Hess in the movie (the picture is based on a true story) a glowing second chance. For a group of orphaned South Koreans show up, badly in need of succor from the unremitting Communist attacks; and thrown in for good measure is beautiful Anna Kashfi, as their caretaker. So how could a preacher with a massive guilt complex resist playing Good Samaritan?

The picture was not dealt with as kindly as it deserved to be in 1957, being termed "Diabetes with Choral Music" and "sentimental slop." One critic called it "earnest and somnolent," adding that "Its mixture of drama, comedy, religion and war heroics is indigestible despite professional handling." Yet another reviewer, one John Gillett, sourpussed "The film seems to infer that heroic self-sacrifice, a little homely Eastern philosophy and a capacity for combining battle experience with an awareness of spiritual values are enough to overcome all emergencies."

Seen recently after some thirty-six years, the film holds up surprisingly well: Director Douglas Sirk struck a nice balance between do-gooder religiosity and admittedly boy-scoutish idealism and tough, down-to-earth human realism and battle action. Rock Hudson—who always had a gentle, nurturing, kindly side to his nature, both personally and professionally, that has not been publicized as it should have been (see *All That Heaven Allows,* for one, as evidence of *that*)—gets across rather touchingly the guilt that a basically decent man felt for the results of his German mission, an unintended side-product of doing his duty. And he also is a tough survivor, now on his second war and again determined to get the job done—namely, equipping pilots to fight a successful air war against the North Korean Communists.

Anna Kashfi and her brood of Korean orphans respond well to Hudson's efforts to find them a safe haven—a mission not easily accomplished, considering the many dangers that the war has brought about. The picture then takes up the sky pilot's essential dual mission: training the new fliers and rescuing the orphans. At the end, one feels that the

BATTLE HYMN   Rock Hudson evacuates children from a Korean orphanage.

149

Hudson character has in fact both struck a workable inner balance between ancient guilt and present positives, and found a peace of mind that he very much deserves.

Dan Duryea, Don DeFore, and Jock Mahoney are among the men serving under Hudson who react as per their individual natures to his dual mission and the problems it entails. Photographer Russell Metty is as skilled at limning in affecting visual terms the nurturing and sustaining elements as he is in visualizing some rough combat and confrontation scenes.

Rock Hudson once told me that *Battle Hymn* and the aforementioned *All That Heaven Allows* (in which he was a sensitive, decent young gardener who got gossiped about because of his love for older widow Jane Wyman) were two of his all-time favorite pictures, and it is easy to see why. For in both he is allowed to show his better side—the idealistic, decent fellow who was never really corrupted by Hollywood success. (The later revelations of his private-life homosexuality when he was taken ill with, and in 1985 died of, AIDS only add dimen-

BATTLE HYMN   As Dan Duryea looks on, Hudson checks a map for the destination of Anna Kashfi and her orphans.

BATTLE HYMN   Don DeFore, Hudson, and Duryea realize it won't all be smooth sailing. Jock Mahoney stands to the rear. Seated are Phil Harvey and Stanley Cha.

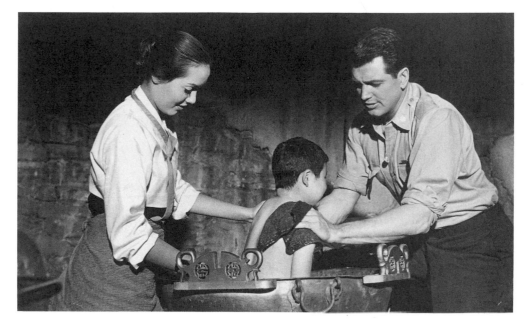

BATTLE HYMN   Kashfi and Hudson bathe a Korean orphan, Jung Kyoo Pyo.

sion to performances like *Battle Hymn*, in which, healthy and hearty at thirty-one, he gave us his best and truest instincts.)

45

PATHS OF GLORY

UNITED ARTISTS / BRYNA

1957

CAST:

Kirk Douglas, Adolphe Menjou, Ralph Meeker, George Macready, Wayne Morris, Richard Anderson, Timothy Carey, Joseph Turkel, Suzanne Christian.

CREDITS:

Stanley Kubrick, director; James B. Harris, producer; Calder Willingham, Jim Thompson, and Stanley Kubrick, screenplay; based on the novel by Humphrey Cobb (which in turn was based on a true story); George Krause, photographer; Gerald Fried, music; Eva Kroll, editor. Running time: 86 minutes.

Paths of Glory is one of the finest war (or rather antiwar) films ever made, and its power, poignancy,

PATHS OF GLORY   Kirk Douglas ponders an unwelcome order.

151

PATHS OF GLORY   Under heavy siege.

PATHS OF GLORY
Douglas in the thick of
trench warfare.

PATHS OF GLORY   Douglas confronts a cowardly Wayne Morris.

153

and pointedness have only seemed to increase over the years since its release in 1957. Director Stanley Kubrick is in top form here (it's his fourth feature film), working on a screenplay with Calder Willingham and Jim Thompson from a searing novel by Humphrey Cobb.

The acting is quite memorable, with Kirk Douglas trenchant as a colonel who sees through all the French high-command politics and injustices in the World War I of 1916. Adolphe Menjou has never been better as a dissimulating, scheming general, and George Macready, that ever able character actor, has a role tailored exactly to his measure as an overbearing militarist whose unbalanced measures eventually misfire on him, leading to his disgrace.

It seems Macready, flattered by Menjou into believing he has higher honors in store, has egged his enlisted men on into an impossible venture—attacking a German stronghold called the Anthill. The fortress, too strong for standard attack strategy, counters all onslaughts by causing multiple casualties. Though the French wounded and dead pile up, Macready keeps ordering his troops to advance, and when some of them resort to justifiably self-protective battlefield strategies he has three of them, from different companies, sent up for court-martial, the charge being that they proved cowardly under fire and must stand as examples to forestall further such behavior.

But in his excess of maniacal zeal, Macready has made a mistake fatal to his own future: He has ordered that his own men be fired upon when they do not try to move out of the trenches and resist enemy fire as expeditiously as he would wish.

Kirk Douglas, as the seething Colonel Dax, defends his men, sees through the crass politicking and craven expediences of the French high command, and serves as counsel for the accused in the court-martial—which, being rigged and politicized as it is, winds up condemning the men to death by firing squad.

PATHS OF GLORY   Pompous commanding general George Macready discusses the campaign with Douglas and Richard Anderson.

An enraged and bitter Douglas, determined to exact revenge, reveals to Menjou Macready's order to fire on his men, presents irrefutable proof, and—to his great satisfaction—sees Menjou order Macready to submit to a major inquiry. But his satisfaction in obtaining justice is short-lived, as the wily and cynical Menjou offers him Macready's command and intimates that he had informed on his superior in order to further his own fortunes. After rebuffing the offer and telling off Menjou, Douglas returns to combat duty.

There are many memorable scenes in this four-star film; the neurotic reactions of the soldiers to stress-filled combat action that has gone on too long (with machine guns rat-tatting and shells bursting and other men's bodies falling on them, they register all-too-believable reactions). The assault, hopeless as it is, is choreographed for maximum effect and, as the casualties mount, is rousing and horrifying at the same time. The court-martial scenes are taut and compelling, and when the three men, disparate types all, face the firing squad, the scene takes on a tautness and tension that are first-rate.

There is a lovely scene at the very end, featuring a bunch of hell-raising French soldiers in a night spot who initially make fun of a diffident German blonde being touted as a singer. But when she sings her simple, sweet song, the men quiet down, listen intently and respectfully, and then shed tears while humming along as her accompaniment. The disillusioned Douglas, a witness to this scene, goes back to duty with his faith in human nature reaffirmed.

Menjou is marvelous as the cynical general who calls the shots, and Macready superb as the manic catalyst to the evils that follow. Ralph Meeker is stoical as one of the condemned, and Joseph Turkel combative and disruptive as another, but Timothy Carey is best of all as the third, who goes to his death clinging tearfully and childishly to a nurturing priest.

Wayne Morris is also compelling as a cowardly, craven, buck-passing officer. In this remarkable film the futility and downright insanity of war is set forth especially vividly, and the corruptions of high command politics (in *any* country, not just France—and in all eras and all wars) are gotten across forcefully and compellingly.

The unpalatable but eminently self-evident truths and lessons in *Paths of Glory* were so strong that the picture was banned in France for a number of years, and even was declared verboten (for a short time, until wiser heads prevailed) on U.S. military bases. Kirk Douglas had fought from the beginning to preserve the original script's integrity and what he conceived (rightly) to be its needed message. When he found that the script had been tampered with by some commercial-minded types, he demanded that the original be used and, because he had the clout to make that happen, the message of that first draft of an admirable script came out loud and clear. Douglas has always declared *Paths of Glory* one of his favorite pictures, and certainly it has attracted a large cult following in the decades since it was made. War is Hell, it says—but war is also sinister, corrupt, cynical, and manic.

46

THE BRIDGE ON THE RIVER KWAI

COLUMBIA

1957

CAST:

Alec Guinness, William Holden, Jack Hawkins, Sessue Hayakawa, James Donald, Geoffrey Horne, André Morell, Percy Herbert, Ann Sears.

CREDITS:

David Lean, director; Sam Spiegel, producer; Pierre Boulle, Michael Wilson, and Carl Foreman, screenplay; based on the novel by Pierre Boulle; Jack Hildyard, photographer; Malcolm Arnold, music; Peter Taylor, editor. Running time: 161 minutes. (CinemaScope / Technicolor.)

A famous adventure story as well as war film, *The Bridge on the River Kwai* focuses on British prisoners in a Japanese POW camp. None of the main characters is exactly who he appears to be. The commandant, Colonel Saito (Sessue Hayakawa), at first seems to be a barbarian, but his gruff manner hides a more sensitive nature. Saito had wanted to become an artist, but his father disapproved and he

THE BRIDGE ON THE RIVER KWAI   Guinness faces off with Sessue Hayakawa.

THE BRIDGE ON THE RIVER KWAI   Guinness is led to his cage.

became an engineer instead. He is under orders to force the prisoners to build a bridge over the nearby river so that the railroad can extend from Bangkok to Rangoon and on into India. If it isn't completed by a certain date—the twelfth of May—he will "lose face" and will have to kill himself.

"Commander" Shears of the United States Navy (William Holden), the only American POW, turns out to actually be a private who exchanged clothing with a dead officer (figuring he'd be better

THE BRIDGE ON THE RIVER KWAI   Alec Guinness, William Holden, and Jack Hawkins against the background of the Bridge in a publicity shot (the three are never seen together in the film).

treated) after his ship was bombed. He seems highly irresponsible and callous, but comes through when devotion to duty is called for.

British Colonel Nicholson (Alec Guinness) seems an admirably stubborn officer who insists that Saito stick to the rules of the Geneva Convention. He refuses to order his officers to join his other men in menial labor, and because of this he is isolated in a suffocating enclosure for days at a time. But his stubbornness is only a mask for dubious class-dis-

THE BRIDGE ON THE RIVER KWAI   James Donald and Guinness discuss the situation.

tinction attitudes, and his staunch British pride forces him into activities that could be viewed as treasonous.

After a test of wills between Saito and Nicholson, the latter decides that if his troops must build a bridge, it will be the best damned bridge that has ever been built. Although the medical officer (James Donald) suggests to the colonel that they may be aiding the enemy, Nicholson dismisses the notion. He is going to show these savages what British ingenuity and know-how can accomplish. He also feels that building a bridge they can be proud of will keep up his men's morale.

Shears manages against all odds to escape through the jungle surrounding the camp, only to learn that he had been "loaned" to the British service to lead a contingent back to where he has just escaped from. The camp is too distant for bombers to be of use, so the strategic bridge must be destroyed by a team of sappers. Accompanied by stiff-upper-lip Major Warden (Jack Hawkins) and young Lieutenant Joyce (Geoffrey Horne), Shears arrives at the site just after the completion of the bridge. After successfully planting mines to blow it up, Shears is appalled to find that Nicholson has discovered the mines and is leading Saito right to

THE BRIDGE ON THE RIVER KWAI   Guinness against the background of the bridge, his and his men's handiwork.

158

THE BRIDGE ON THE RIVER KWAI   Geoffrey Horne and Holden bring the wounded Hawkins up to date.

them. Too late, Nicholson realizes the terrible thing he has done; both he and Saito are killed, and the bridge is destroyed as a train carrying enemy supplies stretches across it, hurtling the train into the river. Shears and Joyce also are killed.

With its striking cinematography by Malcolm Arnold, and location shooting in Ceylon, the hugely popular *Bridge* is a handsome picture to look at. It also is consistently exciting and absorbing under David Lean's taut direction. There are many memorable sequences, starting with Colonel Nicholson's arrogant march into the camp at the head of his ragtag but whistling group, which sounds off with "Colonel Bogey's March" (both the scene and the music have become famous), and proceeding to the initial confrontation between Guinness and Hayakawa that begins with Saito threatening to shoot the prisoners but ends with his slapping Nicholson's face instead.

Another film scene has young Joyce confronting a frightened Japanese soldier in the jungle and finding himself unable to kill the boy, who is his counterpart. Major Warden has to stab the

Japanese, and as the body drops to the ground we see a picture of the soldier's loved ones lying beside it. The climax, while exciting and suspenseful, is not as dramatically handled as it could have been, and also suffers because of the crucial absence of music.

A more problematic aspect of *Bridge* is the characterization of Nicholson. Although Guinness won a Best Actor Oscar for his work in the film, even he isn't quite able to make the batty, foolish colonel—who builds a fine bridge for the enemy instead of trying to sabotage it—entirely believable. This basic contrivance at the core of the whole story doesn't succeed in sinking the film or negating its stirring entertainment values, but it does render much of the goings-on rather implausible. The final moment, with the medical officer surveying the wreckage and bodies from a hilltop and declaring "Madness! Madness!"—and that final shot of a dove!—might have worked thirty-seven years ago, but today seems only hokey.

Sessue Hayakawa, who first won stardom in American films in 1914, had earlier played a "sym-

159

THE BRIDGE ON THE RIVER KWAI   Holden gets a death grip on an enemy he has come upon.

pathetic" camp commandant in the earlier reviewed *Three Came Home*—a movie about a Japanese POW camp for *women*. He was excellent in these and other films, but the American public had to be considered very tolerant of these "sympathetic" portrayals of our World War II enemy, given the cowardliness of their sneak attack upon Pearl Harbor and their other wartime malfeasances and atrocities. William Holden strikes a jarring note in this British production, his "Hollywooden" acting style at odds with that of the other players. Unfortunately, he's only one of the elements in this movie that don't always ring true.

Nevertheless, *Bridge* is a good picture, well worth seeing, and on that the Oscar purveyors certainly agreed. *Bridge* won a Best Picture Oscar; statuettes also went to the direction, cinematography, editing, and scoring, and to the Guinness performance. *Bridge* also won for Best Screenplay, which was attributed to Pierre Boulle, who wrote the novel that the film was based on. (The screenplay was actually written by two blacklisted writers, Carl Foreman and Michael Wilson, who in the 1980s were posthumously credited by the Motion Picture Academy.)—*W. S.*

THE BRIDGE ON THE RIVER KWAI   Guinness tangles with knife-wielding Horne at the climax.

160

47

IN LOVE AND WAR

20TH CENTURY–FOX

1958

CAST:

Robert Wagner, Jeffrey Hunter, Bradford Dillman, Dana Wynter, Hope Lange, Sheree North, France Nuyen, Mort Sahl, James Bell, Murvyn Vye.

CREDITS:

Philip Dunne, director; Jerry Wald, producer; Edward Anhalt, screenplay; based on the novel *The Big War*, by Anton Myrer; Leo Tover, photographer; Hugo Friedhofer, music; William Reynolds, editor. Running time: 111 minutes. (CinemaScope / Deluxe Color.)

IN LOVE AND WAR   Jeffrey Hunter, Robert Wagner, and Bradford Dillman contemplate their future.

In Love and War, based on an Anton Myrer novel, was made in 1958, when World War II was thirteen years in the past. It has an objectivity some of the flag-waving war epics of the 1941–45 period could not boast, and some of its sentiments, as set forth in the screenplay of Edward Anhalt and delineated tellingly via the directorial touches of Philip Dunne, convey distinct reservations about war as a national pursuit.

Jerry Wald gave it solid production values, and Leo Tover photographed it realistically and forcefully. The combat scenes of marines in action in the South Pacific are well-staged, and the Hollywoodisms are largely kept in abeyance.

Basically, this is the story of three leathernecks from the San Francisco–Monterey area—and specifically of their individual reactions to the demands, disciplines, and stresses of both their earlier marine life and their later performance in the Pacific. Jeffrey Hunter is the patriot who thinks the war worth fighting and is determined to give it his best shot; Robert Wagner is the slacker who wants to get through the war in one piece, and Bradford Dillman is a son of the rich who feels he must give his best as a matter of principle.

All three get as much attention for their love lives as for their martial activities—hence the title. Wagner carries on a romance with Sheree North; Hunter marries steady, sensible Hope Lange while on leave; and Dillman, having commenced with Dana Wynter, winds up with exotic, lovely France Nuyen.

The difference in temperament among the three marines is highlighted in their romantic as well as military lives. Wagner, who seems more boy than man in his approach to women (as hapless North discovers) is the least likely marine around until he sets his course more purposefully. However, even in his later scenes he doesn't seem the best of marine material, and so his superior officers and buddies alike are left to get across, subtly but definitively, their reservations concerning him.

161

IN LOVE AND WAR   Enroute, they rest and read.

IN LOVE AND WAR   Wagner and Hunter weather combat conditions.

Hunter is the All-American boy gone gung-ho marine, and while his character as drawn is the least complex of the three (and at times he seems almost too good to be true), he is the type that would have lent itself well to the more simplistically propagandistic World War II pictures of the early 1940s.

Dillman is obviously out to prove (and does) that boys of wealthy background and good family can make fine marines if they are correctly motivated. His shift from Dana Wynter to France Nuyen smacks of a more "democraticizing" approach on the part of the screenwriter, but his scenes with both ladies are well carried off. This was Dillman's first year in films after his initial 1956 Broadway hit as the young Eugene O'Neill character in *Long Day's Journey Into Night*, and he is most effective in his role. (Wagner and Hunter had been in films longer, usually joined at the hip in Fox films, but they do not seem any more real and true in their roles than does their newcomer confrere.)

The assorted romancings get more-than-usual time for a war picture, but once the war sequences in the Pacific take over, the action is fast, the choreographing of the fighting true and real, and the overall martial ambience well-staged. Wald and company seem to have taken extra pains to convey war realistically, probably to balance out the romances earlier in the picture. All the actors share equally in praise for the acting, with Dillman holding the edge. He seems to mean, and fit in with, the combat heroics he is called upon to perform, and indeed injects his scenes with realism.

Comedian Mort Sahl, in his first film, makes a fine marine in a role that, as one critic commented, "was written especially for him—and from the sound of it, by him." Sahl provides moments of levity and other humorous relief that are welcome when the action gets too serious—and grim.

A TIME TO LOVE AND A TIME TO DIE John Gavin argues with a buddy (Klaus Kinski), who wants to kill the prisoners.

48

A TIME TO LOVE AND A TIME TO DIE

UNIVERSAL-INTERNATIONAL

1958

CAST:

John Gavin, Lilo Pulver, Jock Mahoney, Don DeFore, Keenan Wynn, Thayer David, Dana (Jim) Hutton, Klaus Kinski, Agnes Windeck, Erich Maria Remarque (in a personal appearance, in a small role).

CREDITS:

Douglas Sirk, director; Robert Arthur, producer; Orin Jannings, screenplay; based on the novel by Erich Maria Remarque; Russell Metty, photographer; Miklos Rozsa, music; Ted J. Kent, editor. Running time: 132 minutes. (CinemaScope / Eastman Color.)

In 1958, Universal-International unveiled its World War II version of the *All Quiet on the Western Front* theme—again from a novel by Erich Maria Remarque, who appeared in a small role. This time around, the war activities are mixed with a tender love story. Bittersweet in its progression, the tale, of course, ends in futility and tragedy.

John Gavin, certainly one of the great male beauties of the screen, was in this period being groomed by Universal as a Rock Hudson rival and/or successor, and he gets the Big Star buildup in this as a decent, kindly German soldier on furlough from the miseries of the Russian front. The scenes from that terrible campaign have been graphic and horrifying, and it is small wonder that our hero is facing a first-class burnout when the blessed reprieve comes through.

Back in his hometown in Germany, he finds that his old residence has been bombed out and his family has disappeared. Then it's on to his lonely peregrinations around his once-beautiful town, now reduced to rubble and frightened people and straitened wartime conditions. In his effort to locate his parents, he runs up against old acquaintances who arouse both happy and unhappy memories, corrupt German officers who party in luxury while the townspeople endure the rigors and privations of wartime, and the Gestapo and other suspicious Nazi bigwigs. He also meets a girl (Lilo Pulver), and a tender romance develops that results in a quick marriage before he must leave again for the front.

163

As in the famous *All Quiet*, no happy ending either is presaged or transpires, and thus it is sad but not unexpected when, cheered and distracted by the warmth of a letter from his young wife, he carelessly lets down his guard to do a prisoner of war a kindness by letting him go, and the man grabs a gun and shoots him. In a scene most reminiscent of *All Quiet*, he dies as his hand releases the letter, which floats gently away on a nearby stream. (In *All Quiet*, Lew Ayres's character reaches for a butterfly, and we see his hand tense and drop to earth as a bullet hits him.) The scene in which John Gavin dies was generally regarded in 1958 as a form of *homage* to the ending in the 1930 masterpiece.

While the film gives much footage and attention to the Gavin-Pulver love story, the horrors of war, both on the battlefield and on the home front, are set forth graphically and brutally. The demoralization of the German civilian population under fire, the corruption of officials and officers of the armed forces, the black-marketing and other offshoots of war, all are gotten across forcefully.

In the early battle scenes on the Russian front, the exhaustion and fear and tension are palpable in the soldiers. Death may be imminent, but an apathy has come over many of them—a quiet, dulled awaiting of the inevitable. Gavin's character is at that time seen to be one of the lucky soldiers: Having served sufficient time in combat, he is sent on furlough, and thus is given at least a brief lease on life and hope.

Gavin, then thirty years old, was to go on to the presidency of the Screen Actors Guild, and then to a career in diplomacy (he was Ambassador to Mexico under President Reagan). He had been an

A TIME TO LOVE AND A TIME TO DIE   Returning to war's devastation in his hometown.

A TIME TO LOVE AND A TIME TO DIE   Gavin and girlfriend Lilo Pulver failing to sneak past the landlady.

air intelligence officer with the navy in the Korean War. Bright and sensitive and extremely handsome, he was to know his finest hour in *A Time to Love and a Time to Die*. A gentle, self-effacing fellow in private life, he was far from a forceful, dynamic, take-charge actor onscreen, but in this film he is well cast. For the role is perfectly tailored to his measure, being that of a young soldier of decent instincts and manly affirmations who wants to do his duty while hurting as few people as possible. That he finds life is not that simple, and that therefore he must rise to its occasions, is one of the profound sadnesses that bedevil his psyche. Because he is a good person, as portrayed in the film, his death at the end is all the sadder, and the sense of waste is

profound. He is well supported by Lilo Pulver, and (as German soldiers) Keenan Wynn, Don DeFore, and Jock Mahoney; and Remarque (who plays a small role as a schoolteacher) once again gets across his hatred for war and his horror at its random cruelties and futilities.

Jim Hutton (then Dana Hutton) made his film debut in this movie.

166

49

PORK CHOP HILL

UNITED ARTISTS

1959

CAST:

Gregory Peck, Harry Guardino, Rip Torn, George Peppard, James Edwards, Bob Steele, Woody Strode, Robert Blake, Martin Landau, Norman Fell, Bert Remsen, Harry (Dean) Stanton, Gavin McLeod.

CREDITS:

Lewis Milestone, director; Sy Bartlett, producer; James R. Webb, screenplay; Sam Leavitt, photographer; Leonard Rosenman, music; George Boemler, editor. Running time: 97 minutes.

Lewis Milestone, of *All Quiet on the Western Front* fame, acquitted himself most creditably some twenty-odd years later with his Korean War action drama, *Pork Chop Hill*. Yet again he offers solid, highly individualized characterizations and rousing, tough-action scenes that, as in the earlier film, carry their own cutting edges of irony. James R. Webb seems to have understood the director's intentions, for he has carried them out with a screenplay that ably complements Milestone's long-held-and-sustained contempt for war, and especially its human cost and intellectual bankruptcies. Photographer Sam Leavitt, and Leonard Rosenman, who supplied highly effective mood music, also fell in with the general plan (as did production designer Nicolai Remisoff), and the felicitous result demonstrated how well a film can turn out if all creative hands, guided by an original concept and inspiration (Milestone's), work together instead of against each other—in other words, a positive combination of artistic teamwork rather than egoistic one-upmanship.

As in his fine film *A Walk in the Sun*, Milestone gets across both war's essential pointlessness and command corruption. Gregory Peck, a commander who believes in following orders however he may question them, is ordered to take what his higher-ups insist is a strategic hill whose conquest will, he is told, change the course of general operations for

the better. Actually, the hill has little strategic value, but is a key morale factor.

It turns out that the taking of the hill, however briefly or lengthily Peck and his men can hold onto it, will aid the American general staff at the truce confabs that are already in progress; they can speak

PORK CHOP HILL   Gregory Peck is the intrepid American commander.

PORK CHOP HILL   Peck barks essential orders to Sgt. Norman Fell.

from strength, demonstrating their military capacities in tough engagements.

The entire attempt, so costly in human lives and the sufferings of the wounded, is shown under Milestone's aegis as a consummate act of essential futility designed to fatten up the unrealistic egos of phonies and blowhards at the top of the military command.

In the true incident on which the film was based, the commander of the assault, green and inexperienced, made something of a mess of the engagement. But Milestone, to his great resultant anger, had to suffer some prerelease tampering on the part of higher-ups designed to make Peck into a sort of John Wayne gung-ho type, and the assault on (and all-too-brief conquest of) the hill a major victory—which it was far from being. Peck is even given a jingoistic speech at the end, a voice-over in which he proudly proclaims "Millions live in freedom today because of what they did."

Milestone later publicly declared that both the gung-ho nonsense and Peck's metamorphosis (via cutting and photographic emphasis, into a John Wayne clone) ran contrary to both his intentions

168

PORK CHOP HILL   The commander and his men take extreme measures.

and the underlying concept of the film. However, even given the tampering and jingoism, *Pork Chop Hill* is a very powerful war drama—rugged, realistic, and true. Milestone's was too strong a personality to be truly subverted via tampering by mediocrities guided by what they conceived would be audience reactions rather than by the individualized instincts of the true artist that Milestone was applying to his work.

There is much in the film that is biting, unsparing, and—tampering notwithstanding—contemptuous of war in all its phony grandiosities and futilities. The contempt for human life, the foolish grandstanding, the mock heroics, the battle and engagement plans designed to feed egos rather than advance overall military objectives, are on fitting display here.

Gregory Peck, a rather passive, albeit agreeable and stalwart actor who has rarely shown fire and passion and spirit (as he did, *occasionally*, in films like *Duel in the Sun*), had matured considerably at age forty-three, and this is one of his strongest, toughest, and indeed most impassioned portrayals. Harry Guardino, George Peppard, Rip Torn, and the

PORK CHOP HILL   Peck rallies his men in holding the hill.

other actors playing soldiers under his command are grittily true in their portrayals. War is not shown here as gung-ho glamour, but rather as a futile, often mad and pointless pursuit in which the individual soldier is the one who pays—often with his life.

50

THE HORSE SOLDIERS

THE MIRISCH COMPANY / UNITED ARTISTS

1959

CAST:

John Wayne, William Holden, Constance Towers, Althea Gibson, Hoot Gibson, Anna Lee, Russell Simpson, Ken Curtis, Denver Pyle, Strother Martin, Hank Worden, Stan Jones, Carleton Young.

CREDITS:

John Ford, director; John Lee Mahin and Martin Rackin, producers-screenplay; based on the novel by Harold Sinclair; William Clothier, photographer; David Buttolph, music; Jack Murray, editor. Running time: 119 minutes. (Deluxe Color.)

At the height of the Civil War, a contingent of Union soldiers, led by tough taskmaster Col. John Marlowe (John Wayne) makes its way into Confederate territory with the aim of taking Newton Station in Baton Rouge, which supplies the forces of Vicksburg with ammunition. Many of Marlowe's fellow officers disagree with his decisions, and he is constantly bickering with the regiment's medical officer, Maj. Hank Kendall (William Holden), particularly when Kendall takes time out to deliver a Negro baby instead of attending to wounded soldiers. "You took an oath to the army," Marlowe tells him. Kendall reminds the colonel that he also took a Hippocratic oath and therefore can't refuse anyone who is in need of his services.

The underlying reason for the friction between the two men is Marlowe's fundamental distrust of doctors; a team of them "killed" his young wife when they operated for a tumor that didn't exist. (The two men eventually come to blows, but this aborted sequence is disappointingly brief.)

Eventually Marlowe and his men arrive at the estate of Greenbriar in Mississippi, which is run by a determined Southern woman, Miss Hannah Hunter (Constance Towers), who initially tries to throw them out but later turns cordial in the hope of obtaining secret information for the Rebels. Later learning of her deception, Marlowe has no choice but to take her and her maid (track star Althea Gibson) along as captives.

Hannah proves a nuisance to Marlowe, given her constant escape attempts, but eventually a grudging understanding and affection—and finally love—blooms between the two. After a brutal battle at Newton Station, Kendall does his best to patch up horribly injured soldiers from both sides; he and Marlowe come to respect each other after many bitter arguments. Giving Hannah a kiss, Marlowe rides off with his men into battle while both wonder if they will ever see each other again.

The Horse Soldiers was John Ford's only film about the Civil War (except for his brief segment of *How the West Was Won*). That, plus the fact that John Wayne is the star, make it a notable war film for buffs—but it should never be confused with a truly great picture. The first half of the film is too "cute" by far; you begin to wish Marlowe would simply shoot Miss Hunter (who constantly tries to betray him and his men) and be done with it.

Far too many scenes lack that ring of "truth," and moments that might have been affecting in other pictures seem merely hokey and ill-advised in this one. Hannah's Negro slave talks back to her in a highly unrealistic (for the times) fashion, and when the indentured woman is accidentally shot, Wayne uncharacteristically tells her mistress: "You must know how we feel about [her]." Too, a scene in which a dying young soldier says to Wayne, "Just hold onto me—and write my Mom," comes off like a parody of similar scenes in other movies, to say nothing of Wayne looking distinctly uncomfortable "doing the Walt Whitman bit." Nor is the "romance" between Yankee Marlowe and Rebel Hunter all that convincing.

By 1959, age fifty-two, Wayne had become a rather ossified caricature of himself in many of his pictures, and director Ford was not able to elicit a more subtle performance out of him here.

THE HORSE SOLDIERS   John Wayne contemplates the terrain.

THE HORSE SOLDIERS   Basil Ruysdael (right) leads the cadets.

Knocking a guy out with just one punch, Wayne is back to being the icon instead of a realistic human being. And Constance Towers is fiery but limited as Hannah Hunter. Holden comes off best as the medical officer, a part he was well suited for.

There are, however, several good scenes in the picture's second half. For example, the battle at Newton Station is exciting and well-staged. But the movie's best moments have to do with a Southern military academy whose oldest boys, only fourteen, are recruited to form the first wave of attack against the invading Union forces until more seasoned Rebel soldiers can arrive. As they march toward the confrontation, one mother rushes out of her house to grab her son. "He's all I have left," she screams, as the boy struggles to get away from her. Her husband and other sons have already been killed in the war. As the boys swarm across the field toward

THE HORSE SOLDIERS   A heavy conference engages Wayne and (left to right) Willis Bouchey, William Leslie, Richard Cutting, William Forrest, and Jack Pennick as the sergeant major.

Marlowe and his men, the "Reverend" who's in charge of them—the only adult in the bunch—lags far, far behind. But even this compelling sequence turns "cute" when the Yankees refuse to fire on the boys and merely spank them instead! (Indeed, the depiction of soldiers and their actions in war is consistently sanitized and Hollywoodized throughout.)

Nevertheless, this picture presents Wayne as many of his fans love to remember him—and,

THE HORSE SOLDIERS   Wayne makes up a strategy with his men: Walter Reed and Bouchey to his right, and Leslie to his left.

while a lesser John Ford film, it does offer at least some rewards for the Civil War aficionado.—*W. S.*

51

THE LONGEST DAY

20TH CENTURY-FOX

1962

CAST:

John Wayne, Rod Steiger, Robert Ryan, Peter Lawford, Henry Fonda, Robert Mitchum, Richard Burton, Jeffrey Hunter, Richard Beymer, Sal Mineo, Roddy McDowall, Eddie Albert, Curt Jurgens, Sean Connery, Robert Wagner, Paul Anka, Tommy Sands, Edmond O'Brien.

CREDITS:

Andrew Marton, Ken Annakin, and Bernhard Wicki, directors; Darryl F. Zanuck, producer; Cornelius Ryan,

THE LONGEST DAY   Henry Fonda's Brig. Gen. Theodore Roosevelt, Jr., plans strategy.

Romain Gary, James Jones, David Pursall, and Jack Seddon, screenplay; from the book by Cornelius Ryan; Henri Persin, Walter Wottitz, Pierre Levent, and Jean Bourgoin, photographers; Maurice Jarre, music; Paul Anka, theme; Samuel E. Beetley, editor. Running time: 169 minutes. (CinemaScope.)

The real Longest Day was June 6, 1944, when Allied forces invaded Europe at Normandy. This acclaimed black-and-white film depicts the first twenty-four hours of the multinational operation and takes three hours, three (credited) directors,

and a huge international cast to do so. It is admirable both in its attention to detail and in the way it successfully juggles so many characters and locations—compressing them into its seemingly rather shorter running time.

Many of the characters are real-life generals and other soldiers who were instrumental in bringing off the historic invasion. Cornelius Ryan's screenplay (based on his book) also serves to humanize and scale down the story by occasionally focusing on individual GIs, such as Richard Beymer's paratrooper who is lucky at cards the day before the assault and is afraid this might mean he will be fatally

THE LONGEST DAY   John Wayne as Col. Benjamin Vandervoot surveys the scene with subordinates Steve Forrest (to his right) and Tom Tryon and Stuart Whitman (to his left).

*un*lucky during the invasion. (He does survive the first twenty-four hours, at least.)

The film begins and ends with a haunting shot of an overturned helmet on a deserted beach as Beethoven's *Fifth Symphony* plays in the background. The credits roll over this same frame in the ending shot (there are no credits as the picture begins).

We are first introduced to German officers who are smug in their assertion that the Allies will not dare invade occupied France because the weather is so bad and the waters of the channel so inhospitable. But the Allied forces realize they can delay no longer and, with some reservations, the orders are given by General Eisenhower to proceed. When the Allied troops hit the beaches hours later, the German officers can scarcely believe what their own men are telling them, even though they can hear the sound of explosions miles away from their commandeered plush estates.

What follows is a series of thrilling, expertly staged tableaux: the British glider assault on Normandy, with the aircraft stealing down to the beaches like silent birds of prey; the special force of U.S. troops desperately scaling a cliff while Germans fire upon them and cut the ropes that they are climbing; a woman in the French resistance struggling with a German soldier on a trestle as he tries to warn an approaching train that the Allies have mined the tracks; an American GI (Sal Mineo) thinking he has come across a comrade when he hears a correctly coded clicking signal, unaware it is actually the sound of a German officer cocking his rifle (Mineo is killed moments later).

A truly outstanding sequence—a recreation of an actual event during the invasion—features Red Buttons as an American paratrooper whose chute is caught on a church steeple. Instead of landing in the countryside as intended, the troops have come down in the middle of a German-infested town. As Buttons struggles to free himself, he can only watch helplessly as his comrades successfully reach the

THE LONGEST DAY   Wayne, Forrest, and Whitman take time off for chess.

178

ground—only to be mercilessly mowed down by German soldiers. Seeing all this from Buttons's point of view adds an immediacy and intensity to the sequence, which—while not as well-edited—reminds one of the classic scene from the following year, in Hitchcock's *The Birds*, in which Tippi Hedren is forced to watch the terrible things happening to the townspeople while she is helplessly trapped in a phone booth. Added suspense occurs when Buttons's parachute starts slowly tearing; he winds up on the ground with a broken foot, but alive.

The battle scenes are stringently rehearsed and flawlessly executed, particularly in sweeping crane and plane shots that go on for several minutes without a cut—for example, German soldiers strafing the beaches and otherwise firing upon the Allies. And, in a superb sequence, the Allies invade a town: First the soldiers are shown crossing a bridge, firing at snipers; then the camera pulls back to reveal an old building at a crossroads, where more fighting occurs; and *then* it pulls up even farther, over a roof from which German soldiers are firing on the Allies—all in one shot! For this sequence, involving about a hundred extras, carefully timed explosives, and spurts of gunfire, *weeks* of rehearsal were involved.

There are, inevitably, some missteps in the film, and some mercifully rare Hollywoodish moments of comedy relief, and, too, some of the big-name actors—Wayne and Mitchum, for instance—seem to be just walking through the picture. (With such a large cast, hardly anyone gets a lot of onscreen time, and there are no true "stars" as such.) Aware that the public—even war film aficionados—might have trouble sitting through a three-hour movie (*Gone With the Wind* notwithstanding), the producers decided to increase the picture's appeal by filling it with well-known (although alphabetically listed) actors. The trouble is that counting the famous faces—even in tiny parts—becomes rather tiresome and (worse) distracting after a while.

THE LONGEST DAY   John Crawford and Henry Fonda plan a breakthrough.

Some of the big names seem much too fat and old to be leading men into combat (Wayne, for instance). Others are simply miscast (Eddie Albert, Roddy McDowall), and still others border on the ludicrous (Tommy Sands, Fabian, Paul Anka), although Anka acquits himself reasonably well as an American soldier. (He also contributed the picture's theme song.)

Certain moments defy belief, such as when a group of French nuns walk calmly through a combat area and its fusillade of bullets (none of which hits home) in order to attend to the wounded. Surely even nuns are capable of *running*!

The main problem with *The Longest Day* is, perhaps, an unavoidable one, due to historical circumstances. June 6, 1944 was hardly the end of the war: The Germans didn't surrender until nearly a year later (May 7, 1945), so the picture is left without a suitable climax. Still, other films have ended with men going off to fight further battles (*Retreat, Hell!* for instance) and managed to achieve rousing conclusions nevertheless. *The Longest Day* just sort of quits when the twenty-four hours are over, and

with a very flat and sudden windup at that. We see Richard Beymer as a lost American soldier, and Richard Burton as an injured flight officer, sharing a cigarette in a courtyard, wondering who "won." (Beymer out-acts the hammy Burton!) Then we cut to Robert Mitchum, throwing away his old stogie and happily finding a new one in his pocket. He lights it and walks off with some of his men. And that's *it*. Whatever the historical realities, surely they could have come up with a more dramatic conclusion than that!

In spite of this ending (and other flaws), however, *The Longest Day* is a genuinely absorbing and extremely well-made epic in the grand style, fully deserving of its Oscars for special effects and cinematography, and appealing to war fans and film buffs alike.—W. S.

52

THE VICTORS

COLUMBIA

1963

CAST:

George Hamilton, George Peppard, Vince Edwards, Eli Wallach, Melina Mercouri, Romy Schneider, Jeanne Moreau, Albert Finney, Peter Fonda, Senta Berger, Elke Sommer, James Mitchum.

CREDITS:

Carl Foreman, producer–director–screenwriter; based on the novel *The Human Kind*, by Alexander Baron; Christopher Challis, photographer; Sol Kaplan, music; Alan Orbiston, editor. Running time: 175 minutes. (Panavision.)

The Victors follows the fortunes of an American infantry unit from the initial Sicilian landings to the fall of Germany. Made in 1963 and ably and realistically directed by Carl Foreman, the film has an attitude toward World War II, then nearly two decades in the past, that is fittingly ironic and detached. Its strong sense of human waste and of the

THE VICTORS Infantryman George Peppard slogs along determinedly.

THE VICTORS   George Hamilton, Peppard, and Vince Edwards
rest after a tough engagement.

THE VICTORS
Concentration camp
horrors along the
infantry route.

THE VICTORS Peppard makes off-duty time with Melina Mercouri. Both actors died in 1994.

everlasting futility of war is underlined over and over—this time, repetition working in its favor, for the strong underlying antiwar premises bear reinforcing.

Foreman got fine performances out of actors giving more than their usual efforts, including George Hamilton (more realistic and forceful than in the usual roles assigned him in that period), George Peppard, Eli Wallach, and Peter Fonda. There is plenty of time for soldierly womanizing in this, and among the women the infantrymen encounter along the way—sometimes for better, sometimes for worse—are Elke Sommer, Melina Mercouri, Romy Schneider, and Jeanne Moreau. The film runs a taut yet leisurely and detailed 175 minutes, and gets across tellingly the initial enthusiasm of the relatively untried troops as their peregrinations militarily across a Europe disintegrating before their eyes under the horrors of war gradually harden, jade, and then disillusion them.

Each soldier, portrayed tellingly in individual vignettes and character studies, meets his fate by the time Germany is reached; none survives. Romy Schneider effects a crumbling of green, idealistic

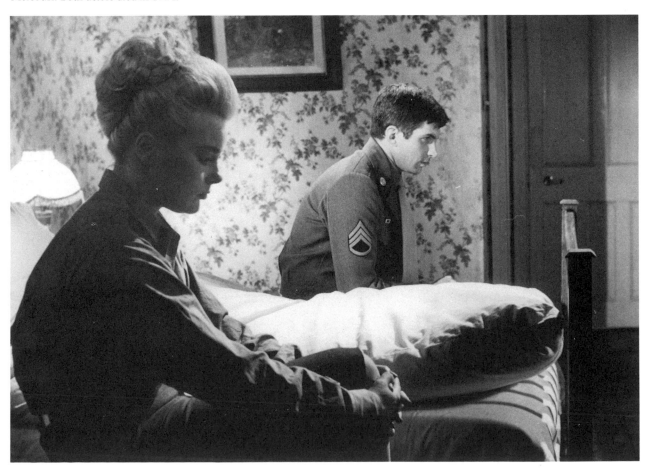

THE VICTORS Elke Sommer and Hamilton weather a bedroom impasse.

THE VICTORS   Mercouri and Peppard hold a romantic liaison.

George Hamilton's morale, scorning his relatively gentle and cleanly boyish persona in favor of that of a soldier she considers more hip and tough. She is the initial agent in Hamilton's transformation into a disillusioned, hardened veteran who, by the end, believes in nothing but self-preservation—and even in that he fails.

George Peppard, a more worldly guy, dallies with racy Melina Mercouri, a black-market queen and proprietor of an off-limits, anything-goes establishment. Others among the highlighted soldiers are left at least a bit happier than usual—if not particularly inspired—by their occasional ladies, but the endless engagements of war and the constant death and suffering they witness in battle leave these men, who are on their own undeviating path toward death, greatly depleted in spirit toward the end. At fadeout time, the last of the original group meets an undignified as well as untimely end from the knife-thrust of a drunken Russian soldier (played briefly but sharply by Albert Finney) amid the horrors of occupied Berlin.

The story certainly belonged in the drab black-and-white hues in which it was told, for it eschews "glamour." Foreman obviously being determined to portray war in all its tedium, violence, mud, dirt, and human waste, emotionally as well as physically. The director judiciously injected considerable World War II news footage that, while grainy at times, in most instances blends with the deliberate drabness and grayness of Christopher Challis's photography.

Along the way from Sicily to Berlin, the boys-prematurely-turned-men encounter horrifying concentration camps with near-skeletal inmates, dead bodies by the road (both military and civilian), the whiz of machine-gun bullets, attacks from the air, the cries of the wounded, and the exasperated commands of officers determined to exact the last smidgens of energy from their ever-more-tiring and nearly rebellious men.

Foreman in a later interview commented that as of 1963, eighteen years after the end of World War II, audiences were ready for an objective, unvarnished, realistic view of that six-year conflict and the frightful tolls it had exacted on people and nations—and that, he said, was what he set out to give them. His technique of making points first with telling images, followed by actions that reinforce and repeat those images, added force to the film, he felt. "Sometimes repetition, properly implemented, can add to the overall conviction," he said. *The Victors* illustrates this approach compellingly. It is a greatly underrated film.

53

DR. STRANGELOVE

OR

HOW I LEARNED TO STOP WORRYING AND LOVE THE BOMB

COLUMBIA

1964

CAST:

Peter Sellers, George C. Scott, Sterling Hayden, Peter Bull, James Earl Jones, Keenan Wynn, Tracy Reed, Slim Pickens.

CREDITS:

Stanley Kubrick, producer-director; Terry Southern, Peter George, and Stanley Kubrick, screenplay; based on the novel *Red Alert* by Peter George; Gilbert Taylor, photographer; Laurie Johnson, music; Anthony Harvey, editor. Running time: 93 minutes.

One of the great black war comedies with its own distinctive, cynical edge, *Dr. Strangelove*, now thirty years old, continues to get better by the decade. What seemed to more conservative souls far-out japing in 1964 now appears even more applicable in the surrealist 1990s. Based on a book by Peter

George, the Stanley Kubrick film, which carries the additional monicker [*or*] *How I Learned to Stop Worrying and Love The Bomb*, bears some resemblance to the more serious *Fail-Safe*, released the same year, but has a lighter, more facetious, yet wackily ironic touch. Offbeat and original in concept, it was not then (and is not now) likely to reinforce one's faith in politicians or statesmen-diplomats who have put themselves in charge of the world and its hapless denizens. And even the sixties' obsession with nuclear danger from the Soviet Union is not dated, given the danger of a resurrected and militant Russia that these days is bothering the heads and nervous systems of statesmen from Berlin to London to Washington.

The plot is simple in structure, yet complex in psychic nuances. A Strategic Air Command general, acting purely on his own, orders an atomic attack on Moscow. Then triple-play action and interplay is tensely, sharply set up among the initiating, wacked out general, the bombers winging it to the Soviet Union, and the war room at the Pentagon—where the chief executive is frantically trying to head off the now-imminent Inevitable.

The dialogue is comical, biting, trenchant, and satirical to the *n*th degree. Peter Sellers is on hand as the triple-treat / triple-role megastar of the film. He plays the President of the United States, a British RAF officer, and one Dr. Strangelove, a German scientist in the employ of the United States who sports inbred Nazi manners and stances and seems more than a bit daft.

George C. Scott is the wild-and-woolly general who exploits the crisis to push for the total annihilation of the Russian Bogeyman. Sterling Hayden distinguishes himself as a wacko *par excellence* general who won't be stopped from bombing the hell out of the Russians; he is an anticommunist gone berserk and more than a little insane, blaming the commies for each and every negation in the world of 1964. That, incidentally, was a year when America's fear of the Soviet Union, and its obsession with nuclear deterrence (along with some extremist Attack-Is-the-Best-Form-of-Defense views), were at their all-time high. Thus the picture, a four-star rater with many critics and vastly popular with audiences here and abroad, registered in spades. In fact, the entire title of the picture, long-drawn-out as it was, entered the language as a catchall phrase for extremist, illogical stances political, diplomatic, and militaristic.

Receiving an Oscar nomination as Best Picture, *Dr. Strangelove* is regarded today as one of the top of-

DR. STRANGELOVE   Hayden and Sellers talk out their plans.

DR. STRANGELOVE   Slim Pickens, as intrepid bomber pilot Maj. "King" Kong (right), discusses with his men, in a businesslike manner, their horrific mission.

ferings of director Stanley Kubrick, an artist who has never been afraid to take on controversial (indeed, supericonoclastic) subjects and make them ring with truth and emotion. His contempt for technology's spectacular advances in the *wrong* direction for the *wrong* reasons and on behalf of the assorted and widespread human stupidities that promote all these addlepated hydras of alleged "forward-looking theses," is abysmal—and certainly justified.

Some critics have felt that Kubrick pressed his views too extremely, but no one questions that Kubrick's heart was in the right place. Nor did he give his audience a cop-out ending: The world *did* come to an end, and somehow it all seemed good riddance, along the lines of "If you can't reform them and bring them up-to-snuff, then put 'em to sleep and assure cosmic quiet and peace"—the long rest that the tortured universe is held, by some pundits of both the right and the left persuasions, to badly need.

Scott's gung-ho militarist bogged down with bureaucratic dithering is something to see, his performance being what can only be termed comically operatic. Comically operatic is also the overall term for this end-it-all extravaganza so brilliantly orchestrated by Kubrick and recorded for posterity by photographer Gilbert Taylor.

DR. STRANGELOVE   The nuclear warheads are replete with 1964-style goofy graffiti, Pickens inspecting.

Arnold, music; Derek Parsons, editor. Running time: 90 minutes. (CinemaScope.)

54

THE THIN RED LINE

ALLIED ARTISTS

1964

CAST:

Keir Dullea, Jack Warden, James Philbrook, Kieron Moore, Ray Daley, Robert Kanter, Merlyn Yordan.

CREDITS:

Andrew Marton, director; Sidney Harmon, producer; Bernard Gordon, screenplay; based on the novel by James Jones; Manuel Berenguer, photographer; Malcolm

Adapted from one of James Jones's lesser novels, *The Thin Red Line* deals with the American campaign on Guadalcanal in exciting, trenchant terms. This film is a real sleeper, underrated both in its own time and since. It not only is a fine battle film, but also constitutes a study of relationships between men undergoing the stress of combat, in this case a company of raw recruits, most of whom are fated to die during one or another of the several battles depicted.

Keir Dullea is the intrepid private, green but tough and individualistic, who runs afoul of a veteran, combat-smart sergeant, Jack Warden. The interplay between these two takes up most of the personal phase of this womanless drama. There seems to be genuine antagonism between Dullea, an intelligent, sensitive young man who can summon gung-ho attitudes and approaches when needed, and the sadistic, one-track-mind Warden.

However, as it so often the case in such pairings and/or confrontations, love and hate prove to be two sides of the same coin—and, after much combat action and assorted other stressful situations, Warden dies in the arms of Dullea after saving the latter's life.

Dullea and Warden offer interesting contrasts characterizationally, the private being intense and introspective, the sergeant alternating between easygoing cynicism and almost sadistic leadership. Warden won't tolerate hesitations or falterings among his recruits; he recognizes that they are untried, and far more vulnerable than more-seasoned men would be; he tries to show patience with their gaucheries, and realizes he has been cast as older brother/father/what-have-you as much as leader of a pack of fighting boys/men. What would today be called "tough/love" is one of his standard approaches to the recruits under his command, but they often translate his tough orders and aggressive stances as cruelty and insensitivity.

James Jones, himself a veteran of the Pacific fighting, shows the Guadalcanal engagement for what it was: a mass exercise in butchery. He deplores, unsentimentally yet compassionately, the waste of young lives, the extinction of hopes for a future in peacetime, the false heroics that often conceal overcompensative fright and self-loathing. Jones understood the male psyche in wartime as well as any writer or commentator of the World War II period, and director Andrew Marton and screenwriter Bernard Gordon do full justice to his intentions. *The Thin Red Line* may not be on the level of *From Here to Eternity*, but it does convey not only Jones's sincere intentions but also some strong autobiographical emanations. One is left feeling that Jones is drawing his main characters from life—his own life, his own experiences—and felt the work deeply and intimately as he wrote it.

The other men depicted in the Guadalcanal engagement, or at least this miniature of it, get across the assorted intrepidities and desperations of deter-

THE THIN RED LINE   Keir Dullea gauges the enemy position while neck deep in a Guadalcanal swamp.

THE THIN RED LINE   Dullea gets a stranglehold on an enemy soldier.

other—the sense of dedication, of a mutual pulling-together—is also most eloquently displayed.

mined but callow recruits trying to rise to the occasion in the midst of chaos, death, woundings, shellfire—all the usual panoply of destruction. James Philbrook, Ray Daley and Robert Kanter really deliver the goods here: We feel we are looking at actual servicemen caught in an inescapable crucible of destruction, and not mere actors making faces and choreographing their actions to a watchful director's command.

War is shown at its worst, as only James Jones can show it. But the love of comrades for each

55

BATTLE OF THE BULGE

WARNER BROS. / UNITED STATES PICTURES

1965

CAST:

Henry Fonda, Robert Ryan, Robert Shaw, Dana Andrews, Telly Savalas, George Montgomery, Ty Hardin, Pier Angeli, Barbara Werle, Charles Bronson, James MacArthur, Werner Peters.

CREDITS:

Ken Annakin, director; Philip Yordan, producer; Philip Yordan, Milton Sperling, and John Melson, screenplay; Jack Hildyard, photographer; Benjamin Frankel, music; Derek Parsons, supervising editor. Running time: 167 minutes. (Cinerama or Ultra-Panavision [70mm] / Technicolor.)

Originally made in the Cinerama process, *Battle of the Bulge* was later shown in more conventionally reduced ratios. For 167 action-packed, drama-driven minutes, it gives yet another slant on the famous engagements of December 1944 that saw the Germans rallying for one last strong counterattack before retreating into their own country and, within months, to total defeat. But, like cornered rats, they set out to fight hard, and cause considerable loss of American lives before they are through.

Robert Shaw is highly effective—and lethal—as the German commandant determined to show the Americans and other allies that entrance into Germany itself will not be won easily. Shaw is one of the main dramatic pillars on the German side; his single-minded intensity as he conducts his operations is compelling acting. In the Ardennes, the Allies find themselves slowed down by the crack German Panzer operation under Shaw's command. His battle of wits, and variegated strategies, as deployed on the Allies, are fascinating to watch.

Some critics had reservations about the star-packed *Battle of the Bulge*, with one calling it a "bloody and unbowed war spectacle, quite literate and handsome but deafeningly noisy and with emphasis on strategy rather than character." Another

BATTLE OF THE BULGE   A town finds itself awash in battle action.

Germans are planning a strong, retaliatory, and desperate winter counterattack that will call for the deployment of all available Allied resources. Fonda is excellent as the loner whose careful analyses and researchings prove correct in the end. His stubborn maintenance of his unpopular views compels admiration among even his adversaries, and when he is justified at the conclusion, there is an empathetic admiration for his cool determination and sterling courage in upholding his beliefs.

Robert Ryan, as the American general, etches a firm, stoic, granitic characterization of the kind that originally won him notice with critics and audiences. He is cautious, careful, wary about premature moves, and analytical—but, once convinced of a correct strategy, he moves with the dispatch and force of the trained soldier he is. As played by Ryan, the commander is the archetype of the soldier who combines action and analysis in equal measure.

BATTLE OF THE BULGE   German commander Robert Shaw plans a renewed offensive.

sneered, "This over-inflated war drama about an important event cannot triumph over the banal script. Read a good book on the subject instead." But to this viewer, the character aspects were ably supplied by the Robert Shaw portrayal (and those of others); and the Yordan–Sperling–Melson script, as directed by the able and empathetic Ken Annakin, gave equal and expert play to character delineation and action. Some of that action is quite terrifying and riveting indeed, as whole towns and populations are wiped out, and field breakthroughs are undertaken, in both advance and retreat positions, with clipped dispatch—strong pyrotechnics being applied to battle, positioning, and strategic encountering.

The pitting of Shaw on the German side against Allied commander Robert Ryan and his alert, intrepid aids Henry Fonda and Dana Andrews, is truly a battle of wills and strategic planning. Fonda is a maverick colonel whose views are anathema to the top Allied brass, as he is convinced that the

BATTLE OF THE BULGE   Tanks wreak fiery devastation on the countryside.

190

BATTLE OF THE BULGE
Commanding general
Robert Ryan (second
right) and his aide, Henry
Fonda (foreground left),
orchestrate a counter-
attack.

BATTLE OF THE BULGE Shaw and Barbara Werle take time out
for mutual comforting.

Dana Andrews is thoughtful and compelling as another of Ryan's senior officers whose main objective is to *think* through—and *act* through—the campaign dilemmas posed.

The assorted skirmishes, minor engagements, and battles all are orchestrated ably by director Annakin, who obviously worked well with the three scripters, getting across their concepts while adding some rousing approaches of his own. There seems to have been an able synchronization of all creative hands in the mounting and presentation of this picture. Too, Benjamin Frankel's evocative music helps promote the various ambiences and moods effectively.

Barbara Werle and Pier Angeli handle the romancings well, though they are decidedly second-fiddle to the main goings-on, as are their relatively brief scenes. Last, but once again certainly not least, all the individual soldier vignettes are gotten across sharply.

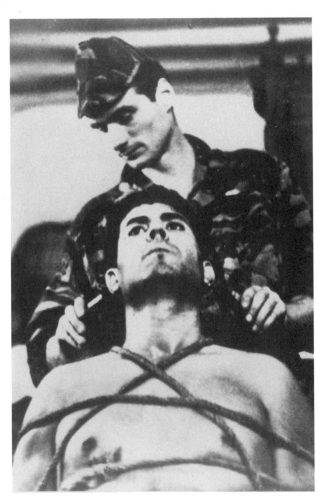

THE BATTLE OF ALGIERS   The French apply torture.

56

THE BATTLE OF ALGIERS

CINEMA V / CASBAH FILMS (ALGIERS) / IGOR FILMS (ROME)

1965

CAST:

Jean Martin, Yacef Saadi, Brahim Haggiag, Tommaso Neri, Samia Kerbash, Fawzia El Kader.

CREDITS:

Gillo Pontecorvo, director; Antonio Musu and Yacef Saadi, producers; Franco Solinas, screenplay; Marcello Gatti, photographer; Ennio Morricone and Gillo Pontecorvo, music; Mario Serandrei and Mario Morra, editors. Running time: 135 minutes. (CinemaScope.)

With graphic realism, *The Battle of Algiers* deals with the Algerian revolt against the French in the 1954–62 period. Actors were blended with real-life participants from the streets by director Gillo Pontecorvo. This drama-documentary blend was notable for its fierce and authentic-looking combat scenes. (A reel of footage showing French torture methods applied to Algerian rebels was later deleted from British and American showings of the film.) Without having to rely on a single foot of conventional newsreel footage, Pontecorvo made the violent doings seem so lifelike that he won a Best Film award at the 1966 Venice Film Festival, as well as a Best Foreign Film Oscar nomination.

The wealth of effective detail and protracted footage of violent acts undertaken almost surreally gave the picture an anarchic, hallucinatory vividness that was much commented upon by international critics. Certainly *The Battle of Algiers* set the pace for much of the political cinema that proliferated in the late sixties and throughout the seventies.

192

THE BATTLE OF ALGIERS
Onlookers at a shooting.

The liberation of Algeria itself is covered in an epilogue; in the main footage one particular phase of the guerrilla operations is made to symbolize all revolutionary operations throughout the nation. As the years went on, the FLN (as the rebel group was known) recruited many more adherents from the initial rebellion of 1954. Nothing seemed to stop them, though the exasperated and ever-more-beleaguered French overlords applied every measure that came to mind: midnight seizures, stepping-up of the torturing of captured rebels, and sudden raids when least expected and in quarters that felt themselves surely "off limits."

The film goes on to depict the organized crime in the Casbah of Algiers, much of it allied to rebel causes and hence politicized, resulting in numerous woundings and killings. Sometimes innocents get caught in this endless war of attrition, but obviously these and other circumstances seem to the rebels sad but inevitable byproducts of the overall struggle for freedom from French suzerainty. When the French colonel on the scene decides that more drastic means are required and starts decimating the FLN from the roots up, the latter takes such brutal revenge that the journalistic outcry in France changes the policy, and redirects the conduct of what both sides recognize is a full-fledged war.

THE BATTLE OF ALGIERS   A sudden alley ambush.

THE BATTLE OF ALGIERS   The military storm the barricaded civilians.

As one critic put it: "Pontecorvo refuses to caricature the French or glamorize the Algerians; instead, he sketches the way a guerrilla movement is organized and the way a colonial force sets about decimating it."

There is far more action than talk in this film—possibly by a ratio of nine to one. The constant action; the murderous rhythms; the sharp, sinister images caught by Marcello Gatti's photography and Ennio Morricone's apposite and full-throated and alarumed scoring—all give *The Battle of Algiers* a haunting (indeed, frightening) individuality among films of its kind. That is, if there *are* films of this particular kind, texture, and quality.

Most effective and memorable of all are the character studies of people on the street, on balconies, on stairways, in alleys. Pontecorvo sketches these people individually in swift, sharp strokes; he gets photographer Gatti to zero in on them, taking close, uptight shots—some of them from below—that in one flash limn both a life and a background. One feels that one knows these people, that their lives are precious even though the opposing forces think of them as pawns, or even as nuisances. For this is

194

THE BATTLE OF ALGIERS   The troops demanding immediate surrender.

195

a man's war, and women and children had better make themselves scarce if they know what's good for them.

Anyway, that's what the film seems to be telling us, and in eloquent, persuasive terms. *The Battle of Algiers*, winner of many awards in Europe and America, is a film with something to say, and it says it loud and clear. One of its loudest, clearest messages: War may be Hell, but if it's the only way to get one's objective, *get to it!*

57

BEACH RED

UNITED ARTISTS

1967

CAST:

Cornel Wilde, Rip Torn, Burr DeBenning, Patrick Wolfe, Jean Wallace, Jaime Sanchez, Genki Koyama.

CREDITS:

Cornel Wilde, producer-director; Clint Johnston, Donald A. Peters, and Jefferson Pascal, screenplay; based on the 1945 novel *Red Beach*, by Peter Bowman; Cecil R. Cooney, photographer; Antonio Buenaventura, music; Frank P. Keller, editor. Running time: 105 minutes. (Deluxe Color.)

In 1967, actor–producer–director Cornel Wilde had himself a sleeper with *Beach Red*, which depicts the taking of a Japanese-held island by American forces in 1943. The film is not so much entertaining as riveting. Wilde directed it tautly and without frills, and it is a brutal indictment of war, showing it at its unvarnished worst. So strong was the presentation and treatment, and so graphic are the visuals, that it had to be watered down to be made acceptable to mass television—yes, even in the violence-prone 1990s.

This film is a neglected masterpiece. One critic called it "harrowingly brutal, almost like a horror movie, with severed limbs washing up on the beach. Although Wilde deals exclusively in pacifist clichés, the film has a genuine primitive power."

Time has only enhanced the favorable critical reaction to this picture, which passed through the system relatively overlooked in 1967 but now, in the 1990s, has picked up something of a cult following.

The usual old saws of casting and character are avoided. As one reviewer put it, "No tough-talking sergeant with a heart of gold. No green kid proving himself a man under combat conditions." It is true that the main characters tend to be individual exemplars of points of view rather than fully characterized persons; they may not have the stuff of life in them. But what they stand for makes a strong impact, and under Wilde's directorial guidance the points are well made.

Wilde plays a captain who is devoted to both his wife (played by real-life wife Jean Wallace) and the life she makes possible, yet knows he must do a job in this man's war and so is not out to shirk his responsibilities. Rip Torn is a depraved type, a sergeant who gets sadistic kicks from the brutal, inhuman action. Then there is Patrick Wolfe, a green kid of eighteen, son of a clergyman, who dreams of being reunited with his girlfriend back in the States. At even his tender age he has come to learn that war can truly be hell. Burr DeBenning is a crude, rough, ill-educated outsider who has found a home in the army and will follow its—and his—fortunes straight to extinction if need be.

It is not to say that these people do not register as human beings; they do. But the movie is so written and directed that, for once, the rules are broken and archetypes come on more forcibly and directly than do standard humanized types so common in war films. It is as if, by reversing the usual rules of characterizational portraiture, Wilde hoped to strengthen the antiwar message he is sincerely endeavoring to portray. Surprisingly, the reverse gimmick works—to a point, anyway.

But this is not a picture designed to entertain, a diversion to be savored and then forgotten like a banana split. It is out to make a lasting impression—to linger in the collective audience consciousness. And, as a result, there is no pandering to popular concepts of "entertainment," and certainly "escapisms" are eschewed, and so are "light moments," "relief," and "easy laughs." Hence the message is gotten across, with increasing force, that war is a damned dirty business, evil in its effects, demoralizing in the acting-out of its necessities, deadening in its finalities.

Wilde directed the combat scenes with inspired detachment; these men come on as genuinely experiencing and suffering from their individual fates.

BEACH RED Cornel Wilde and his men in the thick of the action.

BEACH RED Wounded, he's still in charge.

BEACH RED He comes to the aid of a dying serviceman.

The graphic depictions of woundings and dismemberments, as mentioned before, make *Beach Red* a questionable candidate for mass TV. For the violence and human carnage depicted here lack the pace and "glamour" and theatricalism that audiences of the 1990s expect along with all that. Nothing here is sugarcoated—it is all salt and paprika.

Beach Red, viewed a quarter-century after its making, looms larger than ever as a real, true, graphically delineated war film of sterling caliber—and very much to Wilde's credit as its instigator and catalyst.

58

THE GREEN BERETS

WARNERS-SEVEN ARTS / BATJAC

1968

CAST:

John Wayne, David Janssen, Jim Hutton, Aldo Ray, Raymond St. Jacques, Bruce Cabot, George Takei, Jack Soo, Patrick Wayne, Mike Henry, Jason Evers, Luke Askew.

CREDITS:

John Wayne and Ray Kellogg, directors; Michael Wayne, producers; James Lee Barrett, screenplay; based on the novel by Robin Moore; Winton C. Hoch, photographer; Miklos Rozsa, music; Otho Lovering, editor. Running time: 141 minutes. (Panavision / Technicolor.)

John Wayne was sixty-one when *The Green Berets* was released, and he was starting to show the wear-and-tear of the numerous action and war films in which he had appeared for nearly forty years. He was also politically anathema in some circles for his gung-ho stance on Vietnam, a war that had become increasingly unpopular on the home front and the object of frequent protests, some of a violent nature, in the late sixties and early seventies.

Wayne was a staunch conservative who believed in the domino theory, which proposed that the Soviet Union was trying to drain our strength in one "small" war after another, as well as test U.S. mettle in locations of the Soviets' choosing, such as Korea in 1950–1953. Wayne also felt that if we didn't resist the communist encroachment, we would lose the Cold War. Wayne was also convinced that if we *had* to fight in such places as Vietnam (as earlier in Korea) we should *fight to win* and that the hesitations of various administrations in Washington had needlessly prolonged such conflicts.

Such stands and opinions as Wayne articulated were naturally unpopular in liberal circles with many demanding that we abandon *our* nuclear arsenal while at the same time permitting the Russians to keep *theirs*. Of course many war pro-

THE GREEN BERETS   Aldo Ray and Edward Faulkner flank Wayne as he gets tough.

testers of the time either missed or deliberately evaded the point that *both* superpowers should abandon, once and for all, the nuclear ratrace. Outspoken Wayne also had waxed impatient with the continuing attacks on Joe McCarthy and Roy Cohn, feeling that while some "innocents" might have gotten caught in the "purges" of the 1950s, a good many Communist fellow-travelers *were* getting caught in the McCarthy-Cohn net—hence the dismay of some liberals wrongly sympathetic to them.

Given his political views Wayne ran up against the prejudices of the liberal press when his *Green Berets*, a tribute to the Special Forces who fought so valiantly in Vietnam, was released.

Actually the film has much merit. The action pyrotechnics are in the best Wayne tradition, and he even co-directed, (sharing credit with Ray Kellogg.)

THE GREEN BERETS   Wayne gets the salute.

199

The standard military characters are trotted out doing their usual thing. Jim Hutton is an unmilitary type who goofs off in the supply room. Aldo Ray is the typical cutup (endemic in such films) who pulls out his usual bag of tricks; Jason Evers is the All-American young officer who, as one critic put it, belonged more in a toothpaste ad. Luke Askew does yet another turn on the naive but well-meaning country yokel, and Mike Henry is described by one critic as "the beefy soldier who takes several enemy soldiers with him as he dies and dies and dies!"

The Green Berets admittedly is ridden with the usual situations and formulas of the genre. Cliches abound—though the old saw that a cliche has to have some measure of truth and strength and validity in it to qualify as a cliche in the first place, certainly applies in this case.

Wayne, as always, is out to entertain his audiences, and he ladles out a goodly share of suspenseful situations, rousing combat-action sequences and the like, and the acting in many instances is individualized, highly professional and eminently suited to the vehicle. The camera work is smooth, the pacing fast, the movement tense and well-timed.

Anyone willing to leave individual political persuasions and biases out of his reaction to *The Green Berets* will credit it with its honest and fair critical due, such as well-presented and choreographed battle sequences and more than its share of well-acted and lively situations and gimmicks. Even to 1994 eyes, *The Green Berets* presents a sheaf of assets.

59

THE BATTLE OF BRITAIN

UNITED ARTISTS

1969

CAST:

Laurence Olivier, Robert Shaw, Michael Caine, Christopher Plummer, Kenneth More, Susannah York, Trevor Howard, Ralph Richardson, Patrick Wymark, Curt

THE BATTLE OF BRITAIN   Volunteer firemen try to control the fires and general devastation after a German bombing raid on London.

Jurgens, Michael Redgrave, Harry Andrews, Nigel Patrick, Ian McShane, Robert Flemyng, Edward Fox, Nicholas Pennell.

CREDITS:

Guy Hamilton, director; Harry Saltzman and S. Benjamin Fisz, producers; James Kennaway and Wilfred Greatorex, screenplay; based on the book *The Narrow Margin*, by Derek Wood and Derek Dempster; Freddie Young, photographer; William Walton and Ron Goodwin, music; Bert Bates, editor. Running time: 131 minutes. (Panavision / Technicolor.)

A stirring account of Britain under fire as the Germans conduct their lethal air raids in 1940 is offered in *The Battle of Britain*. An all-star cast creates fun as find-the-celebrity games result from sudden appearances by such well-known names as Laurence Olivier, Michael Redgrave, Robert Shaw, Michael Caine, and Christopher Plummer. Olivier is impressive as Sir Hugh Dowding, the fighter command's head, and Trevor Howard is taciturnly competent as the air vice-marshal.

The Battle alternates between personal vignettes

THE BATTLE OF BRITAIN Nicholas Pennell watches Edward Fox and Ian McShane play chess as they await the signal to man their planes.

THE BATTLE OF BRITAIN A squadron of German Heinkels is inspected by the Nazi staff officers at their base in Northern France.

and marvelous dogfight air action across the British skies. The film cost a reported 12 million and lost some $10 million worldwide, but it was a worthy effort nevertheless, with director Guy Hamilton and photographer Freddie Young in there pitching all the way. The aerial action is breathtaking, and Hamilton nicely balances the personal dramas with the war maneuvers.

The RAF top brass is shown debating the strategies, pondering the decisions that will eventuate in dire loss of life and questionable results. One of the serious problems faced by the British in 1940 was a shortage of both planes and pilots, most of whom had to be hastily trained.

Olivier, in what time he is given, offers a fine portrait of a responsible commanding officer worn down by quick decision-making and hopeful that his instincts will carry him through some tight situations when so much depends on his judgment and expertise. Howard looks solemn throughout—as well he should, for an accumulation of even minor mistakes and miscalculations could spell the beginning of the end for Britain as a combat power.

The relentless air action by the Germans over Britain is captured harrowingly, and the destruction in the English cities is rendered graphically and brutally.

One is left with a profound admiration for British endurance in the face of an initially overwhelming

THE BATTLE OF BRITAIN   Trevor Howard as the air vice-marshal who commands the group.

THE BATTLE OF BRITAIN Michael Redgrave and Laurence Olivier ponder a crisis.

203

204

German superiority in aircraft and personnel. As whole neighborhoods are destroyed and people are left homeless, the human capacity for survival against heartbreaking odds is an inspiring spectacle to contemplate. There are telling little passages in this film, too. For example, one brief scene, in which two British fliers are trying to enjoy a quiet chess game although knowing they are about to put their lives on the line in the skies against lethal enemy combat expertise, is both touching and inspiring in its evocation of the human capacity for discipline and self-composure. There are few stiff-upper-lip clichés throughout—just a lot of people in variegated pursuits doing what has to be done to ensure the survival of their nation and their way of life.

Some marvelous photographic dexterity is displayed in the shots of the aerial action; the cross-cutting and exciting dives and sweeps are caught breathtakingly. Unfortunately, at times the abrupt shifts between such frenetic combat action and quiet human interplays on the ground do interrupt somewhat the flow of what is overall a hypnotically fascinating depiction of war's ultimate indignities and horrors.

Many of the actors who appear in this film, made some twenty-four years after the end of World War II, actually participated in either the action or the strategic planning at the time, if not in both. It is interesting to discern in their faces the conscious—and unconscious—memories of the worst crisis their country ever faced. It was a crisis surmounted only after six years of stress and trauma in a war that lasted two years beyond the prior national trial, the World War I of 1914–18. Hence this account of the 1939–45 high points of World War II—and certainly the Battle of Britain is one of those salient high-water marks—ranks with the best of the graphic, grittily recalled cinematic re-creations of war.

60

PATTON

20TH CENTURY–FOX

1970

CAST:
George C. Scott, Karl Malden, Stephen Young, Michael Strong, Frank Latimore, James Edwards, Lawrence Dobkin, Michael Bates, Tim Considine, Karl Michael Vogler.

CREDITS:
Franklin Schaffner, director; Frank McCarthy, producer; Francis Ford Coppola and Edmund E. North, screenplay; based on the books *Patton: Ordeal and Triumph*, by Ladislas Farago, and *A Soldier's Story*, the autobiography of Gen. Omar N. Bradley; Fred Koenekamp, photographer; Jerry Goldsmith, music; Hugh S. Fowler, editor. Running time: 171 minutes. (70mm. [Dimension 150] / Deluxe Color.)

Patton is as realistic a war picture as one could want, and its central character—the tyrannical, bad-tempered, egoistic Gen. George S. Patton—is about as dimensional a man as has ever been portrayed on the screen. George C. Scott makes this legendary World War II general come fully alive, and he is shown as the exemplary commander he was while

THE BATTLE OF BRITAIN   Aircraft over the White Cliffs of Dover.

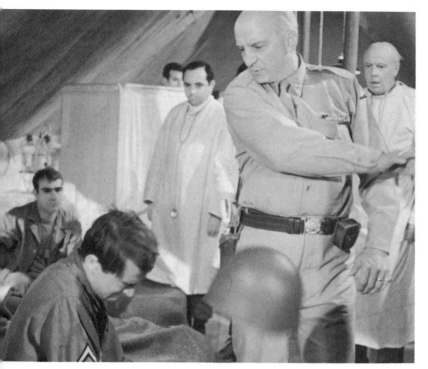

unstintingly and uncompromisingly displayed as insensitive, martinet-ish, brutal, and violent. Patton despises men he conceives to be cowards, and in one case does not hesitate to physically assault a man he feels is not soldierly. Karl Malden is equally believable as a more balanced Gen. Omar Bradley, who understands Patton's complex nature while deploring his excesses.

Bradley's attitude toward Patton is similar to Abraham Lincoln's toward Gen. Ulysses S. Grant—namely, that while he may have personally obnoxious traits and deplorable attitudes at times, he *fights* to *win*.

Audacious, imaginative, no-nonsense, forceful, and ruthless in demanding the best in the men under his command, George C. Scott's Patton

PATTON Letting a PFC (Tim Considine) have it.

PATTON Getting into the tank action.

PATTON   Getting a right-royal reception.

arouses conflicting reactions in his troops: awe, respect, anger at his methods, bewilderment in the face of his character changes. Scott is so dedicated to doing justice to Patton that you feel he has gotten not only under the skin of the original but also has *become* him.

The picture won a number of Academy Awards, but Scott—in what many felt was an unnecessarily contrary gesture—refused his Oscar, declaring (among other things) that he did not feel his portrayal caught the truth of the man. It was an opinion many of his admirers among the public and the critical fraternity felt was totally wrongheaded and unduly modest. Others felt, though, that Scott—a man who, like Patton, often displayed a violent temper and an egoistic, contrary nature—was merely "showing off" in his usual style.

Scott, as actor and man, has often been admired but not particularly liked. As one actor who worked with him in *Patton* said, "I wouldn't have wanted him as a father in real life; he would have been a killer ball-breaker!" (It would be interesting to get the reaction of Scott's son, actor Campbell Scott, to

PATTON
Contemplating the
next move.

that statement. If anyone should know, *he* should!) Scott as Patton is compelling and riveting in what is perhaps one of the all-time great film performances, whether haranguing the troops, leaving them both cowed and electrified; or slapping one of his soldiers he feels is a slacker; or disagreeing with fellow officers; or cutting buffoons down to size; or decrying cowardice and what he conceives to be gross incompetence.

The film's battle sequences are put over convincingly, authentically, and well, but the Patton personality, as filtered through Scott's own formidable mystique, is the Main Event in this film. The story material was based on Ladislas Farago's *Patton: Ordeal and Triumph*, and on *A Soldier's Story*, Omar Bradley's autobiography. The picture, shot in a variety of locations (including such disparate sites as England, Morocco, Greece, Sicily, and Spain), won a total of seven Oscars—Best Picture among them.

Scott appeared in *The Last Days of Patton*, a television sequel, some sixteen years later. He seems to have had a change of heart by that time, regarding both his Oscar and his attitude toward the role, because he played in the sequel as convincingly and thoroughly as in the original—indeed, displaying a kind of retrospective relish in delineating the general's complexities and perversities.

Throughout *Patton* it is Scott's preternatural energy as an actor that carries the action and the human interplays alike. He is rousing and perfectionist and disciplined in the battle scenes, demanding as much of himself as of his men. Impatient with the hesitant and fearful, he refuses to suffer fools—either gladly or in any other mood, accepts no nonsense from anybody, and takes issue with his fellow officers whenever one of his views or strategies is overruled (or, in his view, traduced). A fine, riveting war picture electrified and magnified enormously by a fine, riveting star performance by Scott: That was—and is—*Patton*.

61

M*A*S*H

20TH CENTURY–FOX

1970

CAST:

Elliott Gould, Donald Sutherland, Tom Skerritt, Sally Kellerman, Robert Duvall, Jo Ann Pflug, Rene Auberjonois, Roger Bowen, Gary Burghoff, Fred Williamson, John Schuck, Bud Cort, G. Wood.

CREDITS:

Robert Altman, director; Ingo Preminger, producer; Ring Lardner, Jr., screenplay; based on the novel by Richard Hooker (pseud. Dr. H. Richard Homberg and William Heinz); Harold E. Stine, photographer; Johnny Mandel, music; Danford B. Greene, editor. Running time: 116 minutes. (Panavision / Deluxe Color.)

Iconoclastic, forceful Robert Altman's first major hit was *M*A*S*H* back in 1970, and its antiwar comedic spoofing and brazen irreverence are as fresh today as a quarter-century ago. Following the black comedy doings of a wildly iconoclastic, no-holds-barred medical unit on constant call during the Korean War, it proved a stomach-turner for some, a visceral belly-laugh for others, depending not just on the viewer's political persuasion but on his or her concept of humor.

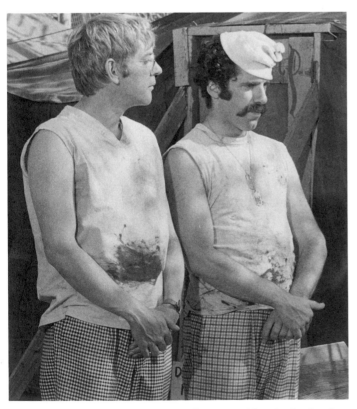

M*A*S*H   After their latest butchery, Donald Sutherland and Elliot Gould as Hawkeye and Trapper John are bloody but unbowed.

The play won an Oscar for screenwriter Ring Lardner, Jr., although in actuality the script was a pastiche of spontaneous inspirations concocted by writer and cast as they went along. A 1973 rerelease also proved popular, with music by Ahmad Jamal added (the original had a Johnny Mandel score). Later it was a long-running hit TV series, which many joked ran longer than the war itself.

The gore and the sex alternate wildly. The endless operations are performed with what appears to be efficiency and dispatch, but the absence of emotion and the jaded attitudes of doctors and operating crews indicate how the stresses of war have dehumanized, the constant repetition of trauma and death leaving all comers benumbed.

Some of the reviews of the time nailed down the film's individualistic appeal in cynical 1970, when yet another war everyone was fed up with kept refusing to terminate, and exasperation was giving way to ennui—albeit of a highly cynical kind. One critic termed *M*A*S*H* "a foul-mouthed, raucous, antiestablishment comedy combining gallows humor, sexual slapstick, and outrageous satire."

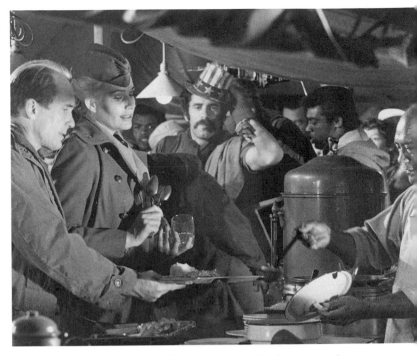

M*A*S*H   Robert Duvall, Sally Kellerman, and Gould take time out for chow.

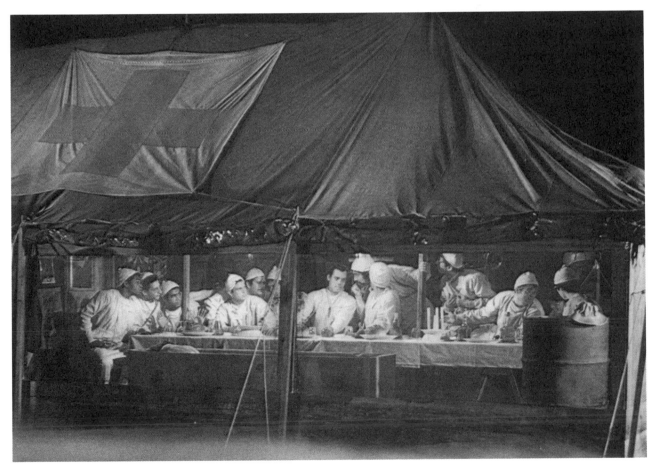

M*A*S*H   The boys create a Last Supper travesty.

And from another: "[The picture is] bloody funny, a hyper-acute wiretap on mankind's death wish."

M*A*S*H, which stands for Mobile Army Surgical Hospital, is set within minutes of bloody battles along the Korean 38th parallel. Elliott Gould (as Trapper John McIntyre), Donald Sutherland (as Hawkeye Pierce), Tom Skerritt (as Duke Forrest) and others head a team of medics. Gould is super-cool, efficient, and utterly sardonic as he takes on wave after wave of horribly wounded and muti-lated soldiers, fixes them up as best he can with some fancy repairing and stitching, and then sends them on, assembly-line fashion, to other areas—presumably those on the way to hospitals back home. Like the others, Gould has become totally calloused by a surfeit of suffering, in a cause which he thinks bankrupt and grossly overextended com-bat-wise.

Working twelve to fifteen hours at a stretch, the team lets off steam both sexually and bibulously once released for relaxation. The language is coarse and profane, the doings larkish and indeed buf-foonish—but the point is gotten across, however satirically, in spades: War is hell, and it is better to laugh than cry—to let off steam than to simmer until one explodes.

The entire cast works in wonderful synergy to convey the futility and waste and mechanical reac-tions that come with oversaturation in suffering, and overexposure to the military butchering oper-ation. Gould is delightfully wacky and waggish; in fact, in *M*A*S*H* he demonstrates his first-rate comic abilities as well as in anything else he has done. Sutherland, too, gets across a character be-fuddled by the insanities of war, and hypnotized by its sounds and furies, yet sufficiently self-possessed and detached to find laughs amid the endless vari-eties of negation. Jo Ann Pflug is a sexy army

M*A*S*H   Gould, Sutherland, and Bud Cort plot more iconoclastic mischief.

nurse, efficient both on the job and off, and Sally Kellerman, Robert Duvall, Tom Skerritt—and the amusing Rene Auberjonois (as the unit's padre)—get across their own individual ideas of how Burnout Transcendent can be translated into Foolish Fun and Iconoclastic Idiocy.

Amid the wild comedy and assorted inanities, a point is being made: Sometimes the human mind, spirit, body—soul, for that matter—need the release of utter wild hilarity and buffoonery and to-hell-with-it nihilism, just to keep functioning. In an insane world, the better part of valor goes without saying: Don't even try to lick 'em—join 'em!

*M*A*S*H* is a masterpiece of kaliedoscopic comic moods, spontaneous eruptions of high spirits, and antiestablishment spoofings, all rendered as effectively as is humanly possible under inhuman conditions.

62

KELLY'S HEROES

METRO–GOLDWYN–MAYER

1970

CAST:

Clint Eastwood, Telly Savalas, Don Rickles, Donald Sutherland, Carroll O'Connor, Stuart Margolin, Dick Davalos, David Hurst, Hal Buckley, Gavin McLeod.

CREDITS:

Brian G. Hutton, director; Gabriel Katzka and Sidney Beckerman, producers; Troy Kennedy Martin, screenplay; Gabriel Figueroa, photographer; Lalo Shifrin, music; John Jympson, editor. Running time: 148 minutes. (Panavision / Metrocolor.)

This offbeat 1970 war film starring Clint Eastwood is interesting in that it gives rather sharp and unromantic insights into *some* soldiers' capers during World War II. During the course of the serio-comedic action, an American platoon captures a German officer, David Hurst, who happens to be stashing away some $16 million in gold bullion.

The guys decide this is Damn Nazi money, so it's okay to dispose of it as they will. Before reality asserts itself, the picture is a fun-filled catalogue of dogface japes, sporadic combat action during which the guys show there is mettle and valor beneath the clowning, and fusses-and-fumings over the Nazi wealth.

The picture is also a collection of character studies. Clint Eastwood, in his earlier Great Stone Face phase, is the wall against which the other, more mercurial cast members dash their mercurial feelings. Telly Savalas offers some paprika and personality-plus as one of the more forthright soldiers, as does Donald Sutherland, as the unit's beatnik "philosopher." Don Rickles, Gavin McLeod, and Carroll O'Connor get across a variety of types in their assorted moods, manners, bitchings, and happy-time moods.

Some critics liked *Kelly's Heroes*, praising its vitality and high spirits, as ably directed by Brian G. Hutton and sharply photographed by Gabriel Figueroa—who proved as good with the close-ups and long shots during the combat scenes as during the more buffoonish episodes. One pundit sneered that the picture must have been made "for no possible reason other than a chance to use the Yugoslav army at cut rates." Cut rates or no, the Yugoslav forces—this was in the relatively-blessed-and-benign 1970s, before the Croats and Serbs began going at it—ably acquit themselves, and some of them turn out to be good bit-actors, too.

Yet another critic cluck-clucked at the "over two hours of consistently devastating explosions, pyrotechnics, and demolition." But the film does have vitality, and it presents troops as they often were in this or any other war—clownish boys sometimes, worked-up combat do-or-die-ers at others, and always lively and high-spirited.

The theft of the bullion takes place during a lull in the fighting, and the guys seem to think it's all a lark. Their commander, Hal Buckley, only wants a rest between engagements, and short of raping or otherwise abusing the civilian population—definite no-nos in this man's platoon—he doesn't really give a damn how they amuse themselves. That the amusement turns out to be to the tune of a $16 million gold cache is, of course, a development unforeseen. Savalas, senior noncom in the outfit, while initially reluctant to get involved in what constitutes a theft despite wartime conditions, finally jumps into the act, gleefully outdoing the others.

The combat scenes are well done, Lalo Schifrin's

KELLY'S HEROES   Clint Eastwood in the thick of the action.

KELLY'S HEROES   Gavin McLeod (with cigar, left), bearded Sutherland, Stuart Margolin (background), Perry Lopez (foreground), Eastwood, and Telly Savalas take a breather with the platoon.

musical alarums-and-excursions often give the goings-on a portent and an importance they don't really warrant, and Eastwood (as the Kelly of the title) and his acting troupe all give fine accounts of themselves.

The chief recommendation of *Kelly's Heroes* to serious students of war films is its larkishness, its depictions of the lighter, more human sides of American fighting men in Europe, and its array of highly individualized characters who, whether beating the hell out of Germans in combat or robbing them blind, are full of life-force and sly clevernesses. One is left with the feeling that if these boys survive the war, they will make great lawyers, bankers—or deluxe con men and state-of-the-art Wall Street crooks.

KELLY'S HEROES   Rickles, Eastwood, and Sutherland survey the Nazi treasures.

Philippe Forquet, John Savidant, Susan Wood, Andrea Checchi.

63

WATERLOO

PARAMOUNT / DINO DE LAURENTIIS / MOS-FILM

1971

CAST:

Rod Steiger, Christopher Plummer, Orson Welles, Jack Hawkins, Virginia McKenna, Dan O'Herlihy, Michael Wilding, Rupert Davies, Ian Ogilvy, Sergei Zakhariadze,

CREDITS:

Sergei Bondarchuk, director; Dino De Laurentiis, producer; H. A. L. Craig and Sergei Bondarchuk, screenplay; Armando Nannuzzi, photographer; Mario Garbuglia, production design; Nino Rota, music; E. V. Michajlova, editor. Running time: 132 minutes. (Panavision, Technicolor.)

Napoleon's final defeat on the Belgian battlefield of Waterloo (near Brussels) in June 1815 is depicted colorfully and with strength by Russian director Sergei Bondarchuk in this lavish historical drama lensed in the USSR and Italy, with interiors shot at Dino De Laurentiis's Rome studios. De Laurentiis

pulled out all the stops to make this lavish drama as authentic and striking as possible. While the Russian version ran over four hours, the prints shown in the West most often run 132 minutes.

Bondarchuk, who also guided the sumptuous Russian version of *War and Peace*, features an international cast, with Rod Steiger particularly striking and forceful as Napoleon, and Christopher Plummer stolid and sure as the Duke of Wellington. Orson Welles, though he appears only briefly, is a believably dour Louis XVIII, the restored Bourbon king who secures a lasting claim to the French throne only after Napoleon's Waterloo defeat. Dan O'Herlihy is Marshal Ney, loyal friend and aide to Napoleon; and Virginia McKenna, Michael Wilding, and Jack Hawkins (as General Picton) also stand out in a notable assemblage of acting talent.

Having been defeated in 1814, and exiled to the island of Elba, Napoleon has made an almost in-

WATERLOO Rod Steiger as Napoleon hoists a drink to his troops while Andrea Checchi attends.

WATERLOO Napoleon suffers a stomach attack on the battlefield.

WATERLOO Led by Lord Gordon (Rupert Davies), the Scottish regiment marches into battle against the French troops.

WATERLOO Christopher Plummer's intrepid Duke of Wellington is poised to win the engagement.

stant comeback as Emperor of France. Once the master of Europe, with major nations enlisted as his allies after he has conquered them, he *now* has all his former associates among the European powers firmly determined to dislodge him once and for all from his throne. At Waterloo they succeed. Napoleon abdicates, and this time is exiled to St. Helena, where he remains to die in 1821.

The many events leading up to the crucial encounter: the partying, the troop maneuvers, the conferences among the statesmen, and some superficial romancing between young couples that is given relatively short shrift—all are gotten across skillfully.

The lavish historical backgrounds are called into play, and disparate types who flourished on the international scene at the time are depicted both individually and strikingly. In Brussels on the eve of the historic battle there is a lavish ball, at which Plummer's Wellington receives the news that Napoleon is marching for a final major engagement. The field of Waterloo is the deciding encounter site. (The Prussian and Scottish military particularly distinguished themselves.)

WATERLOO   Louis XVIII
(Orson Welles) wonders
what Napoleon is up to.

WATERLOO   Napoleon surrenders his sword.

WATERLOO   The battle rages fiercely.

The battle itself, while confusing in spots (perhaps because of the American truncation) and in minor engagements, is staged rousingly and with panache. Troops of the many nations are engaged in the complicated strikes, feintings, retreats, and countermaneuvers. Considering the complexity of the orchestrations of battle, Bondarchuk and his able photographer, Armando Nannuzzi, do an able job of it; and the multinational "troops" perform with a realistic intensity so strong that one is given occasion to wonder why more accidents did not result. The Technicolor and Panavision effects are most striking, and in the final hour given over to the battle the screen becomes virtually alive.

Wellington towers over all the other victors, and Plummer makes him live again, infusing an interesting blend of the stoical and the determined in Wellington's approach to his task. But the hit of the picture is Steiger, incorporating his "Method" approach into an utterly believable portrait of a complex leader who cannot accept that his time on the stage of history is past. Steiger alternates between brooding silence and outbursts of titanic rage. When his always-troublesome stomach is aggravated by the stresses of battle, he retires briefly, only to burst back into action. Eventually he realizes the hopelessness of his situation, and leaves the battlefield a beaten, morose man.

Browne, associate photographers; John Addison, music; Anthony Gibbs, editor. Running time: 175 minutes. (Panavision, Technicolor.)

64

A BRIDGE TOO FAR

UNITED ARTISTS / JOSEPH E. LEVINE

1977

CAST:

Dirk Bogarde, James Caan, Michael Caine, Sean Connery, Edward Fox, Elliott Gould, Gene Hackman, Anthony Hopkins, Hardy Kruger, Laurence Olivier, Ryan O'Neal, Robert Redford, Maximilian Schell, Liv Ullmann.

CREDITS:

Richard Attenborough (with Sidney Hayers), director; Joseph E. Levine, producer; William Goldman, screenplay; based on the book by Cornelius Ryan; Geoffrey Unsworth, photographer; Harry Waxman and Robin

A Bridge Too Far was Richard Attenborough's attempt to join the Big War Film Leagues. Creditable as the film was, however, it indicated that Attenborough was more at home with other subjects. The story of a 1944 military operation conducted by the Allies against the Germans in Holland, with paratroopers dropping behind the lines and six bridges targeted to be seized, this movie has Dirk Bogarde on display as the ranking Allied officer. Good actor though he is, he still doesn't seem the type of stalwart, intrepid officer to take on such a daunting task. For the Germans are fighting back like cornered rats, and what at first seemed a snap turns out to be anything but. In the long run, in fact, *both* sides come away losers from this abortive attempt by the Allies to break through into Germany—at least in 1944.

Based on Cornelius Ryan's epic recounting, *A*

A BRIDGE TOO FAR   The Germans shoot at Allied paratroopers.

A BRIDGE TOO FAR   Allies and Nazis fight for a Dutch bridge.

Bridge Too Far features some thrilling paratroop drops, and there is lots of realistically simulated killing and wounding, advancing and retreating, supplemented by stock footage of genuine warfare. (The several original newsreel cuts from 1944 add authenticity to the opening sections, but the grainy quality of the originals contrasts rather shabbily with the fresh-looking footage of the 1977 photographers. This raises the question: Why use grainy newsreel stuff when the same action can be portrayed more dramatically and effectively—and more "prettily"—via freshly staged scenes?) But the scenes where the Allies try to storm and take the six Dutch bridges have a genuinely unalloyed dynamism and excitement of their own.

As Bogarde and other officers state, this operation constituted a massive Allied attempt to shorten the war by bringing the enemy to its knees via an Allied march straight to the German border and beyond, with the aid of behind-the-lines paratroop drops and field troops securing and/or bombing strategic bridges. The title obviously arises from the attempt to do too much too soon, going for one bridge—or two or three bridges—too far for cohesive operational support.

Through all of this parade a host of well-known

A BRIDGE TOO FAR   Ryan O'Neal and Michael Caine ponder the failed operation.

names, from now-you-see-him-now-you-don't brief shots to standard "bits" that indicate little about the people being characterized. We do make out that Ryan O'Neal is a rather stolid, get-the-job-done type; that Elliott Gould is the troop clown, cracking jokes and cutting up (which he doubtless would have been doing had he actually been on hand, no doubt); and Robert Redford show-offy and hypermacho as a guy who can lead and still get things done (or so he believes.)

Attenborough is not in his usual form here, as if his initial enthusiasm for the project waned half way through and he could find no honorable way to pull out of it. Some of his situations and setups are between perfunctory and throwaway, but the action scenes—the storming of the bridges, the paratroops descending into fields in the face of murderous fire from German ground troops—ring true enough.

One critic praised *A Bridge* lavishly as "a conscientiously-wrought, intrepid tale of war, heroism and courage among the common soldiery that delivers a punch to the heart as well as the eyes." Individual scenes were highly praised, as when intrepid American soldier James Caan carries a badly wounded buddy clear across a field where snipers are lurking—and firing.

Laurence Olivier, at seventy on hand as a sort of elderly good-luck charm, is just that—charming and courtly, intelligent and alert. But he looks like he wandered in from a set next door, or into a studio across the street, for that matter, so perfunctory—almost absent-minded—is his stint. Michael Caine and Edward Fox manage to look reasonably alert and cool-cat, but then they were somewhat younger men.

Attenborough obviously had second thoughts about films of this nature: In the years that followed, he sought other material.

65

THE DEER HUNTER

UNIVERSAL / EMI FILMS

1978

CAST:
Robert De Niro, Christopher Walken, John Savage, Meryl Streep, John Cazale, Chuck Aspegren, Rutanya Alda.

THE DEER HUNTER   John Cazale, Chuck Aspegren, Robert De Niro, John Savage, his bride Rutanya Alda, Christopher Walken, and Meryl Streep experience only temporary happiness and felicity at Savage's wedding.

THE DEER HUNTER Savage and De Niro try outwitting the enemy after escaping from a POW camp.

THE DEER HUNTER De Niro and Walken enjoy deer-hunting trips as macho excursions.

CREDITS:

Michael Cimino, director; Barry Spikings, Michael Deeley, Michael Cimino, and John Peverall, producers; Deric Washburn, screenplay; from a story by Michael Cimino, Deric Washburn, Louis Garfinkle, and Quinn K. Redeker; Vilmos Zsigmond, photographer; Stanley Myers, music; Peter Zinner, editor. Running time: 182 minutes. (Panavision / Technicolor / Dolby Stereo.)

The Deer Hunter is an atmospheric, often compelling, but overlong and sexually and emotionally ambiguous film that commanded a lot of attention in 1978 but has been subject to critical revision since. No doubt it has its moments of power and poignancy, along with repellent realism and more than a touch of cynicism, as it traces the before-during-and-after-war-experience fortunes of three men from a Pennsylvania steel town who find their lives forever changed by Vietnam. And the assorted vicissitudes of the leads—Robert De Niro, Christopher Walken, and John Savage—are recounted vividly and intensely. Too, the film is highlighted by some superb acting and splendid photography, even though Michael Cimino's direction is spotty—sometimes brilliant, other times careless. But the uncertain script fails to make any particularly coherent point, and still could use a good editor to chop at least an hour of its stupefying 182 minutes.

Some scenes and shots go on forever, and the characters aren't fully developed. One never really gets into the head of De Niro's character, aside from less-than-subtle indications that he feels more than

THE DEER HUNTER   Walken, De Niro, Aspegren, Savage, and Cazale in a relaxed moment.

friendship for buddy-in-peace-and-war Walken. We never get to find out what makes these people tick, and at the end, when the surviving members of the cast sing "God Bless America," we are not sure if we are being given an honestly patriotic finish or a touch of irony.

De Niro's character carries the "star" elements, and the film is actually built around him. His macho qualities are fully on display, as are those of his costars, and the deer hunt that figures early in the film is supposed to underline their "manly" attributes (some critics termed it "a ritual of manhood.") So is Savage's wedding, which is pictured in great detail—especially the post-wedding party. Then it's off to 'Nam and these harrowing sequences, including the attempted escape by Savage and De Niro from a prisoner-of-war camp; their combat experiences; the dead and dying contrasting with the frenetic activities of those attempting to survive.

De Niro, the strongest mentally and emotionally of the three, survives the war fairly intact, but Walken is drastically affected; he won an Oscar for Best Supporting Actor for his graphic depiction of a man going to pieces. The famed Russian roulette scene, in which the men with ironic, suicidal intentness play the game with the one bullet in the gun, is perhaps overrated as a symbol of nihilistic

destructiveness and point-of-no-return cynicism, but Cimino makes it pay off in dramatic terms.

Whatever its faults, and however controversial its approach, *The Deer Hunter* had a sufficiently influential cabal behind it to win the Best Picture Oscar for 1978. Director Cimino also won an Oscar, as did those responsible for editing and sound.

The cast is excellent: De Niro especially, in his depiction of a macho guy with homoerotic leanings who is determined to survive no matter what; Walken plumbing the depths of a sensitive and vulnerable survivor of Vietnam's horrors; Savage, less traumatized than Walken but carrying his own burden of emotional disengagement. Chuck Aspegren carried with him his own stamp of authenticity because he was a real-life steel worker from Gary, Indiana. Meryl Streep has her first significant role here, Rutanya Alda is touching and sweet as Savage's young wife, and John Cazale is also effective as one of the boys' pals.

Inchoate though its message may be, and confused as are its intrinsic motivations, *The Deer Hunter* (though, as before noted, crying out for an hour's cutting) is for the most part provocative, powerfully directed, and cinematically riveting. Deric Washburn got an Oscar nomination for his screenplay, as did Vilmos Zsigmond for his photography, and Streep for her supporting performance.

66

THE BOYS IN COMPANY C

COLUMBIA

1978

CAST:

Andrew Stevens, Stan Shaw, James Canning, Michael Lembeck, Craig Wasson, Scott Hylands, James Whitmore, Jr., Lee Ermey, Noble Willingham.

CREDITS:

Sidney J. Furie, director; Andrew Morgan, producer; Rick Natkin and Sidney J. Furie, screenplay; Godfrey Godar, photographer; Jaime Mendoza-Nava, music; Michael Berman, Frank J. Urioste, Allan Patillo, and James Benson, editors. Running time: 125 minutes. (Panavision / Technicolor.)

The Boys in Company C depicts tellingly, grittily, and realistically the transforming of green recruits into fighting marines. Stan Shaw is particularly outstanding as the former junkie turned leader whose men entrust their lives to him. Among the recruits are such disparate types as Andrew Stevens, a hotshot on the athletic field who turns junkie and combat-zombie under the stresses of the war; Michael Lembeck, a callow sports enthusiast and hustler who matures into selflessness and comradely give-and-take; and Craig Wasson, who sheds the hair and beard of the flower child he was for the disciplines of gung-ho marine dedication. Also on hand is James Whitmore, Jr., whose understanding marine officer inspires the men to dedicated combat expertise.

The picture, shot in the Philippines, is full of locker-room humor and racy talk (edited down in some later versions), but as seen in the original version the grunginesses and scatology only increase the realistic sense of being *there*, *with* the men, undergoing the *same* stresses and conditions-under-fire that *they* do.

Of course each of the boys in Company C reacts to the stresses and challenges of war in his own individual ways. Some find themselves overwhelmed and/or dulled and/or stupefied by their stresses; others mature from boys into men, and surprise themselves when their "reach and grasp" run equal, so to speak.

THE BOYS IN COMPANY C   Andrew Stevens is hardened for combat.

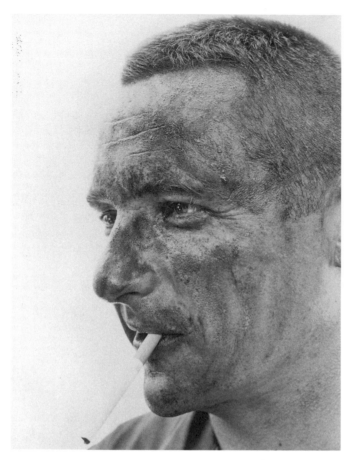

THE BOYS IN COMPANY C   James Whitmore, Jr., plays an officer who understands men.

Because the picture is couched in enlisted men's terms and is seen from their perspective, its intimate context inflicts no windy philosophizing about geopolitical issues on the audiences, and no Raymond Massey type shows up in full uniform to introspect about the why and how of war. We simply accompany these boys through the various stages of their training and combat experiences, and we rejoice over individual triumphs, and sympathize—sometimes even empathize—with their failings and defeats, along the well-known lines of there-but-for-the-grace-of-God-go-I.

Not that these intrepid marines invite condescension or that brand of sympathy that is, more often than not, contempt in disguise. We feel we know these Company C boys: We understand them; we accept them as initially flawed human beings who react to the hardening conditions on hand according to their individual natures—though marines all they certainly prove to be.

Stan Shaw gets top acting honors as the natural-born leader who whips the boys into combat readiness. His character is certainly neither saint nor angel—he has been heavily into drugs; his earlier history has cynicized him; he is a hustling opportunist. But purpose, esprit-de-corps camaraderie, and a darker form of idealism, rooted along one-for-all-and-all-for-one lines, bring about a plumbing of his resources for maximum results. His character and rugged determination rub off on the men following him, and their eventual all-encompassing

THE BOYS IN COMPANY C   Michael Lembeck is transformed by his combat experiences.

aim is not to disappoint him but rather to live up to his expectations to the degree that their varying individual capacities permit. This former ghetto dope-pusher who had thought the Vietnam "deal" would enhance his "commerce" is suddenly caught up in something higher, more all-encompassing: the safety and efficiency of his men, the necessity of Getting That Job Done in a savage and unfamiliar setting.

Godfrey Godar's photography catches the ambience of the fighting scene, the tired yet excited features of the men, the grime and grunge of their environment. Sidney J Furie's direction is sure and strong; he makes his characters live, and he individualizes them sharply—and in some cases poignantly.

The Boys in Company C proves itself yet another of those unexpected "sleepers" that blush unseen like the proverbial rose, then burst into prominence when revisionists bring them to the fore—often much too long after a number of years have passed.

THE BOYS IN COMPANY C   Craig Wasson finds the stresses of war both galvanizing and inspiring.

THE BOYS IN COMPANY C   Wasson is grief-stricken when a child is killed during a Viet Cong offensive.

225

signer; Carmine Coppola, music; Richard Marks, supervising editor. Running time: 153 minutes. (Panavision / Dolby Stereo.)

67

APOCALYPSE NOW

UNITED ARTISTS

1979

CAST:

Marlon Brando, Robert Duvall, Martin Sheen, Frederic Forrest, Albert Hall, Sam Bottoms, Larry Fishburne, Dennis Hopper, G. D. Spradlin, Harrison Ford, Tom Mason, Scott Glenn, Colleen Camp.

CREDITS:

Francis Coppola, producer-director; John Milius and Francis Coppola, screenwriters; based loosely on the novel *The Heart of Darkness*, by Joseph Conrad; Vittorio Storaro, photographer; Dean Tavoularis, production de-

Director Francis Coppola was later to say of his controversial 1979 Vietnam war epic, "It's more of an experience than a movie. At the beginning there's a story. Along the river the story becomes less important and the experience more important."

The picture took several years to complete and was later dubbed by wags "Apocalypse Later." One commentator noted that it featured "vivid scenes along the way and some interesting parallels with Conrad's *Heart of Darkness*, but these hardly atone for the director's delusion that prodigal expenditure of time and money will result in great art."

The action takes place in 1968. A renegade army officer (Marlon Brando) has gone insane and has taken over a Cambodian island, where he has set himself up as a deified dictator. Joseph Conrad's novel is the basic source of the story, though in his version a man named Kurtz (also Brando's name in the film) has gone mad after ruthlessly conquering an African territory—and Coppola and John Milius

APOCALYPSE NOW   Sheen, in search of power-mad Colonel Kurtz (Brando), arrives at a moment of truth. Dennis Hopper, left.

APOCALYPSE NOW   Under helicopter cover, U.S. patrol boats stage an amphibious landing on a coastal village under Viet Cong control.

APOCALYPSE NOW   Troops gather at a river's edge to enjoy a USO show at a remote camp in the Mekong Delta of Vietnam.

took off from Conrad's premise, establishing a horrifically realistic Vietnamese ambience and *mise-en-scène*.

In the movie, a Special Services captain, played by Martin Sheen (he replaced Harvey Keitel), sets off through the forbidding Cambodian jungle to track down and exterminate "with extreme prejudice" the mad Brando. Along the way he is given full doses of war's horror. Among the characters are Robert Duvall's Lieutenant Colonel Kilgore, who has become psychologically and emotionally depleted by the war's stresses and surrealistic absurdities and loves "the smell of napalm in the morning." One compelling sequence has the half-demented Duvall leading his helicopter operation against the enemy while Wagner's rousing-manic "Ride of the Valkyries" blasts from loudspeakers.

An ironic note is struck when, after leading the successful and grimly destructive leveling of a Viet Cong–controlled village, Duvall presides over a nocturnal beach party, strumming along unconcernedly on his guitar as if he had just come back from an office or a factory rather than a grim carnival of destruction.

Martin Sheen's captain finally beards Brando's madman in his lair, but the result is as intellectually obfuscated as it is grim. Brando, who shaved his head to complete baldness as the power-hungry, unbalanced Kurtz, is compelling in the footage he is given, getting across the sadistic power-lust and unhinged viciousness of an intelligent man gone bananas. Sheen is also fine. During the shooting, after sets and equipment were completely destroyed by an unexpected and sudden typhoon, Sheen suffered a severe heart attack (he recovered) and

227

APOCALYPSE NOW   Helicopters and tanks go into action.

many of his scenes had to be shot with doubles.

The film was shot primarily in the Philippines; Vittorio Storaro's excellent photography later won an Oscar for him. The picture won the Grand Prize at the Cannes Film Festival and got eight Oscar nominations, winning for photography and sound.

Some twelve years later, in 1991, Coppola's wife, Eleanor, produced a documentary called *Heart of Darkness; A Filmmaker's Apocalypse*, which gives much valuable information about the *Apocalypse Now's* conception and production.

According to one commentator, *Apocalypse Now* used the Vietnam war "as a metaphor for a vision of war as a demonic voyage into the deepest pit of hell." Certainly Sheen's adventures and tribulations on his way to Brando's lair qualify as dances with the devil, with every variety of combat vicissitude limned in graphic detail and with merciless clarity and detachment. The film is yet another of those that depict the Vietnam war as one of disillusioning futility and nihilistic waste calculated to cynicize even the most trusting, patriotic, gung-ho souls. But nowhere in films of this type is the point made that had we *fought to win*, instead of dithering about with false feints and withdrawals the war might have been far shorter and served a truer purpose.

68

THE BIG RED ONE

UNITED ARTISTS / LORIMAR

1980

CAST:

Lee Marvin, Mark Hamill, Robert Carradine, Bobby DiCicco, Kelly Ward, Stephane Audran, Serge Marquand, Siegfried Rauch.

CREDITS:

Samuel Fuller, director-screenplay; Gene Corman, producer; Adam Greenberg, photographer; Dana Kaproff, music; David Bretherton and Morton Tubor, editors. Running time: 113 minutes. (Metrocolor / Dolby Stereo.)

Director-writer Samuel Fuller had always wanted to make a film of his military experiences in World War II, to follow up (or as a "prequel" to) his earlier *Steel Helmet* and *Fixed Bayonets*, both about Korea. This deeply-felt evocation of his four-year experience concerns the varying fortunes of four "wet-nosed" foot soldiers and their intrepid sergeant in many areas of war, from North Africa through Europe.

Fuller, at the time of the film's release in 1980, told interviewers that the picture had taken two years to fully formulate, but that three decades of thought and feeling and selectively recalled reminiscence had gone into its eventual evolvement.

With its story of the First Infantry Division's campaigns in the North African–European theaters of war, most of the action takes place in the years 1942–45, when the overall drive among the Allies intensified into getting the war won, the job done.

John Wayne had originally planned to do a film on the subject some years before, then backed out. Other producers got into the act, but Fuller was determined to get his individual concept across without concessions to star power or fancy directorial approaches. There was considerable discussion of the appropriate locations in which to shoot it, but producer Gene Corman finally reached an agreement with the Israelis to shoot it in their land. The terrain chosen complements the film's intent ably, for it is bleak and forbidding, a true evocation of what soldiers went through, with no glamorizations or short cuts.

Lee Marvin's wonderful characterization as the

THE BIG RED ONE Lee Marvin gets ready to strike.

THE BIG RED ONE   The casualties mount.

strongest among the fighting men proved there was no Star Ego on hand to blunt the total effect. Everyone fit into his role with truth and underplayed integrity. Fuller announced in early publicity that he was not out to show the Face of War glamorously or theatrically or dramatically, but with raw power—and the response of viewers and critics alike indicated that he succeeded in full measure.

The men depicted here are out neither for glory nor for ego-enhancing exploits, and certainly not to prove their courage and resourcefulness—though these qualities are certainly called into play again and again. Rather, as Fuller stressed, they are out to demonstrate mutual caring among comrades, and a firm aim (in some cases not terminally successful) to survive this most terrible of all wars.

The infantry soldiers are shown as they were in real life: dirty and tired, tense and bleary-eyed. They gripe when that's called for, and express with cheers and laughs their satisfaction with whatever small positives come up. Mutually protective and otherwise concerned for one another, they are as prudent as hellish circumstances permit them to be.

Lee Marvin truly lost himself in his role, as Fuller had hoped he would. He *is* a tired military man out to get the job done, grabbing a meal or a little sleep only when time and circumstance permit. He *is* weary, disillusioned, aware of the grim surroundings. The line "Ours not to wonder why; ours but to do and die" might well apply to him—except that he wants to do and *live*, if he possibly can, and among his comrades at that, until his job *is* done.

Etching fine individualized portraits of men in war, humble, self-effacing, and devoid of actorish flourishes, Mark Hamill, Robert Carradine, Bobby DiCicco, Kelly Ward (the platoon members), and the others are content simply to *be*, getting inside the skin of their roles with telling, truthful impact.

The Big Red One has it all: the battles, the wounded, the dying, and the dead. It would be to denigrate the film to say it has combat newsreel verisimilitude. Rather, it may be said that it captures the verisimilitude of life—and of death—among men at war, in flesh-and-blood terms.

230

THE BIG RED ONE   Mark Hamill, Bobby Di Cicco, Kelly Ward, and Robert Carradine (right) take a breather with Marvin.

69

GALLIPOLI

PARAMOUNT / ASSOCIATED R & R FILMS

1981

CAST:

Mel Gibson, Mark Lee, Bill Kerr, Robert Grubb, David Argue, Tim McKenzie, Bill Hunter.

CREDITS:

Peter Weir, director; Robert Stigwood and Patricia Lovell, producers; David Williamson, screenplay; Russell Boyd, photographer; Brian May, music; William Anderson, editor. Running time: 111 minutes. (Panavision, Eastman Color.)

Australian director Peter Weir set out to make what he conceived to be his magnum opus in *Gallipoli*, an acclaimed film about World War I which would bring stardom to Mel Gibson. That he largely succeeded in his expressed aims is testified to by the affirmative response worldwide to his rousing and touching film. (The picture also was notable for its period verisimilitudes, for its zeal, and for its photography.) Two close and idealistic Australian friends from Perth, Gibson and Mark Lee, set off on a journey from their native land to the Dardanelles, where they meet their fate at Gallipoli, in one of

GALLIPOLI   Robert Grubb, Mel Gibson, Mark Lee, and David Argue are out for new adventures in war.

GALLIPOLI   The boys explore the ancient pyramids of Egypt.

the most celebrated battles of World War I. The year is 1915.

A combined force of New Zealand and Australian troops, numbering about 35,000, is out to capture Istanbul and thus control the strategically important Dardanelles. They face a formidable enemy in the Turks, who are overtly ruthless and covertly sly and treacherous. Because the generals from Down Under have bungled their timing, the Turks are enabled to strengthen their defenses. The result: a drawn-out stalemate that in time proves attritional to both sides.

While it is an allied effort, the Gallipoli engagement drags on (again through a combination of military and espionage bungling) into protracted fighting that pulls into the front lines the mixture of Australians and New Zealanders, who find them-

selves bearing an unfair share of the fighting and casualties. Although they end up decimated, their courage and valor create a legend that endures (in fact, to this day). As one critic put it, "Gallipoli is as much an essential part of the Australian ethos as, say, the Alamo is to Texas: a military defeat that became rationalized over the years into a moral victory."

Certainly *Gallipoli* testifies to soldierly valor and mutual supportiveness in combat. The hardy, enduring, stoically courageous qualities inherent in the Aussie and New Zealander temperaments are on striking display here, and the film made a star of Mel Gibson—not only because his handsome and manly attributes proved ideal for cinema, but also because in his hardihood and no-nonsense manner he came to symbolize the ideals and aspirations and attitudes of the Boys from Down Under.

Lee matches Gibson all the way as the buddy who goes through hell with him, culminating in a freeze-frame death of one of them at a crucial point in battle. The sense of waste is conveyed by this fitting ending, for the entire engagement, depicted so eloquently and tellingly, seems to symbolize the waste—and futility—of youthful ideals and dreams. The many young men who died at Gallipoli seem to have left their spirits to somehow guard the essence of that spot where they lived and died so valorously: Visitors to the site, some eight decades afterward, have spoken of a strange impression of spiritual life coursing the terrain.

Bill Hunter, Robert Grubb, Tim McKenzie, and Bill Kerr all offer individualized portraits of the Down Under temperament as exemplified in war. They are matter-of-fact on the surface, intent and serious within. They know how to laugh, but there is a rueful note to their humor, as if they know their time for joy and life is short. They get across a sense of poignant victimhood—for they are, after all, the victims of higher-level bungling which brings their best efforts to naught.

Though Gallipoli was not a victory, it was to serve for decades as a symbol, and as a statement—that statement being that the valor of men in battle somehow compensates for any negations and miscalculations in the overall effort. Men, it says, find ultimate bonding in shared suffering, in a common purpose; many become one, and—even when purchased at the price of suffering and death—that Oneness can become a glory in itself.

GALLIPOLI   Gibson and Lee reach their appointed destiny.

GALLIPOLI   Gibson on a crucial mission.

234

70

REVOLUTION

GOLDCREST / VIKING / WARNER BROS.

1985

CAST:

Al Pacino, Donald Sutherland, Nastassja Kinski, Joan Plowright, Dave King, Annie Lennox, Steven Berkoff, Jesse Birdsall, Graham Greene, Robbie Coltrane, Dexter Fletcher, Sid Owen.

CREDITS:

Hugh Hudson, director; Irwin Winkler, producer; Robert Dillon, screenplay; Bernard Lutic, photography; John Corigliano, music; Stuart Baird, editor. Running time: 125 minutes. (Technicolor / Dolby Stereo.)

Ever since it was made, no one has been quite sure what motivated Al Pacino to appear in a movie about the American Revolution of 1775–83. Certainly in this one he appears to be Scarface in a time warp, and one expects wildly careening automobiles and machine guns to show up at any time amid the dusty roads and ubiquitous horses and other eighteenth-century relative primitivisms. Pacino is however an undeniably vital actor, and though his reach exceeded his grasp here, he is to be commended for essaying a period role that gave him a wide characterizational range, however ill-advised and misdirected it might have been in this instance.

Certainly Donald Sutherland, Joan Plowright, and others in the cast seem more solidly set in the period, though no match for the aforementioned Pacino star presence, vitality, charisma, or whatever you want to call it. Anyway, Pacino gets energetically into the spirit of the story for which, as one critic put it, he is "two centuries too contemporary" and here he is on display as a trapper whose boat—and son—get conscripted by the Continental Army. Nastassja Kinski is a Tory scion of a particularly rebellious kind, and Donald Sutherland is on hand as an English officer with a thick accent difficult to decipher. However, being a professional, he nevertheless does get across (as always), via colorful scowls and stances and smiles and jeers, what his character is up to.

REVOLUTION Al Pacino finds himself conscripted into the Continental Army.

There is a lot of faithful historical period detail in this movie. Even the action scenes (and they *are* rousing) coexist and mesh fairly well with the more intimate, personal sequences. As Tom Dobb, Pacino (with his New York patois) seems hardly a Yankee of English descent, but nevertheless provides sufficient energy and star forthrightness—known to some as star charisma—to cut a wide swath through the tumultuous events of our emergence as a nation free of British rule. And, when roused to action and out to "get 'em," Pacino performs with his usual energy and fierce reaction to any and all issues and situations. Dexter Fletcher is winning and winsome as his son Ned, and Sid Owen upholds the character of the older Ned consistently and well. Both look more Yankee English than their "dad," but that point has already been belabored sufficiently.

Kinski is attractive as a renegade upper-class young woman who inspires the "tender sentiment" in Pacino. As one Daisy McConnahay, Kinski looks no more like a Tory miss than Pacino does, but she fits nicely into the period doings, flouncing her eighteenth-century skirts and petticoats and other assorted undergarments, or what passed for them in 1776, and looking pertly knowing as she perceives the reaction she has inspired in Pacino's Tom.

After a while the personal story takes a back seat to the battles and engagements of the Revolutionary War, and while we are largely spared a succession of Famous Actors playing Famous Historical Characters, the historical detail and the cannons, muskets, flashy uniforms, fancy hats (for men and women both), and whatnot all are trotted out professionally and with a dispatch that sometimes seems as hasty as it is efficient.

Since the Revolutionary War has been neither overworked nor a popular screen subject for some

REVOLUTION   Father and son Dexter Fletcher face an uncertain future together.

REVOLUTION   Buddies in arms. Sid Owen, Pacino.

decades now, it was nice to see somebody attempting it circa 1985, and—considering all the opportunities for martial exploits, pyrotechnics, and assorted "alarums and excursions"—it is conceivable that this 200-years-past war may yet come into its own as a more frequent cinematic subject.

All in all, Pacino and company get a plus for trying to give us something off the beaten path of history, and the action sequences, as directed by Hugh Hudson and photographed by Bernard Lutic, certainly demonstrate a dutifully and scrupulously applied professionalism.

71

PLATOON

ORION

1986

CAST:

Charlie Sheen, Tom Berenger, Willem Dafoe, Forest Whitaker, Francesco Quinn, John C. McGinley, Kevin Dillon, Richard Edson, Reggie Johnson, Keith David, Johnny Depp, Chris Pedersen.

CREDITS:

Oliver Stone, director-screenplay; Arnold Kopelson and A. Kitman Ho, producers; Robert Richardson, photographer; Georges Delerue, music; Claire Simpson, editor. Running time: 120 minutes. (CFI Color.)

Oliver Stone, a seasoned and disillusioned veteran of the Vietnam War, won an Oscar for his realistic depictions of that conflict in *Platoon*. Under Stone's shrewd and trenchant direction, Tom Berenger, Willem Dafoe, Charlie Sheen, and others gave the best performances of their careers. The movie also won Academy Awards as Best Picture, and also for film editing and sound, with Supporting Oscar nominations going to Berenger and Dafoe.

This otherwise superior picture had one relatively minor flaw—the framing of the story via Sheen's letters home to his grandmother. Apart from the fact that such realistic brutalities as experienced in combat are hardly the subjects a soldier would cover in detail with his grandmother, of all people, to say nothing of the awkwardness of the framing device (uncharacteristic of the hard-bitten, realism-*uber-alles* mentality of Stone, who also wrote the screenplay), *Platoon* is a down-and-dirty, no-holds-barred depiction of the horrors-and-hazards-galore hellishness of Vietnam combat.

Sheen's character is new to Bravo Company, 25th Infantry, and he comes to the tough outfit with some boyish illusions still intact. He emerges at the end a seasoned soldier, *sans* illusions, almost without hopes, concerned only for his survival—though one is given occasion to wonder what his post-Vietnam experience would be should he survive, so macerated are his emotional and mental processes at the conclusion.

Two contrasting leaders, played by Berenger and Dafoe, embody radically different approaches to combat: Both sergeants, they bring their individual personalities and mystiques to the dirty business foisted on them. The Berenger character is cold, ruthless, opportunistic, viciously intent on getting the job done along ends-justify-the-means lines. That of Dafoe is a combat-shrewd soldier who hasn't yet sacrificed his humanity to the cruel exigencies of war, so tries to show compassion and flexibility in various situations while getting on with the job.

There is reason to believe that Stone was subconsciously revealing the dualities and dichotomies of his own nature via the projection of memories and associations that were so intimately a part of his own past in combat. Stone has always elicited contrasting reactions from both film pundits and audiences: Some respect and admire his tough, nononsense survivalism, and his determination to put his own imprint on his work; others find him excessive, maniacally obsessed, and dehumanizingly egoistic and cruel. Whatever the truth (and it is probably an admixture, as in all such men), Stone gets across with uncompromising truth, the realities of what he and his buddies went through, the guts of *Platoon* being rooted in his own experiences and reactions.

Unsure of what sort of ending he wanted, Stone

PLATOON   Charlie Sheen (left) and Francesco Quinn carry Chris Pedersen to safety.

shot two: In one, the Good Guy lives and triumphs; in the other, he perishes. Realism won out, as it does in all Stone films. The director-writer put his "men" through some brutally grim and intense advance training in the Philippines, with the government providing equipment and weapons and other accoutrements for the film. When they got to the nitty-gritty shooting, Stone let it fly fast and furious. His own strong but unmistakably homoerotic approach has men obeying without protest, mourning for lost buddies, bonded in a determination to survive.

Stone's love for his comrades, and the almost orgiastic glee with which he shows the fighting, dying, bonding, and wounding that constitute their individual fates, give *Platoon* a tensile force and deeply felt addressal that smack of the real thing, on all counts. It is this fathomless subjective commitment which Stone brings to it that raises it to the level of cinematic art.

Berenger gets across the essential evil inherent in his character, and Dafoe limns the fundamental goodness and balance in his. Between them, the characters show Good Oliver Stone and Bad Oliver Stone perhaps more clearly than he intended—or might have wished. The photography is excellent, the production values impeccable. Another homoerotic clue to Stone: He keeps Samuel Barber's haunting, insistent "Adagio for Strings" running all through the film, as its musical leitmotif.

PLATOON   Berenger (center) has been dehumanized by his experiences.

239

PLATOON   Dafoe is the center of negative attention, held back by Keith David. Others include (from left) Sheen, Corey Glover, Pedersen, and Forest Whitaker.

72

FULL METAL JACKET

WARNER BROS.

1987

CAST:

Matthew Modine, Adam Baldwin, Vincent D'Onofrio, Lee Ermey, Dorian Harewood, Arliss Howard, Ed O'Ross, Kevyn Major Howard.

CREDITS:

Stanley Kubrick, director; Stanley Kubrick and Philip Hobbs, producers; Stanley Kubrick, Michael Herr, and Gustav Hasford, screenplay; based on the novel *The Short*

Timers, by Hasford; Douglas Milsome, photographer; Anton Furst, production design; Abigail Mead, music; Martin Hunter, editor. Running time: 116 minutes. (Color.)

A year after Oliver Stone's fiercely trenchant *Platoon*, Stanley Kubrick decided to resurface and get into the Vietnam-depiction act with *Full Metal Jacket*. While in retrospect, it plays second fiddle to the more deeply felt Stone work, it nevertheless is forceful and strong in its own right. Under Kubrick's direction, Matthew Modine gives one of the signature performances of his career as a young marine hardened into a combat-wise-and-ready gung-ho-er under the tough Parris Island training drill instructor Lee Ermey.

Ermey has but one objective: to metamorphose his green recruits into remorseless, determined fighting men. He dominates the first half of this film—but dies, ironically, at the hands of a weak and inept and ridiculed recruit (played with dimensional subtlety by Vincent D'Onofrio), who—upon being pushed an inch too far—becomes a demented killer. The scene where D'Onofrio goes berserk, killing Ermey while gun-teasing Modine, who is frantically trying to calm and disengage him, is notable for its suspense.

The training scenes in this first half of *Full Metal Jacket* are models of disciplined, no-nonsense, militaristic movie-making—and then it's on to part two, with Modine applying all his hard-earned and faithfully internalized military techniques to the tensions and horrors of the Vietnam fighting. Modine's transformation under combat conditions is compellingly gotten across: He shows some interesting (if self-satirizing) ambivalences as he wades through the thick of the fighting, wearing a "Born to Kill" inscription on his helmet and sporting a "Peace" button on his jacket at the same time.

Certainly the incidents depicted in part two of *Full Metal Jacket* illustrate the dehumanizing effects of protracted combat fighting, indifference escalating into contempt regarding the civilian population, and ditto for ambivalent attitudes toward Vietnamese women. One sees also the growing callousness in the face of the deaths of soldiers and civilians alike.

The strength of Modine's performance lies in his gradually changing character as played in the film. Well-meaning, boyish, naive, and half-formed in his personality at the beginning, he comes through at the film's end as tough, realistic, survival-obsessed, and—despite the disillusioning knowledge of human nature under stress that he has acquired—not only somehow still balanced, but also hopeful for the future.

The other actors playing combat marines all get across their types well, though Kubrick—not having had Stone's hands-on, *there* experiences, does not portray their individual natures as tellingly and

FULL METAL JACKET   Lee Ermey as the gunnery sergeant chews out the recruits.

FULL METAL JACKET Tough fighters out to give 'em hell.

FULL METAL JACKET Dragging a wounded buddy out of harm's way.

(strange-but-true adjectives to use for Stone) sensitively and compassionately. Among the outstanding performances are those given by Adam Baldwin, Dorian Harewood, Arliss Howard, Ed O'Ross, and Kevyn Major Howard.

The heat of the jungles, the muted stupefaction of hapless civilian types, the fear and tension, the myriad horrors of the unexpected—all these and more tax not only these marines' mental balance but also their spiritual and emotional makeup.

Kubrick (in this case *like* Stone) does manage to suggest that many of these men will come back to the States permanently altered in mind as well as body, and that the stresses they underwent will cast a pall over their lives, in many cases preventing normal adjustment to peacetime. So individually etched are the performances that an observant audience can easily decipher which will end up in service hospitals permanently, which will go all-out druggie or grapple with semisuccessful marriages and truncated civilian careers.

73

CASUALTIES OF WAR

COLUMBIA PICTURES

1989

CAST:

Michael J. Fox, Sean Penn, Don Harvey, John Leguizamo, John C. Reilly, Thuy Thu Le, Erik King, Sam Robards.

CREDITS:

Brian DePalma, director; Art Linson and Fred Caruso, producers; David Rabe, screenplay; based on a real incident recounted in a *New Yorker* article by Daniel Lang, subsequently a book; Stephen H. Burum, photographer; Wolf Kroeger, production designer; Ennio Morricone, music; Bill Pankow, editor. Running time: 113 minutes. (Panavision / DeLuxe Color / Dolby Stereo.)

Casualties of War was a change of pace for director Brian DePalma, who had made his mark with vivid thrillers like *Body Double* and *Dressed to Kill*, as well as such violent action movies as *Scarface* and *The Untouchables*. Generally more interested in style than substance, DePalma decided in this to bite off no less than the Vietnam conflict, as well as a true incident that might be considered a byproduct of that war: the rape and murder of an innocent Vietnamese girl by a group of American soldiers.

DePalma received a lot of heat from Vietnam veterans over this picture, but the film does not try to say that these men's behavior is typical of American troops during the 'Nam conflict—and in fact the

CASUALTIES OF WAR   Sean Penn and Michael J. Fox come under fire.

CASUALTIES OF WAR   Penn and Erik King are happy at the thought that they have only a few weeks of combat duty left.

basic story (some maintain that DePalma "embell-ished" the original incident) could have taken place during *any* wartime period. Besides, the film runs even deeper than its surface storyline, indicting the whole macho system of war and soldiering, and be-coming quite unsettling at times in its implications. While short of being a masterpiece, *Casualties of War* is at least a memorable film and one of the direc-tor's best.

DePalma has also gotten into trouble with femi-nists who object to the antifemale violence in his murder mysteries, so it's ironic that he chose to make a film about the outraged reaction of one sol-dier (Michael J. Fox) to his buddies' kidnapping and sexually assaulting a woman who has done no harm to anyone.

DePalma's direction of David Rabe's stark screen-play is assured and never affected. Sean Penn (one of our greatest actors) as the soldier who initiates the kidnapping, is as excellent and chilling as ever. Fox, on the other hand, seems out of place, espe-cially at first, and though the power of his portrayal eventually grows, he's never really quite up to the level of his comrades. While his weaker perfor-mance doesn't ruin the picture (and in fact his pres-ence may make the unpleasant proceedings more

palatable), he never gets across the terror and lone-liness of his situation.

Refusing to take part in raping the girl, the Fox character tries first to effect her freedom, then save her from being murdered. To get even with him, his "buddies" plant a bomb in their bathhouse, hoping to blow him up. Here he is, in a foreign country where the enemy is out to kill him, and his own "friends" are trying to do the same. Can there be any greater sense of desolation and betrayal? Yet Fox fails to get all this across. He never seems more then perturbed.

DePalma does not show the rape itself in graphic detail, placing it, instead, in the background of the shot. The woman's murder as she tries to flee across a railroad trestle is more graphic—and needed to be.

Another powerful sequence concerns a goofy guy in camp who bothers the hell out of everyone

CASUALTIES OF WAR   Fox refuses to join Penn when Penn abuses a Vietnamese girl (Thuy Thu Lee).

until he is blown apart when he steps on a mine at the side of the road. DePalma's camera does not spare us the gruesome result. "He was dead before he got here," sneers one callous fellow warrior. The sight of the troops slogging past the broken, twisted body of the dead soldier who was killed *in an instant* without anyone even caring (and these are his own men!) is extremely disturbing. Even more disturbing is that some audiences have found the whole sequence *funny*.

Very powerful stuff—and a far cry from *Sergeant York* and its ilk. But while realistic enough, reflecting as it does its time, and the corruption of standards and personal conduct in the military, it can never detract from the heroism and exemplary performance of many other servicemen.—*W.S.*

74

GLORY

TRI-STAR PICTURES

1989

CAST:

Matthew Broderick, Denzel Washington, Cary Elwes, Morgan Freeman, Jihmi Kennedy, Andre Braugher, John Finn, Donovan Leitch, John David Cullum, Bob Gunton, Cliff De Young, Jane Alexander, Raymond St. Jacques.

CREDITS:

Edward Zwick, director; Freddie Fields, producer; Kevin Jarre, screenplay; Freddie Francis, photographer; James Horner, music; Steven Rosenblum, editor. Running time: 122 minutes. (Technicolor, Dolby Stereo.)

GLORY   Matthew Broderick plans to "toughlove" the troops into discipline.

GLORY The 54th Regiment parades through the streets of Boston.

My test for a really exceptional picture goes like this: Is the current on emotionally throughout the running time? Does the film cast a spell, right through to the end? Does it exude those most precious qualities, sincerity in its making and an obvious emotional commitment by all hands? Well, to me at least, *Glory* certainly fills the bill, meeting all the requirements for a four-star picture.

Matthew Broderick has his best role to date as Col. Robert Gould Shaw, scion of a wealthy and prominent WASP family of Boston abolitionists who accepts with alacrity the command of the 54th Regiment of Massachusetts Volunteer Infantry—the first military unit of blacks raised during the Civil War. Before that war had run its course, over 185,000 blacks had served in the Union Army, more than 37,000 of whom died in action.

If ever a picture was designed to improve—indeed, help to cement—relations between blacks and whites, this is the one. Edward Zwick directed as an obvious labor of love. Freddie Francis photographed with expertise and commitment born of loving devotion. James Horner's music latches onto

246

GLORY   Broderick leads his men through murderous artillery fire.

GLORY   The men charge the Confederate-held Fort Wagner.

and perfectly complements the ongoing emotional currents and rhythms set by both director and photographer.

The brilliant Denzel Washington, also in one of his finest hours, won for himself the 1989 Best Supporting Actor Oscar for his wonderful performance as a runaway slave who is the recalcitrant, rebellious man in the unit until his character undergoes a transformation. Compelling indeed is Mr. Washington as he is flogged for a malfeasance early in the picture. When they strip him, his back is already replete with welts, white and scarred. The camera stays on his face as he is whipped afresh, and his manly stoicism, his refusal to register pain, is reflected only in a tear or two given up by his eyes.

Morgan Freeman, another excellent actor, was never better as the sergeant who guides Washington to true soldierhood, showing him the meaning of manhood through combat. Distinguished for bravery, Washington nevertheless refuses to bear the colors—but in the final battle, caught up by loyal feelings toward his comrades, he picks them up from a fallen fellow-soldier and waves them high. His relationship with Broderick's character progresses from hatred to reluctant admi-

247

GLORY   Jihmi Kennedy (left), Denzel Washington, and Morgan Freeman confront jeering white Union troops.

ration to firm loyalty. Here is a man who has suffered the worst evils of slavery, redeemed by that love of comrades of which Walt Whitman wrote so eloquently. No longer dehumanized by injustice and persecution, Washington's "new self" soldier is at his most eloquent when he tells a group of his comrades in a revivalist gathering, on the eve of the battle that will spell doom for half of them, that what matters most in what they face is *to be a man*.

Broderick etches a winning and persuasive portrait of a rather callow officer who hardens under the necessity of training his black soldiers to fight the enemy professionally and well. And *he* fights for his *men*: When they are refused shoes (although many of them have lacerated feet), because they are not to be allowed (at first) to fight, he raises holy hell, the men get them. When they are told they will be paid $10 a month as against the $13 that white soldiers will get, he tears up his own paycheck in sympathy. He teaches a slow, nervous recruit to load his rifle in one minute's time—emphasizing that speed of that kind will one day save his life. When a fellow officer objects that he is pushing his men too hard, Broderick declares—and with deep truth—that he is ensuring their welfare in battle in the best way he knows.

At first put off by this diffident young commander (he is only twenty-three), the black soldiers gradually come to hold him in the highest regard—and the transformation in them is understandable, for within the frame of this slight, humble figure beats the heart of a lion.

Cary Elwes is also fine as Broderick's second-in-command, who starts out doubting Broderick and winds up his stout adherent and comrade. Elwes is a scandalously neglected actor; he has been giving superb performances for ten years in roles often unsuitable, but here at last he gets a role tailored to his measure. (One can only speculate as to what an admirable lead in, for instance, *The Age of Innocence* he might have been. In the day of studio nurturing, he'd have been a major star long ago.)

All the black actors are excellent as they perform their dramatic metamorphoses from self-denigrating, put-upon also-rans to expert, well-disciplined fighting men. And, after Broderick has rescued his regiment from hard-labor contingents, and countered the contempt and condescension of his white superior officers (by threatening to reveal their crooked malfeasances), he wins for them the chance to fight.

In their first engagement, Broderick's troops

248

emerge victorious, though of course suffering casualties. Their joy over their victory is both touching and galvanizing to witness. And then they are given the task of leading the Yankee assault on the almost impregnable and formidable Fort Wagner in South Carolina. And in that great and glorious charge, in which half of them die, they meet their finest hour. Broderick falls on the battlefield, and his enraged men fight their way into the fortress itself—where, as the twists of war would have it, they all too soon are overcome by the hard-fighting defenders.

And then comes the film's most touching moment. The contemptuous Confederates, who hate the idea of black fighting men, and hate their white commanders, pick up the Union bodies, to bury them in a mass grave—officers and men, white and black, together. And when Broderick's body is rolled in on top of his fallen black troops, he lands on his back with his right arm outstretched—and a moment after, Washington's body lands in its crook. They will lie together for all eternity, this white colonel and his devoted black comrades and brothers.

Broderick's essential humility and occasional honest self-doubting is affectingly gotten across in his letters to his mother in Boston (Jane Alexander, in an unbilled role). Raymond St. Jacques also appears, in the Boston sequences, as the pioneer black activist Frederick Douglass—a noble, determined figure indeed.

The battle scenes are rousing and eloquently choreographed by cinematographer Freddie Francis, and Zwick's direction proves as honestly loving as it is disciplined and expert. In addition to Washington's Supporting Oscar, the film won for cinematography and sound.

When this writer saw *Glory* back in 1989 with a mixed black and white audience, the members of the moved and tearful audience hugged each other after the conclusion, African Americans and whites embracing. I did my share of hugging. Would that more pictures struck a blow for our common humanity, which transcends race, creed, sexual orientation, and any other cruel divisiveness that *still* afflicts our troubled nation.

75

GETTYSBURG

NEW LINE CINEMA / TURNER ENTERTAINMENT

1993

CAST:
Jeff Daniels, Martin Sheen, C. Thomas Howell, Tom Berenger, Richard Jordan, Sam Elliott, Stephen Lang, Andrew Prine, Kieran Mulroney, Kevin Conway.

CREDITS:
Ronald F. Maxwell, director-screenwriter; based on the novel *The Killer Angels* by Michael Shaara; Kees Van Oostrum, photography; Cary White, production designer; Randy Edelman, music; Corky Ehlers, editor. Running time: 244 minutes. (Color.)

Gettysburg celebrates the famous Civil War battle of early July 1863 in which Union and Confederate forces met outside that little Pennsylvania town in

GETTYSBURG   Martin Sheen (Lee) and Tom Berenger (Longstreet) discuss battle plans.

GETTYSBURG   Hand-to-hand combat at Little Round Top is excitingly portrayed.

an engagement that involved 150,000 soldiers on both sides and left a third of them killed or wounded. This was the most decisive engagement of that war, and when, after several days of fierce fighting, the Southern forces retreated after many casualties, it was an eerie portent of their final and conclusive defeat by the Northern armies two years later.

For this film, some 5,000 Civil War buffs and "re-enactors" restaged the engagement (which had taken place from July 1 to July 3, 1863) on the actual site, the Gettysburg National Military Park. It was the first time a movie crew had been permitted to do so—and in fact the first time this most famous of Civil War battles had ever been captured in detail in a theatrical film.

Based on Michael Shaara's Pulitzer Prize–winning novel *The Killer Angels,* this epic movie captures the essence of the human as well as the military dimensions of the original conflict. Among the more than one hundred speaking parts the principal actors shine, including Jeff Daniels (especially), Martin Sheen, Tom Berenger, Sam Elliott, C. Thomas Howell, Richard Jordan (in his last role), and Stephen Lang.

250

Speaking of the original book, and of the film that resulted from it (all 244 minutes of it), Ronald Maxwell stated: "One of the ironies . . . is that we understand and identify with each one of the characters. We have great sympathy for them; we care about them. We're attracted to them, we admire their zeal, their compassion, their commitment. Every character is quite exemplary, quite likable. At the same time, each and every one of them is ready to kill for what he believes in; each one of them embodies the killer and the angel in the human being."

The film essentially is divided into two parts, separated (in most showings) by an intermission. Part one takes us into the thick of the famous Little Round Top engagement, on a steep, wooded area where Union Col. Joshua Chamberlain (played superbly by Jeff Daniels, in the film's best performance) is commanding a brigade that successfully, and against formidable odds, has repulsed many successive waves of Confederate troops. Had they broken through, the Confederates would have had an open path to Washington. It is during this episode that Daniels, an actor who long since should have been a major star, shines with a determination and purpose and almost mystical leadership charisma that his men are ready to die for—and many do.

GETTYSBURG   Sam Elliott is Brig. Gen. John Buford.

GETTYSBURG   Union and Confederate armies converge at the stone wall during the famous Pickett's Charge.

GETTYSBURG   Stephen Lang (Pickett) salutes Berenger's Longstreet.

In one key sequence, Daniels's Chamberlain wins the loyalty of exhausted and recalcitrant Union soldiers who have refused further combat by addressing them so simply and movingly, and with such an understanding of their—and his—crucible of suffering, that he wins their enthusiastic loyalty. In his piercing yet sensitive eyes, Daniels mirrors the ultimate passion of combat-togetherness, and it mesmerizes his men. So the Union side holds, and the Confederates fall back—as if as much in awe as in fear.

In part two, the concentration is on Pickett's Charge, during which the Confederates make an ultimately disastrous attempt to drive a wedge through the Union center. Martin Sheen (as Confederate Gen. Robert E. Lee) orders this attack over the impassioned protests of his second-in-command, Lt. Gen. James Longstreet, played forcefully by Tom Berenger. Soon some 15,000 hapless Confederate foot soldiers march across a field and are annihilated with deadly precision by better-positioned Union defenders. This is the engagement that decides the battle, sending Lee into Virginia in abject retreat.

The late Richard Jordan is moving as Confederate Brig. Gen. Lewis A. Armistead, who feels that God is truly on the side of his Virginia brigade. All the actors get into the spirit of the period, and while Sheen's Lee misses the nobility of the historical figure, he nevertheless turns in an honest, workmanlike performance.

The most moving scene comes near the end, when Daniels and his aide, C. Thomas Howell, meet after a battle in which so many of their comrades have perished, and go into each other's arms in a warm and lengthy hug. That embrace is joyful as well as affectionate. For these two have *survived;* they have not lost each other; they have lived to fight again, together. The joy, relief, togetherness, camaraderie—the unashamed male bonding—which that hug conveys encapsulates all that men feel for one another under the unifying stresses of combat.

GETTYSBURG Confederate soldiers include Lang, Sheen, and Walter Taylor (seated), Richard Jordan (standing, fourth from left), and Berenger (standing, third from right).

GETTYSBURG   Federal soldiers include C. Thomas Howell (third from left, standing), Kevin Conway (fourth from left, standing), and Jeff Daniels (behind Conway).

Lawrence J. Quirk in uniform.

Lawrence J. Quirk served as an army sergeant in the Korean War (1950–1953). He refers to *Great War Films* as "a true labor of love."

A leading film authority, he has authored some twenty-five books, and is director and founder of the James R. Quirk Film Symposium and Research Center in New York, which tenders annual awards in memory of his uncle, the pioneer editor-publisher of *Photoplay* magazine. Mr. Quirk has written for many publications over a forty-eight-year career, including the *New York Times*, *Cosmopolitan*, *Films in Review*, *Writer's Digest*, *Photoplay*, *Modern Screen*, *Art Films*, *The Theatre*, and his own film periodical, *Quirk's Reviews*. He also has edited major movie magazines.

ORDER NOW!
Citadel Film, Television and Music Books

If you like this book, you'll love the other titles in the award-winning Citadel Film Series, as well as our television and movie books.

From James Stewart to Moe Howard and The Three Stooges, Woody Allen to John Wayne, The Citadel Film Series is America's largest and oldest film book library. With more than 150 titles--and more on the way!--Citadel Film Books make perfect gifts for a loved one, a friend, or best of all, yourself!

A complete listing of the Citadel Film Series appears below. If you know what books you want, why not order now? It's easy! **Just call 1-800-447-BOOK and have your MasterCard or Visa ready.** (Tell the operator code #1529)

STARS
Alan Ladd
Arnold Schwarzenegger
Barbra Streisand: First Decade
Barbra Streisand: Second Decade
The Barbra Streisand Scrapbook
Bela Lugosi
Bette Davis
The Bowery Boys
Brigitte Bardot
Buster Keaton
Carole Lombard
Cary Grant
Charlie Chaplin
Clark Gable
Clint Eastwood
Curly
Dustin Hoffman
Edward G. Robinson
Elizabeth Taylor
Elvis Presley
The Elvis Scrapbook
Errol Flynn
Frank Sinatra
Gary Cooper
Gene Kelly
Gina Lollobrigida
Gloria Swanson
Gregory Peck
Greta Garbo
Henry Fonda
Humphrey Bogart
Ingrid Bergman
Jack Lemmon
Jack Nicholson
James Cagney
James Dean: Behind the Scene
Jane Fonda
Jeanette MacDonald & Nelson Eddy
Joan Crawford
John Wayne Films
John Wayne Reference Book
John Wayne Scrapbook

Judy Garland
Katharine Hepburn
Kirk Douglas
Laurel & Hardy
Lauren Bacall
Laurence Olivier
Mae West
Marilyn Monroe
Marlene Dietrich
Marlon Brando
Marx Brothers
Moe Howard & the Three Stooges
Norma Shearer
Olivia de Havilland
Orson Welles
Paul Newman
Peter Lorre
Rita Hayworth
Robert De Niro
Robert Redford
Sean Connery
Sexbomb: Jayne Mansfield
Shirley MacLaine
Shirley Temple
The Sinatra Scrapbook
Spencer Tracy
Steve McQueen
Three Stooges Scrapbook
Warren Beatty
W.C. Fields
William Holden
William Powell
A Wonderful Life: James Stewart
DIRECTORS
Alfred Hitchcock
Cecil B. DeMille
Federico Fellini
Frank Capra
John Huston
Steven Spielberg
Woody Allen
GENRE
Black Hollywood, Vol. 1 & 2

Classic Foreign Films: From 1960 to Today
Classic Gangster Films
Classic Science Fiction Films
Classics of the Horror Film
Classic TV Westerns
Cult Horror Films
Divine Images: Jesus on Screen
Early Classics of Foreign Film
Great Baseball Films
Great French Films
Great German Films
Great Italian Films
Great Science Fiction Films
The Great War Films
Harry Warren & the Hollywood Musical
Hispanic Hollywood
Hollywood Bedlam: Screwball Comedies
The Hollywood Western
The Incredible World of 007
The Jewish Image in American Film
The Lavender Screen: The Gay and Lesbian Films
Martial Arts Movies
Merchant Ivory Films
The Modern Horror Film
More Classics of the Horror Film
Movie Psychos & Madmen
Our Huckleberry Friend: Johnny Mercer
Second Feature: "B" Films
They Sang! They Danced! They Romanced!
Thrillers
The West That Never Was
Words and Shadows: Literature on the Screen
DECADE
Classics of the Silent Screen
Films of the Twenties
Films of the Thirties

More Films of the 30's
Films of the Forties
Films of the Fifties
Lost Films of the 50's
Films of the Sixties
Films of the Seventies
Films of the Eighties
SPECIAL INTEREST
America on the Rerun
Bugsy (Illustrated screenplay)
The "Cheers" Trivia Book
The Citadel Treasury of Famous Movie Lines
Comic Support
Cutting Room Floor: Scenes Which Never Made It
Favorite Families of TV
Film Flubs
Film Flubs: The Sequel
Filmmaking on the Fringe
First Films
Frankly, My Dear: Great Movie Lines About Women
Gilligan, Maynard & Me
Hollywood Cheesecake
Howard Hughes in Hollywood
More Character People
The Nightmare Never Ends: Freddy Krueger & A Nightmare on Elm Street
The Northern Exposure Book
The Official Andy Griffith Show Scrapbook
100 Best Films of the Century
The 1001 Toughest TV Trivia Questions of All Time
The Quantum Leap Book
Sex in Films
Sex In the Movies
Sherlock Holmes
Son of Film Flubs
Who Is That?: Familiar Faces and Forgotten Names
"You Ain't Heard Nothin' Yet!"

For a free full-color Entertainment Books brochure including the Citadel Film Series in depth and more, call 1-800-447-BOOK; or send your name and address to Citadel Film Books, Dept. 1529, 120 Enterprise Ave., Secaucus, NJ 07094.